Exploring the Engagement and Empowerment of Women

By the Same Author

1. Bihar Tourism: Retrospect and Prospect with Swargesh Kumar
2. Ecology and Quality of Life in Urban Slums: An Empirical Study with Rekha Sinha
3. Ecological Imbalances and Plan Perspectives of A Developing Region with Mukesh Kumar
4. Economics of Social Sector and Environment
5. Monetary and Fiscal Actions in India: An Empirical Evidence with K.D. Prasad
6. Sustainable Resource Development: Policy, Problem and Prescription
7. Women Empowerment and Family Management in Tribal Region with Rekha Sinha

---

About the Editor

Udai Prakash Sinha (*b.* 1956) former Vice Chancellor Central University of Haryana, is currently Professor of Economics, T.M. Bhagalpur University, Bhagalpur. He has authored many books including Planned Development of Resources in a Developing Region (1985), Socio-Economic Dimensions of Integrated Development in India (1991) and IRDP for Weaker Sections (1996). He has been editing 'Journal of Economic Issues' since 2000 published by Planning Forum, and Anga Economic Society, University Department of Economics, T.M. Bhagalpur University. Bhagalpur. He has also completed two UGC Major Research Projects and presently working on UGC sponsored major research project entitled, "Ecological Imbalances and Plan Perspective for Rural Bihar." He travelled extensively throughout India to deliver lectures as a resource person. He has also contributed more than 100 research papers to reputed national and international journals of Economics and other social sciences. 35 Research Scholars have already been awarded Ph.D. degree under his able guidance. Micro-level planning and the regional economics are the areas of his interest and research.

Exploring the Engagement and Empowerment of Women

Multidisciplinary Perspectives

Edited by

U.P. Sinha

CONCEPT PUBLISHING COMPANY PVT. LTD.
NEW DELHI-110059

ISBN-13: 978-93-5125-160-6

First Published 2015

Published and Printed by

Concept Since 1974

Concept Publishing Company Pvt. Ltd.
A/15-16, Commercial Block, Mohan Garden
New Delhi-110059 (India)
T: 25351460, 25351794, *F*: 091-11-25357109
E: publishing@conceptpub.com, W: www.conceptpub.com
Editorial Office: H-13, Bali Nagar, New Delhi-110 015, India.

Cataloging in Publication Data--Courtesy: D.K. Agencies (P) Ltd. <docinfo@dkagencies.com>

Exploring the engagement and empowerment of women : multidisciplinary perspectives/ edited by U.P. Sinha.
pages cm
Includes bibliographical references and index.
ISBN 9789351251606

1. Women in development--India. I. Sinha, Udai Prakash, 1956-, editor.

DDC 305.420954 23

Preface

Women empowerment is a much debated subject in India especially because of the paradox that we find in our society. The paradox is a product of "preaching without practice" where a women is regarded as a goddess and destroyer of evil on one hand and is discriminated against in various dimensions of human activities, on the other. However, the field of women empowerment is undergoing rapid changes in recent times. The change is reflected in academic discourse, social activism and government policy making.

Politically, it has gained new momentum after introduction of one-third reservation of seats for women in grass root governance. Although political empowerment can bring about a sea change (an area examined by Usman Siddiqui and Chanchal Kumar Sharma in this book), there are many other dimensions which can perform a critical role in improving socio-economic status of women, quality and standard of their education being the most important of them all. It is thus no surprise that Governments across the globe are making concrete efforts to empower women and shifting focus from "Women Welfare" to "Women Empowerment".

In India, Fifth Five Year plan focused on three dimensions of women development i.e. health, education and employment. The Eighth Five Year plan made a significant leap forward and emphasized women empowerment as such. The working Group on Empowerment of women has emphasized the strengthening of self-help Groups (SHGs) and community based organisations for the empowerment of women.

Since Women's perspective is continuously evolving, it is imperative that multidisciplinary approach is adopted so that a holistic framework could be developed through analysis of different dimensions. I hope that the publication of this book, which includes many papers by the faculty of Central University of Haryana will contribute to the dissemination of the diversity of ideas on women empowerment.

Finally, I would like to acknowledge the contribution of all the faculty members for their contributions. I recognize with profuse thanks the efforts of Dr. Chanchal Kumar Sharma, OSD to VC and Head, Department of Political Science whose dedication, sincerity and honesty at workplace is unparalleled. I shall be failing in my duty if I fail to acknowledge my gratefulness to the Publishers for attractive layout and timely publication of this book.

Udai Prakash Sinha
Editor

Contents

Part VII
Gender and Sexuality: Unexplored Dimensions

Wrapping up Notes

List of Contributors

Ajai Pal Sharma, Department of Management Studies, Central University of Haryana, Mahendergarh.

Anand Sharma, Department of Management Studies, Central University of Haryana, Mahendergarh.

Anil Kumar, EFL University, Hyderabad.

Anju Beniwal, Department of Law, School of Law, Central University of Haryana, Mahendergarh.

Bir Singh Yadav, Department of English and Foreign Languages, Central University of Haryana, Mahendergarh.

Chanchal Kumar Sharma, Head, Department of Political Science, Central University of Haryana, Mahendergarh.

Chitra Choudhary, Department of Economics, University of Rajasthan.

Divya, Department of Management Studies, Central University of Haryana, Mahendergarh.

Madhukar Sharma, Department of English, Central University of Haryana, Mahendergarh.

Muhammad Usman Amin Siddiqi, Assistant Professor, Department of Political Science, GC University, Lahore, Pakistan.

Pardeep Singh, Department of Law, Central University of Haryana, Mahendergarh.

Rajiv Kumar Singh, Department of Political Science, Central University of Haryana, Mahendergarh.

Rekha Kumari, Department of English, Central University of Haryana, Mahendergarh.

Renu, Department of Economics, Central University of Haryana, Mahendergarh.

Richa Mishra, Delhi School of Management, Delhi Technological University.

Samiksha Godara, Department of Law, School of Law, Central University of Haryana, Mahendergarh.

Sanjiv Kumar, Department of English and Foreign Language, Central University of Haryana, Mahendergarh.

Satish Kumar, Department of Political Science, University of Jharkhand.

Sunita Tanwar, Department of Management Studies, Central University of Haryana, Mahendergarh.

Udai Prakash Sinha, Vice-Chancellor, Central University of Haryana, Mahendergarh.

Introduction

Women Empowerment means ability and capacity of women to set her life's agenda and make choices without any fear or pressure. An 'empowered' woman can freely acquire new skills and knowledge and as a result become more self-confident and self-reliant. Such a woman can not only solve her own problems but can also make a positive contribution towards solving community problems. She can demand and defend her rights in order to realize her full potential at different stages of her life.

Several of the United Nations Millennium Development Goals (MDGs) deal with the situation of women. The target of Goal 3 is the elimination of gender disparity. Goal 4 seeks to reduce child mortality, and Goal 5 aims to improve the health of mothers. But the empowerment of women and the strengthening of their position in society is the aim of the other MDGs as well. Women play a crucial role in the fight against extreme poverty and hunger (MDG 1). Girls and women lag far behind boys and men in progress towards achieving universal basic education (MDG 2). No progress at all can be made in the fight against HIV/AIDS, malaria, and other endemic diseases (MDG 6), unless women are included. And without the participation of women, it will be impossible to ensure environmental sustainability (MDG 7).

Empowering women to participate fully in economic life across all sectors is essential to build stronger economies, achieve internationally agreed goals for development and sustainability, and improve the quality of life for women, men, families and communities.

The private sector is a key partner in efforts to advance gender equality and empower women. Current research demonstrating that gender diversity helps businesses perform better signals that self-interest and common interest can come together. Yet, ensuring the inclusion of women's talents, skills and energies—from executive offices to the factory floor and the supply chain—requires intentional actions and deliberate policies.

In many countries, particularly in South Asia, Girls are less likely to attend school than boys and tend to leave school at an earlier age. To remedy this situation, non-formal education campaigns by the civil society can play a huge role. As the Nobel laureate, Malala said, "If we want the education of girls, we should be united. We should not wait. We should do it now." True to her word, Malala advocated for education in her native Pakistan, where the Taliban had banned schooling for girls. This book includes a special contribution by Muhammad Usman Amin Siddiqi who reflect on such issues in the specific context of Pakistan.

This book highlights various dimensions of women issues and those related to their empowerment. The collection of articles serves to enhance understanding of women issues from multiple perspectives.

U.P. Sinha focuses on the role of education for the holistic development of society. It is argued that education can become the greatest tool for transformation of the plight of women. Women have always been a victim of lack of power-political, economic and social. The key component of their powerlessness is lack of education which has socio-economic causes. It becomes a challenging task when the collective opinion of a particular community militates against education for women. Reforming socially backward world view through laws from above may not always prove successful. Thus, the civil society has a role to play. In India, the government has directed all the central universities to adopt villages in their catchment area and promote fresh thinking among villagers through community service. The Central University of Haryana is making an endeavour to create awareness among the villagers regarding various aspects of women empowerment and particularly regarding women education.

Rajiv Kumar Singh focuses on the issue of women education through a communitarian perspective. He argues that Gender as a class in India has not been able to pose a united front since it is further subdivided by various cross cutting linkages based on caste, religion and economic status. However, spread of education can weaken traditional allegiances and liberate women from shackles of a 'belief system' that keeps her trapped in low potential and performance equilibrium. A woman so liberated can stake claim in power sharing in all dimensions of its various manifestations.

Muhammad Usman Amin Siddiqi points out that political empowerment must not be understood in terms of quantitative measurement of women representation in legislative assemblies, but in terms of quality of socio-political participation of women in political system of the country through indigenous acceptance of society rooted and expressed through norms and values. He argues that political empowerment of women can ensure continuity of socio-economic empowerment of women in society, provided former is a result of latter.

Chanchal Kumar Sharma presents a sketch of the problems and pitfalls of parliamentary representation of women in India. He argues that mere presence of a few women in the parliament will not automatically serve the goal of representation of women as a collectivity. For political representation of women to serve the purpose it is intended to, requires two key prerequisites. One of them is education because education and empowerment are in a constant loop. Second prerequisite is putting robust accountability mechanisms in place because representation in itself is not sufficient unless it is accompanied with accountability mechanisms. A more representative legislature does not guarantee more effective representation of women's interests because "standing for women" is not always the same as "acting for them".

Samiksha Godara takes us through a journey into the initiatives taken by legislature and judiciary in India towards the empowerment of women. She however, believes that although numerous women welfare legislations have been enacted from time to time and a plethora of landmark judgments have been delivered yet the goal of women empowerment has not yet been realized. This outcome requires a cultural revolution of sorts; a change in the collective mindset.

Pardeep Singh argues that in order to include women in the process of growth the government must make an endeavour to address socio-legal problems of the women. **Anju Beniwal** on the other hand puts a premium on the paradigm shift especially from a legal perspective.

Divya and **Richa Mishra** charts the course of diverse life experiences of women as the ones who are restricted to their household chores and the ones who take a plunge and make their mark in the corporate life. **Anand Sharma** takes the discussion further and gives an exposition of the challenges and biases that women confront as a part of their corporate life.

Renu correlates female literacy rate with maternal health and child healthcare. Her view is that an educationally empowered woman can take care of her own health and health of her children as well. This can lead to a significant improvement in health indicators which is one of the indicators of human development.

Chitra Choudhary further emphasizes the role of appropriate health intervention strategies not only to promote the well-being of women but also to empower them.

Sunita Tanwar makes an attempt to understand the life stress and behavioural dysfunction of married working women and a housewife in NCR. Her study indicates that a woman's mind remains under stress due to multi-tasking and attempting to meet various demands of the society in terms of work and behavioural norms. Over a long-term the consistent state of mental stress can lead to behavioural dysfunction.

Bir Singh Yadav highlights that ancient vedic literature if followed in word and spirit can prove to be a guiding light for social transformation and women empowerment. He argues that the most reliable and the best thermometer to assess the level of a society is its outlook and treatment towards women.

Anil Kumar depiction of Indian Woman's Anguish through Kamala Das's Works. Pointing to the connection between society and literature he argues that writers take ideas from their surroundings and disperse them back with new form and direction. In the same process, Kamala Das has expressed her concern about the subjugation of female in our society. Thinking with Kamala Das the author argues that the condition of women in Indian society has remained unchanged even in this so-called scientific age of twenty first century.

Rekha Kumari and **Madhukar Sharma** employ the ideas generated by Arundhati Roy in her book '*The God of Small Things' to justify assertion as an antidote to suppression.*

Sanjiv Kumar reflects on the issue of recognition of transgenders as 'third gender'. Recognition means giving them full and unbiased access to mainstream life and recognizing their rights as normal human beings. However, the dilemma is that the recognition of transgenders as 'third gender' is hard to be digested by those who have deeply internalised the notion of absolutely binary gender propositions.

Satish Kumar makes an attempt to access the role of pornography and relatively easy access to such literature and websites on the multiple issues related to women. These include outlook of young men who are exposed to pornography during adolescence and teenage, which is a highly impressionable age; the self-image of the young girls; the ideas regarding acceptable sexual behaviour; and last but not the least abetment of sex related crimes in the society.

The concluding chapter by **Ajai Pal Sharma** highlights why women empowerment is necessary and how it can be achieved. In nutshell, the books is an attempt to look at women issues through various vantage points. The book has adopted a multi-disciplinary approach to understand problems, depict the plight of women and suggest solutions.

29th May, 2015

U.P. Sinha
Editor

PART I
Education and Women Empowerment

1
Women Empowerment and the Role of Education in India

Udai Prakash Sinha

Mahatma Gandhi stated that the position of women the society is an index of its civilization. "Train a man and you train an individual, Train a woman and you build a nation".

Women form almost half of the population of the world. They are the partners of man. As the holy *Quran* says, "*God has created all his creations in pairs*" (*Quran*, 13:3). For example, Physical and Spiritual, weak and strong, day and night, truth and false, matter and space, fire and ice and sky and earth. All these do not oppose or contradict each other but complement each other. Therefore, God has created man and woman to compensate each other's weaknesses so that they can build up a strong power by combining their individuality. God has created women as equal partner to men but the society has given her secondary place to men. This is true in most part of the world, even in the most modern western world.

One of the several factors that justify the greatness of India's ancient culture is the honourable place granted to women. Historically, women have been accorded very high place in the Indian culture. In the ancient India, it cannot be clearly stated whether equal rights between men and women prevailed or not during the Vedic period. But available sources show that liberal attitudes and practices pertaining to women did exist. Women were actively involved in religious and social matters. They had some freedom to choose their partner in marriage and a widow was permitted to remarry. As India started taking steps towards civilization, social discrimination increased. Though, it improved in the time of Buddha and Mahavira and Jainism and Buddhism emerged as potent religious reform movements. According to Buddha, women's spiritual capacities were equal to men's. Buddhism began as a religion that treated women as equal to men in their capacity for personal and spiritual development. The high status that women enjoyed during early Vedic period gradually started deteriorating in the late Vedic period. Lineage began to be traced in the male line and sons were the sole heirs to family property. As the economic and social status of sons began to rise, the position of women saw a steep decline. The position of women reached an all-time low during the age of the *Dharmashastras*[1]. It is during this age that codes of conduct prescribing behaviour norms for women were evolved. This period saw the exclusion of women from both economic and religious sphere. During the period of *Dharmashastra*, child marriage was encouraged and widow marriage was looked down upon. The birth of girl child was considered as an ill omen and many parents went to the extent of killing the female infants. The practice of *Sati* became quite wide spread because of the ill treatment meted out to widows.

In the medieval India with the arrival of Invaders in the Country from middle-east led to the decrease of that status. Women started to be treated as a secondary member of the society. The *purdah* system which was prevalent among royal families, nobles and merchant prince classes prior to the advent of Muslims spread to other classes also. During the medieval period, practices such as polygamy, *sati*, child marriage, ill treatment of widows already prevalent during the *Dharmashastra* age gained further momentum. The priestly class misinterpreted the sacred texts and created an impression that all these evil practices had religious sanction.

The British influence had a very deep impression on the minds of Indian leaders. The reformist movements of the 19th century brought social reformers Raja Ram Mohan Roy, Ishwar Chandra Vidyasagar, Swami Dayanand Saraswati, Swami Vivekananda, Mahatma Gandhi, Jawaharlal Nehru, and many others, who were in the forefront of the struggle for women emancipation. Gandhi's efforts led to the elevation of the women's status, involving them in the struggle for social progress and political independence. Prominent among them were Sarojini Naidu, Kasturba Gandhi, Kamala Nehru, and Aruna Asaf Ali, who participated in the political arena. After initial hesitation, even Muslims took to modern western education in large number thanks to the efforts of Sir Sayyid Ahmad Khan and others. The Muslim student population in modern high schools was generally proportionate to their numerical strength.

Though the years have taken their toll on the image of an ideal woman, she still holds a revered position, in most Indian homes. They are worshipped in the form of Goddess Laxmi, Durga, Saraswati, Ganga, etc. However, even after so many years of Indian Independence, this low status of women still continues in the country. There are many reasons of the low socio-economic and educational status of women in India. Let us first analyse the status of women in India.

Status of Women in India

Today, women are less than half of Indian population and their numbers are decreasing alarmingly. As per census 2011 of India, the population of males were 6237 lakhs (51.5%) and females were 5864 lakhs (48.5%)[2]. A sex ratio of 950 is considered normal sex ratio but it is below normal right from the year 1941 when it was 945 and decreased from 950 in the year 1931.

Table 1.1: Census-wise Sex Ratio of India[3]

Sr. No	*Year*	*Sex Ratio*
1.	1901	972
2.	1911	964
3.	1921	955
4.	1931	950
5.	1941	945
6.	1951	946
7.	1961	941
8.	1971	930
9.	1981	934
10.	1991	926
11.	2001	933
12.	2011	940

Table 1.1 given above shows that the sex ratios are decreasing. However, in the census 2011, a slighter improvement in sex ratio is

visible, but when we see the child sex ratio, we observe that in the year 2011, it was 914 whereas earlier it was 927 in the year 2001.

Social Status

Indian society is a patriarchal society, in which important rights and power to take decisions are ought to be taken by man. Manu in 200 BC said: "by a young girl, by a young woman, or even by an aged one, nothing must be done independent, even in her own house"[4]. This quotation of Manu forces us to accept that Sex and Gender are two different concepts related to women. The universal validity of Simone de Beauvoir's famous observation[5] that "*One is not born but rather becomes, a woman...*" (267) is reinforced in the light of the methods through which a girl is socialized into feminine submissiveness. What Simone wants to establish is that woman is a cultural construction. It is a known fact that biologically, there are some differences between man and woman and god has given different strength to both of them and we know that each has a different function to perform, so to pronounce one inferior or superior is a stereotype that pollutes and corrupts the psychology of society. It is the add-on of cultural norms to this biological categorization that becomes subversive and results in gender discrimination.

Sociologically, the word gender refers to the socio-cultural definition of man and woman, the way societies distinguish men and women and assign them social roles. The distinction between sex and gender was introduced to deal with the general tendency to attribute women's subordination to their anatomy. For ages it was believed that the different characteristics, roles and status accorded to women and men in the society are determined by sex, that they are natural and therefore not changeable. As soon as a child is born families and society begin the process of gendering. The birth of a son is celebrated, the birth of a daughter is filled with pain; sons are showered with love, respect, better food and proper healthcare. Boys are encouraged to be tough and outgoing; and girls to be homebound and shy. All these differences are gender differences and they are created by the society. Gender inequality is therefore a form of inequality which is distinct from other forms of economic and social inequalities and stems from pre-existing gendered social norms and social perceptions. Gender inequity has adverse impact on development goals as reduces economic growth. It hampers the overall well-being because blocking women from participation in social, political and economic activities can adversely affect the whole society. Many developing countries including India have displayed gender inequality in education, employment and health. It is common to find girls and women suffering from high mortality rates and vast differences in education level.

India has witnessed gender inequality from its early history due to its socio-economic and religious practices resulting in a wide disparity between the position of men and women in the society.

In spite of India's reputation for respecting women, including treating her as a Goddess, history tells us that women were also ill-treated. There was no equality between men and women. This is true of ancient, medieval and early modern times. Women in Indian society are considered as a citizen of secondary status. In the patriarchal society of the country, girls and women face lots of discrimination and hurdles. The decrease in the status of women has been due to the prevalence of patriarchal society in the country. Due to this, girls are not allowed to perform various rituals which can be performed only by the male child. They are treated as the property of the family in which she lives as Manu said "In childhood a female must be subject to her father, in youth to her husband, when her lord is dead to her sons; a woman must never be independent.[6] "So woman is never given freedom and she is always subjected to exploitation of various kinds. As a result one can perceive as difference in the cognitive, connotative, and consumption patterns of women residing in various spheres of social and economic layers. The victims of exploitation and oppression have been largely women of the third world countries in general and lower sections among them in particular.

Socially and culturally, the types of discrimination can be understood as follows:

- Gender specific specialization (work);
- Cultural definition of appropriate sex roles;
- Expectation of role within relationship;
- Belief in the inherent superiority of males;
- Customs of marriage (Bride price/Dowry);
- Notion of the family as the private sphere and under male control; and
- Value that give proprietary right over women and girls.

Man is supposed to earn livelihood and woman is expected to raise children and look after house-hold jobs. Woman is treated as a faired sex, weaker sex and she is expected not to do hard and difficult work. Family of woman are generally expected to give dowry to the family of man and have to bear the cost of giving birth to a girl as if they have committed some crime. Women are also not given property rights as she is not treated as head of the family and as they have to go to some other family and some other place.

Economic Status

The socialisation of girls takes place in such a manner and atmosphere that they are supposed to be conditioned to bear exploitations. As a result of the cultural and economic factors, women face discrimination right from the childhood. If there are two siblings in a family and one of them is a male, then the girl is expected to give due respect to the likes and dislikes of her brother, is given food after the male sibling has his share and also expected to do household chorus. It is held that both in childhood and adulthood males are fed first and better. According to one estimate, even as adult women consume approximately 1000 calories less per day than men. This discrimination continues even after she gets mature and even after gets married. Her contribution to the house-hold chorus is not given importance at all and even not counted in the National Income because work done without taking anything in return/remuneration is not treated as income.

Former President Bill Clinton while addressing the annual meeting of the Clinton Global Initiative (September, 2009) rightly said that "Women perform 66 per cent of the world's work, and produce 50 per cent of the food, yet earn only 10 per cent of the income and own 1 per cent of the property. Whether the issue is improving education in the developing world, or fighting global climate change, or addressing nearly any other challenge we face, empowering women is a critical part of the equation."

There are discrimination against women in the economic activities which can be understood with the help of following points:

- Limited access to cash and credit
- Limited access to employment in formal and informal sector.
- Limited access to education.

As per the latest economic survey of the country, only 49 per cent of the Indian population have bank accounts whereas only 18 per cent of women have bank accounts in their name. This show the women's low level of accessibility to banking services in the country which pose hindrance in their economic development and led to low levels. As per the National Sample Survey Organization (NSSO) data reveals that women account for just 22 per cent of workforce in India. According to the International Labour Organization (ILO)[7], out of 131 countries for which data was available, India ranks 11th from the bottom in Female Labour Force Participation (FLFP). In fact, the National Sample Survey Organization (NSSO) data reveals falling FLFP from over 40 per cent in the mid-1990s, to 29 per cent in 2004-05, to 23 per cent in 2009-10 and 22.5 per cent by 2011-12. This shows that female participation is decreasing continuously from mid-1990s.

The disadvantages facing women and girls are a major source of inequality. All too often, women and girls are discriminated against in health, education and the labour market—with negative repercussions for their freedoms. India's gender gap index was 0.655 in the year 2013 on a 0 to 1 scale, with 0 denoting inequality and 1 equality. Gender Inequality Index increased from 0.553 in 2001. The World Economic Forum has placed India in the 101st position among 136 countries in the 2013 annual report that makes a global assessment of the progress made in bridging the gender gap. India was at 124th position out of 136 countries when it comes the economic participation and opportunity.

Gender gap sub-indexes—India

	Rank	*Score*
Economic participation and opportunity	**124**	**0.446**
Labour force participation	124	0.36
Wage equality for similar work (survey)	86	0.62
Estimated earned income (PPP US$)	125	0.27
Legislators, senior officials and managers	—	—
Professional and technical workers	—	—
Educational attainment	**120**	**0.857**
Literacy rate	123	0.68
Enrolment in primary education	1	1.00
Enrolment in secondary education	111	0.79
Enrolment in tertiary education	107	0.73
Health and survival	**135**	**0.931**
Sex ratio at birth (female/male)	133	0.89
Healthy life expectancy	112	1.02
Political empowerment	**9**	**0.385**
Women in Parliament	106	0.12
Women in ministerial positions	100	0.11
Years with female head of state (last 50)	1	0.72

The rankings are based on four of sub-indices that measure economic participation and opportunity, educational attainment, health and survival and political empowerment. It is in the political empowerment arena that India has scored strong, being ranked 9th.

Educational Status

The World Economic Forum has placed India in the 120th position among 136 countries in the 2013 annual report in terms of educational attainment. As per 2011 census the total literacy rate of India was 74.04 whereas literacy rate for male was 82.14 and female was 65.46. It shows that almost 33 per cent or one-fourth of Indian women are literate.

- Gross Enrolment Ratio (GER)[8] of girls in primary stage was 48.2 whereas for upper-primary stage was 48.77 in 2013.
- GER in secondary education shows that there are 10 percentage point gap between enrolment of boys and girls[9]. As per available data of Gross Enrolment Ratio (GER) for Secondary Education for the year 2009-10, 52.39 per cent of boys and 45.86 per cent of girls combined at the Secondary and Senior Secondary level.
- The national GER for girls in higher education in 2011-12 was 18.9 per cent. The national average of gender parity index in higher education, according to the AISHE report, was of 0.88 which shows that still there are.12 differences between the GER of boys and girls at the National Level. As per AISHE 2010-11[10], enrolment of women at UG level was 42.5 per cent, at PG level was 42.7 per cent whereas for Ph.D. level, it was 39.9 per cent showing vast difference between enrolment of boys and girls at different levels of higher education.
- *Technological Status*: Technology has contributed a lot in the dwindling sex ratio in the country. Sex Ratio was 940[11] for females per 1000 males in the year 2011 which further decreased when we see the child sex ratio. The child sex ratio in the year 2011 was 914 whereas it was 927 in the year 2001. The situation is alarming in parts of Delhi, Punjab, Haryana, U.P. and Maharashtra where the figure is less than 850 girls for every 1000 boys. Haryana tops the list with 830

girls for every 1000 boys. Haryana's Mahendergarh district has got another dubious distinction by recording the maximum fall in the child sex ratio in the country during the past 10 years. The child sex ratio in Mahendergarh, which has the lowest sex ratio in the country, has touched 775 girls against 1,000 boys in 2011, compared to 818 in 2001. Other districts of south Haryana like Rewari, Jhajjar and Bhiwani districts, along with Mahendergarh[12], have also witnessed a downfall in the child sex ratio[13]. The maximum downfall in the sex ratio has been in the states and districts which has developed economically and has good medical infrastructure in place. Due to better health and medical facilities, parents easily got the sex of the foetus determined from the greedy and unethical medical practitioners and then able to abort them, if the foetus is going to be of a girl.

Need for Women Empowerment

Women empowerment in India is a burning issue. If the country takes dream of becoming the superpower and developed nation under Vision 2020, then can we ignore the welfare and development of half of the Indian population, absolutely we can't. Therefore, we have to ensure that the half population of the country is healthy, educated and economically sound.

Challenges

1. *Educational Challenges*—Low Literacy, Low Enrolment of Women at Various Stages (Elementary, Secondary and Higher) and types of Education (Technical, General, Medical, etc.).
2. *Health Challenges*—High Girl Child Mortality Rate, High Maternal Mortality Ratio, Anaemia due to Eating Last and Least, High STD and HIV Risks, Lack of Clean Drinking Water.
3. *Economy Challenges*—Low Paid Jobs, Sexual and Gender Exploitation, Less Mobility due to dependence on family or husband.
4. *Safety Challenges*—High Crime Rate against Girls and Women in Family, Society, Educational Institutions, Employment Organisations, etc.

5. *Culture Challenges*—Biased Culture, Unfavourable Social Norms, Patriarchal Society.
6. *Technological Challenges*—Indifferent Attitude towards Use of Technology due to Less Availability, Unfavourable Social Norms towards Women using Technology.

Remedies of the Challenges Facing Women Empowerment

Women Empowerment is a global issue and discussion on women political right are at the fore front of many formal and informal campaigns worldwide. The concept of women empowerment was introduced at the international women conference held at Nairobi, Kenya in the year 1985. According to Kishore (2008) Empowerment has come to denote women's increased control over their own lives, bodies and environments. In discussions of women's empowerment, emphasis is often placed on women's decision-making roles, their economic self-reliance, and their legal rights to equal treatment, inheritance and protection against all forms of discrimination, in addition to the elimination of barriers to access such resources as education and information.

Women Empowerment and Education

Education is panacea of all the problems India facing today including women discrimination. Education is important for everyone, but it is especially significant for girls and women. This is true not only because education is an entry point to other opportunities, but also because the educational achievements of women can have ripple effects within the family and across generations. Investing in girls' education is one of the most effective ways to reduce poverty. Investments in secondary school education for girls yields especially high dividends. As Jawaharlal Nehru once said "If you educate a man you educate an individual, however, if you educate a woman you educate a whole family. Women empowered means mother India empowered". Education is most important tool in the hands of mankind wishing empowerment of women with the knowledge, skills and self-confidence necessary to participate fully in the development process. Because it enables them to responds to the challenges, to confront their traditional role and change their life. Girls who have been educated are likely to marry later and to have smaller and healthier families. Educated women can recognize the importance of health care and know how to seek it for themselves and their children. Education helps girls and women to know their rights and to gain confidence to claim them. However, women's literacy rates are significantly lower than men's in most developing countries. In today's high-tech world, we can't neglect the importance of education in reference to women empowerment India is poised to becoming superpower, a developed country by 2020.

Education has far-reaching Effects

The education of parents is linked to their children's educational attainment, and the mother's education is usually more influential than the father's. An educated mother's greater influence in household negotiations may allow her to secure more resources for her children.

Educated mothers are more likely to be in the labour force, allowing them to pay some of the costs of schooling, and may be more aware of returns to schooling. And educated mothers, averaging fewer children, can concentrate more attention on each child.

Besides having fewer children, mothers with schooling are less likely to have mistimed or unintended births. This has implications for schooling, because poor parents often must choose which of their children to educate. According to Report[14] of International Commission of Education, popularly known as Delor's Commission 'Learning the Treasure Within' there are four pillars of education which are essential for everyone, these have been explained below:

1. *Learning to Know*: Learning to know involves the development of knowledge and skills that are needed to function in the world. These skills include literacy, numeracy and critical thinking.
2. *Learning to Do*: Learning to do involves the acquisition of skills that are often linked to occupational success, such as computer training, managerial training and apprenticeships.
3. *Learning to Live Together*: Learning to live together involves the development of social skills and values such as respect and concern for others, social and inter-personal skills and an appreciation of the diversity of Indians.
4. *Learning to Be*: Learning to be involves activities that foster personal development (body, mind and spirit) and contribute

to creativity, personal discovery and an appreciation of the inherent value provided by these pursuits.

These four pillars of education are very important for the holistic development of anyone, especially women as these teach them life skills which are very important to survive in today's society based on cut-throat competition.

These capabilities which make a person self-reliant, self-realised can be developed by education. The capability approach, as developed in the work of Amartya Sen in late 1970s, provides a very useful way, given the complexity of diverse societies in the world, to think about social justice and a particular component of social justice, gender equality in education.

Women Empowerment and Higher Education

Universities are the most important higher education institutions. They are the parent body of another higher education institution known as colleges. Colleges are dependent on the Universities. It is University which decide the curriculum of colleges affiliated to it. It also conducts examinations and controls almost every functioning of the University. The role of universities therefore is most important. This role in contemporary times is:

- Balancing of personal development, economic opportunities and social good/citizenship
- Social critic and space of public reasoning (Sen: no 'discussionless justice')

Higher education institutions have a great role to play in the empowerment of women. Ban Ki-moon, the Secretary-General of UN said that universities can play "a significant role in promoting gender equality and women's empowerment. They can provide the training in critical thinking that a functional democracy needs," he said, "They provide a foundation for the economic and medical research that is so essential to society's well-being." And they supply graduates to the workforce. "So, it is essential that this issue of women's rights and women's representation is reflected in your curricula, your appointments, your practices and your partnerships."

Role of a University in Women Empowerment in India

A typical Indian university can help in the women empowerment in India in the following ways by establishing:

1. Women Hostel,
2. Women Studies Centre,
3. Residential Coaching Academy for Minorities and SC/ST/ women,
4. Merit Scholarship Scheme,
5. Indira Gandhi Scholarship for Single Girl Child for pursuing higher and technical knowledge,
6. Capacity Building Cells for Women Managers in Higher Education, and
7. Tuition Fee Waiver for Girl Students.

Steps taken by Central University of Haryana

Central University of Haryana is one of the youngest 15 Central Universities in the Country and was established in the year 2009 by an Act of Parliament. Prof. Mool Chand Sharma, Professor of Law at University of Delhi and Ex-Vice Chairman of University Grants Commission, New Delhi was appointed as the Founding Vice-Chancellor of the University which is situated in an area having lowest sex ratio in the country. Prof. Mool Chand Sharma had a vision to make Central University of Haryana as a world class university with inculcating values like hard work, loyalty, humanity and sensitivity towards women, poor and other weaker sections of the society. He took many steps for the women empowerment by organising first in the series of workshop for *'Addressing Discrimination against Women: Walk the Talk'*. In this workshop all the major players were women and girls students of ITI, Narnaul. These participants shared their opinions and experiences at the workshop as a girl students, as a daughter, as a housewife and as a mother. The workshop raised many serious issues which can be of utmost importance for the policy and decisions-makers. Prof. Rajul Bhargava was the Director of the three day workshop in which then Union HRD Minister sent his message and well wishes.

The issue of women discrimination was again raised by the University when the whole country was in tears after the heinous crime was committed on *Damini/ Nirbhaya* in a moving bus in Delhi. The whole country and the world were debating the issues and challenges of women safety and security and were finding reasons that led to committal of the heinous crimes against girls and women in the country. Central University of Haryana, in order to find out the reasons behind such crimes and the issues and challenges of women empowerment, came out with a unique idea of changing the mind-set of the common man towards the girls and the women and initiated a journey titled *"A Journey for Change-from Narnaul to Delhi"* all the way through various educational institutions of various stages including the school, colleges and university. The Journey included two different programme namely a colloquium on *"Value Education-Imperatives for Change"* and a play enacted by the students of Central University of Haryana depicting the crimes committed daily against girls and women and was started on January 28, 2013 from DAV Sr. Secondary School, Narnaul and covered Government College, Ateli; Holy Child Public School, Rewari; Guru Gobind Singh Indraprastha University, a state university in Delhi; Jahan Ara Bagh Stadium, Jhajjar and Ended at Delhi World Book Fair on February 7, 2013. These stoppages of *"A Journey for Change-from Narnaul to Delhi"* saw participation from the various stakeholders including students and teachers of school, colleges and university, educational administrators like Principal, DEO, Police Officers (SSP etc.), Minister of Education. The President of India Shri Pranab Mukherjee in the meeting of Vice-Chancellors of Central University (2013) appreciated the steps taken by the Central University of Haryana for the empowerment of women.

Following are some of the steps taken by Central University of Haryana for women empowerment:

1. Women Empowerment Cell,
2. Legal Aid Cell,
3. Book Reading Club,
4. Discussion Group,
5. Group for the Promotion of Culture, Arts and Heritage,
6. Skill Development and Capacity Building Cell,
7. Gender Sensitisation cell-sex ratio at CUH is better than Sex ratio of Mahendergarh and the National Sex Ratio, and
8. Provision of Recreation Facilities at CUH—Essential for the Holistic Development-3 Hs: Head, Heart and Hand i.e. development of Mind, Emotions and Physic/Health.

Central University of Haryana (CUH) has done a lot for the empowerment of Women, from its very inception since 2009. It is also said that:

> "यत्र नार्यस्तु पूज्यन्ते रमन्ते तत्र देवता:"।
> Where women are worshipped, there the Gods reside.

Therefore, the time has come to respect women and give them their due place in the society, otherwise a time would come when we will fail as a society, as a country and there would be nobody to save us. The time has come.

Notes

1. Status of Women in India: Problems and Concerns: A study by Centre for Study of Society and Secularism, Mumbai.
2. www.iipsenvis.nic.in/database/figuresataglance_4127.aspx accessed on July 11, 2014.
3. *Source*: Registrar General of India, Census 2011.
4. http://cw.routledge.com/textbooks/9780415485432/10.asp accessed on July 11, 2014.
5. http://philosophynow.org/issues/69/Becoming_A_Woman_Simone_de_Beauvoir on Female Embodiment accessed on July 11, 2014.
6. http://cw.routledge.com/textbooks/9780415485432/10.asp accessed on July 11, 2014.
7. http://timesofindia.indiatimes.com/india/Women-account-for-just-22-of-workforce-in-India /article show/26548372 .cms accessed on July 11, 2014.
8. file:///C:/Users/Vijay%20Kumar/Downloads/FlashBook2013-14.pdf accessed on July 11, 2014.
9. http://www.educationforallinindia.com/secondary-education-in-india-universalizing-opportunity-by-world-bank.pdf accessed on July 11, 2014.
10. http://aishe.nic.in/aishe/viewDocument.action?documentId=141 accessed on July 11, 2014.
11. India_factsheet_economic_n_hdi.pdf (undp) accessed on July 11, 2014.
12. University is situated in this district of Haryana and along with providing education, it also try to sensitize people of the area regarding such vital issues.
13. http://timesofindia.indiatimes.com/city/chandigarh/Haryanas-Mahendergarh-records-biggest-fall-in-child-sex-ratio/articleshow/20219311.cms accessed on July 11, 2014.
14. http://unesdoc.unesco.org/images/0010/001095/109590eo.pdfInternational Commission on Education for the Twenty-first Century.

2

Women Education

A Comparative Study of Hindu and Muslim Community

Rajiv Kumar Singh

Gender as a class generally considered as a homogenous group but in India many criss-cross line (like religion caste, economic status, etc.) divides it in to numerous sub-groups. The twenty-first century is considered as a century of knowledge and scholars like Michel Focault equated knowledge with the power. Knowledge is gained through the education. So, an educationally deprived person is not only devoid of knowledge but also from the power sharing.

Women in India is one such group which deprived from their say in the major socio-political culture due to comparatively low education and this deprivation is not homogenous as many of the patriarchal construct (which have their roots in the religious ethos) affected the different section of women in different ways.

The present paper is based on the field study of Varanasi district in which attempt was made to explore the factors affecting Hindu and Muslim girl child education.

India contains a medley of religious and linguistic groups. These are the two grounds (religion and language) which Constitution of India recognizes for identifying the minority groups in India. Religion is an important source of group identity and social solidarity in India. According to Census 2001 out of total population of 1,028,610,328 of the country, Muslims constitute the second largest religious group in India and thus largest religious minority. The 2001 census enumerated India's Muslim population at over 138 million and by 2006 the Muslim population would be over 150 million. In the term of numbers Muslim concentration is highest in Uttar Pradesh but in terms of percentage only in four States i.e. Jammu & Kashmir (67%), Assam (30.9%), West Bengal (25.2%) and Kerala (24.77%). Muslim population is more than 20 per cent. It is found that Muslim concentration is not uniform and they are concentrated in few pockets/ locality of various districts. The sex ratio among this religious community according to 2001 census is 936. The literacy rate among this community is 59 per cent while among Muslim women is 50 per cent this show wide disparity between male and female.

It is often believed that education which a society provides for its women and their social position are closely interrelated. Improvement in women's social status is generally accompanied by the advance in their education and a corresponding change in its character. That is why 'the movement for improving women's status all over the world has always emphasized education as the most significant instrument for changing women's subjugated position in the society.[1]

The purpose of present research is to explore the role of societal factors determining the educational level of women. Also it is reflection of the progress of social advancement. In the Vedic phase there are instances when women were so advanced in the learning that they challenged men of acknowledged learning in public discussion on philosophical and metaphysical subjects.

In the post Vedic phase of civilization female education received a great setback due to the deterioration of the religious status of women and lowering of the marriage age. The girls gradually lost the privilege of *Upanayana*, the Vedic initiation, and were not considered fit to recite Vedic mantras or perform Vedic sacrifices. In the Vedic period the girls were married at about the age of 16 or 17, but during this period the marriageable age lowered down to 12. Girls in rich, aristocratic and royal families, however, continued to receive a fairly good literary education. Besides, the study of Sanskrit and Prakrit works, they were given a good grounding in domestic arts, culminary arts and fine arts like music, dancing, painting, household decoration and garland making. Educated ladies in cultured families had been known to have contributed to literature.

In the Medieval period percentage of literary among women went down very rapidly during the Muslim rule. Society as a whole became prejudiced against female education. The *pardah* system stood in the way of girls beyond a certain age being sent to schools, through very young girls has some schooling where possible.

In the 19th century, touched by the work done by missionaries and philanthropic Englishmen, several great Indians lent their support to the opening of girls' school and breaking down the traditional popular resistances against women education. Among them, Raja Ram Mohan Roy and Pandit Ishwarchandra Vidyasagar played an important role.

The recommendations of the Indian Education Commission (1882-83) on women education included the support of girls' school from Public Funds, the payment of liberal grants-in-aid, the offer of freeships, the scholarship, the raising up a class of women for teaching girls through various plans, etc. Unfortunately, the government could not assign adequate grants for the purpose due to a period of financial stringency that follow the report of the commission, and therefore, the progress of women education mostly depended on private enterprise. By 1901-02, private effort accounted for 11 out of 12 women colleges, 365 out of 422 secondary schools, 3,982 out of 5,305 primary schools and 32 out of 45 training institutions for women. One significant development during the period was the opening of a career in medicine for women. In 1901-02, there were 76 women in medical colleges and 166 in medical schools. The lady Dufferin fund was created for developing medical education for women.

The period between the appointments of the Indian Universities Commission in 1902 and the transfer of education to Indian control in 1921 showed better progress in the education of women mainly due to the great public awakening and First World War. By 1921-22, there were 19 colleges for women, 675 secondary schools and 21,956 primary schools for girls. The burden still lay heavy on private efforts; though direct government effort had considerably increased. A very significant development of this period was the considerable rise in the age of marriage. This naturally increased the educational opportunities for the girls and their continuance in school and colleges. The demand of educated men themselves to have educated wives gave further period was the establishment of S.N.D.T. Women's University in Bombay by Maharshi D.K. Karve in 196. In 1921-22 there were 197 in medical colleges and 334 in medical schools, 67 in colleges for teaching and 3,903 in schools for teaching. A large number of women took up commercial and technical careers.

Table 2.1: Percentage of enrolment among boys and girls in pre-independence period

Year	*Percentage of Boys Enrolled*	*Percentage of Girls Enrolled*
1881-82	94.4	5.6
1886-87	92.2	7.8
1891-92	90.8	9.2
1896-97	90.5	9.5
1901-02	88.2	11.8
1906-07	87.8	12.2
1911-12	85.7	14.3
1916-17	84.0	16.0
1921-22	82.7	17.3
1926-27	83.3	16.7
1931-32	80.4	19.6
1936-37	77.7	22.3
1941-42	76.8	23.2
1946-47	76.6	23.4

Source: Women's Education in India[2].

Table 2.1 shows the ratio of male and female in enrolment before the independence. There was a decline in between 1921-22 and 1926-27, as this was the phase of national movement when women actively participated in the national uprising. However, rise in the proportion in the next phase Rise in the age of marriage, the teachings of Mahatma Gandhi, the phenomenal awakening of Indian womanhood, introduction of provincial autonomy in 1937 are the few favourable factors that helps in the promotion of women education after 1920. Nonetheless it was also a period of financial stringency and political struggle. In spite of difficulties, women education made considerable progress. In 1946-47 there were 59 arts and science colleges for women 2,370 secondary schools for girls, 21,479 primary schools for girls and 4,288 institutions for professional, technical and special education for women. Owing to greater initiative shown by the State Governments and local bodies, the burden on private effort was considerably reduced and now it accounted for 16.979 women institutions out of a total of 28,196 women institutions. The period also showed an increase in the trend towards co-education. By 1947, a little more than half of the numbers of girls under instruction were studying in a mixed school.

A substantial advance in women's education as also in other sphere of education, as also in other sphere of education, came about only after independence. Figures in below mentioned table already indicates this Table 2.2.

Table 2.2: Women education after Independence

Year	Primary Class	Middle Class	High School	College and Universities
1950-51	53.08 (39)	5.34 (20)	1.61 (15)	0.40 (14)
1973-74	244.01 (62)	45.37 (43)	23.40 (36)	9.0 (31)

Note: Numbers in lakhs; figures in parentheses indicate the number of girls for every 100 boys enrolled.

The figure show remarkable expansion of women education both in terms as well as relatively to the educational advance among men during the last quarter of a century. In spite of this expansion enrolment of girls at all the stages still lags behind that of boys. This is clear from the abovementioned figure (Table 2.2). The rate of dropouts among the females is also quite high at the primary stage where out of every 100 girls enrolled in class I only about 30 reach class V, and almost half of those dropout leave school in class I itself. This has serious consequences for female literacy which has inched from 7.93 percentages in 1951 to 18.44 in 1971 (as against male literacy which raise from 24.95 to 39.51 in the same period which itself is not a very commendable advance).

Muslim Women in India

The invasion of the country by the Muslims in 11th century brought about further deterioration of the position of woman. Restriction on her rights and freedom and her resultant hardships were aggravated. Women were forcibly taken away to be slave or to marry in to Muslim homes. The consequent insecurity and instability further narrowed down woman's social liberties.

On the one hand, the foreign Muslim conquerors attempted to impose their coercive norms on the conquered Hindu population; on the other hand, the Hindu society itself became more and more rigid curtailing thereby the rights and freedom of the lower castes and women. Due to this two fold reason, the post puranic period is one of the darkest periods for women in Indian history. The steady deterioration of her status continued till the nineteenth century. Polygamy and the *pardah* were two most important social institutions of the Muslim conqueror of India. Under the *purdah* system, not only were the women required to live in a secluded apartment in the house, but also they had to dress in apparel which completely covered their body excepting the eyes.[3]

They developed *purdah*, illiteracy, disease, legal discrimination and handicaps but the worst part of their fate is the male dominance in their society and their century old dumbness.[4]

The Hindus did not assimilate the customs like divorce, widow remarriage and a larger share of property for women, which governed the Muslim society. The Hindu society had become so static and rigidified that their contact with the Muslims, whose social relations were relatively democratic, did not prompt them to adopt the democratic elements of the Muslim society. The Hindu society continued its old pattern of life based on the principles and directions of Manu.

The Arya Samaj founded in 1875 focused on reform along the lines of caste, idolatry, polygamy and the seclusion of widows. Its exclusive concern with Hindu women "led it towards intolerance towards both Muslims and Christians".[5] Furthermore, it implicitly addressed itself to middle-class Hindu women, where the above-mentioned practices were limited to a small section of society. Therefore, it effectively sidelined the concerns of poor women, including Muslim women. The social reform debate elicited differing responses from Muslims. Modernist views on women were influenced by Western critiques of Islam – particularly the practice of *purdah*, the lack of women's education, and their discrimination within Muslim law. Modernists argued for the abolition of traditional gender roles, reform in Muslim law, and a greater public role for Muslim women based on the principle of equal rights. Concerns for women's education were also reflected in the newly available print medium. Khwaja Altaf Husain Hali's 1905 novel *Chup Ki Dad* (Voices of the Silent) vividly captured the reality of women's oppression. Hali argued for female education; although he felt this should be imparted at home. Mumtaz Ali and his wife Mohammadi Begum founded a newspaper *Tahzib-un-Niswan* (Women's Reformer) which took up the issues of female education, the age of marriage, the importance of a girl's consent to marriage, polygamy, a woman's role in marriage and *purdah*. Ameer Ali, a Bengali lawyer, author of the celebrated *The Spirit of Islam* (1922) argued against polygamy and emphasized the need for reform in Muslim law. Rokeya Shakhawat Hossain from Bengal (*b.* 1880)–an advocate of social reform–spoke out against the 'excessive absurdities'[6] of female seclusion. She was one of the few whose concerns included the bulk of poor, uneducated Muslim women. Individual and collective efforts notwithstanding, modernist views regarding education for Muslim women were not without their contradictions. Syyed Ahmed Khan urged Muslims to gain a modern secular education. His Islamic Anglo-Oriental College was later to become Aligarh Muslim University. However, his vision of modern education for Muslims did not include women. According to this great Muslim social reformer,

> "There could be no satisfactory education... for Muhammedan [Muslim] females until a large number of Muhammedan males [had] received a sound education."[7]

The *ulema's* position on women was based on the orthodox Islamic tradition symbolized by the notion of women as *fitna* (potential disorder). Accordingly, women's social interaction with men had to be regulated, which in effect translated into a control over female sexuality, and female seclusion from public space. Like the modernists, the *ulema* also favoured women's education but only insofar as it centered on religion (i.e. the *Quran*), family values and the moral virtue of women. This was hardly surprising given their view of the Muslim family as being based on sexual hierarchy and the social control of women.

Education—Gender and Religious Differentials

Despite pressures of religious orthodoxies, social prejudice and class/gender bias, Muslim women at the start of the twentieth century successfully emerged from the isolation of traditional roles as self-aware individuals, determined to claim a greater role in public affairs. The theme of women's education was taken up by all communities including Muslims. At the beginning of the twentieth century regional differences existed in the levels of education for Muslims depending upon their socio-economic location and local needs. Certain reports[8] by colonial authorities sought to create the impression that Muslims were opposed to the idea of Western education and that Muslim women were prevented from being educated. Regional reviews of education, however, refuted such generalizations, pointing to the differing levels of Western education among Muslims, depending upon their socio-economic status. Large disparities existed in levels of Muslim female education, although these levels of participation were not conspicuously lower than among other Indian women. In the late nineteenth century, only 0.97 per cent of Hindu girls and 0.86 per cent of Muslim girls were attending recognized schools, and no Hindu or Muslim girls had passed the matriculation examination in either Bombay or Madras (Now Chennai).[9] According to a study in 1901-02, there were 44,695 female secondary students in British India; this represented 27 out of every 100,000 Hindu girls and four out of every 100,000 Muslim girls. Yet, in the United Provinces there were only four Hindu girls attending secondary public school compared to 28 Muslim girls. Enrolment figures for Muslim girls in 1902 placed them ahead of Hindu girls in the provinces of Bombay, Madras and the United Provinces, while they lagged behind in Bengal and Punjab.[10]

Table 2.3: School enrolment figure for boys and girls, 1897-1902

Province	*Hindu*	*Muslim*
Bengal	2.0	0.8
Bombay	3.7	40.
Central Provinces	1	2.3
Madras	3.1	5.9
Punjab	1.6	0.5
United Provinces	0.3	0.7

Source: Fourth Quinquennial Review of Education, India 1897–1902, Supdt. of Government Printing, Calcutta, 1904, p. 308.

Figures for 1922-27 indicate that even though Muslim enrolment was lower than the average of all other communities, there was a rise in girl scholars in Bihar, the Central Provinces and Orissa.[11] This study found that the Muslim population of British India (1922-27) was 59.5 million or 24 per cent of the total population; and on the whole, Muslim pupils under instruction were also 24 per cent of the total population. The 1931 census figures of illiteracy rates were 91.6 per cent for Hindus and 93.6 per cent for Muslims.[12] By 1937; the average rate of Muslim girls' education throughout India had surpassed the national average.

The post-independence scenario is not much different from the pre-independence period. According to government reports, Muslim women are among the poorest, educationally disenfranchised, economically vulnerable, politically marginalized group in the country. In 1983, the Gopal Singh Committee instituted by the government, declared Muslim as a "backward" community in India.[13] A central feature of this "backwardness" is their exceedingly poor socio-economic status, particularly of Muslim women. Most Muslim women remain "invisible" workers in the informal economy. The Muslim share in public employment is less than 3 per cent.[14] Within this picture of marginalization, it is a predictable certainty that the corresponding figures for Muslim women are further skewed towards the bottom. A lack of information on Muslim women contributes to the reinforcement of cultural stereotypes, serving to obfuscate their life experiences and struggles. Consequently, the notion that Muslim women's status in India is attributable to certain intrinsic, immutable "Islamic" features or that their social status derives solely from Muslim law is widely prevalent.

Field Study

The present research aims to trace out the factors that affect the educational level and awareness among Hindu and Muslim girls in the urban areas of the Varanasi district. Average literacy rate of the district in 2011 were 77.05 compares to 66.12 per cent of 2001. If things looked out at gender-wise, male and female literacy were 85.12 per cent and 68.20 per cent respectively in 2011. For 2001 census, same figure stood at 77.87 per cent and 53.05 per cent in Varanasi district. Total literate in Varanasi district were 2,468,572 of which male and females were 1,426,908 and 1,041,664 respectively. Thus there is a big gap between male and female literacy rate in the district. Traditionally, Varanasi is a seat of learning, however in the past two decades the city transform itself in tune with modern education system and it becomes an important educational hub for the eastern Uttar Pradesh.

Methodology

Varanasi Municipal Corporation is divided in to 90 wards. For the purpose of the data collection 20 wards (roughly 22% of the total) have been selected through the process of purposive random sampling. The wards has been selected on the basis of demographic composition (i.e. having both Hindu and Muslim population). These wards are: Sunderpur, Tulsipur, Nadesar, Shivpurva, Alaipura, Nai Basti, Konia, Kazipura, Lallapura, Sigra, Khojwa, Jangambadi Daranagar, Birdopur, Jalalipura, Luxa, Pan Dariba, Rewari Talab, Dashaswamedh, and Madanpura. Opinion has been taken from the respondents through questionnaire method and the focus is on the girls of 12 to 25 years age and their parents who are continuing their study or dropouts. The sample size of the study is 400 (200 Hindu and 200 Muslim respondents).

Findings

It was found that nearly 60 per cent of the Varanasi population is below than the 5 year age-group. So, the potential for the spread of education and henceforth development is quite strong. The primordial tendencies of discrimination lead to a comparatively less enrolment and high dropout rates among the females. This fact is very much evident from the census data of 1991, 2001 and 2003. The dropout rate after the enrolment in the primary education is almost 50 per cent point in the females. The phase of primary to middle level of education witnesses the highest rate of dropout. Also there is also steep dropout in the male literacy, but in term of percentage and in numbers this dropout is less than the females. Most of the respondents (more than 70%) belongs to the age-group of 14-21. During the study it was found that progressive families are giving more years for education of the girl child.

Caste is still an important factor in the determination of the socio-cultural ethos of the families and education is no exception to it. Most of the Muslim respondents are from the other backward category. Even at the national level Ashraf (high caste Muslims) constitute nearly 15 per cent of the total population while Ajlaf constitutes nearly 82 per cent of the total Muslim population in India.

There is a steep drop in the women education especially from senior secondary to graduation level of the study and this drop is much steeper among the Muslim girls and 17 per cent of the respondents have carried their education up to post graduation level in which 88.23 per cent are Hindus and 11.77 are Muslims.

Caste-wise the data speaks of different picture. Highest percentage of illiterate respondents is from schedule caste categories and in term of volume, the highest rate of dropout is among the other backward classes especially from senior secondary to graduate level and graduation and post-graduation level. It was also found in the study that family size and educational status has a direct relation and in small and medium sized families the urge towards the educational attainment is comparatively more than the larger families.

Parent's education plays an important role in the determination of the educational awareness and attainment of the girl. Although it can't be established as a universal fact, but it can be establish as a significant factor in the determination of educational awareness among the females in general. The mean educational level for both the parents among the muslim is less than the mean of the education among the Hindu girls and findings refers that mean educational attainment of the Muslim girl respondent is less than the Hindu girl respondent. So, it establishes a direct relation between educational level of the parents and their girls' child.

Finding establishes that economic condition plays an important role in the educational attainment of the respondent in particular and the female literacy in general. The average the monthly income of the parents of the Hindu respondent is relatively higher than the average of the monthly income of the Muslim respondents and the mean average educational attainment of the Muslim girls respondent is less than the Hindu girls. This approves a direct relation between the economic conditions of the respondents and their educational attainment.

From the field experiences it can be deduced that since the educational level of the parents of the respondents is low, there income is low and since the income of these parents is low, their children's educational attainment is also low. It is a kind of low income–low education vicious cycle which needs a kind of supportive infusion either from the state apparatus or from the civil society. Second, as from the aforesaid analysis it is evident that monthly income of the parents of the Muslim respondent is comparatively low. So, Muslim respondent educational status is relatively low due to low monthly income.

The preference of Muslim community is more toward the '*Deeni Talim*' or in simple term 'religious education' and not towards the modern educational system. That's why still Madarassa system of education is quite prevalent among the Muslims. Secondly, it is observed that government school is almost absent in the most of the

Muslim dominated area. Thirdly, the educational culture of the government school is much tilted towards the Hindu way of life and there is mark absence of pure secular educational culture, as most of the prayers, worships, celebrations, etc. are mostly influenced by the Hindu religion. It seems a kind of majoritarian hegemony which makes feel religious or cultural minority isolated.

Another important phenomenon that has observed is that many unregistered schools and Madarassas that are established in the Muslim locality, generally imparts a mixture of *Deeni Talim* and *Duniyavi Talim*. These schools are run on charity and donation by the fellow community members.

It was observed during the study that Muslim respondents comparatively face more problems in the continuation of their study than the Hindu respondents. It is clear that economic condition of the respondents and their parents plays an important role in the determination of educational attainment. Basically, it is problem with the most of the respondents of the low income group. Since, the number of Muslims in the low income group is more, the Muslim respondents frequently are more in this group. Among the 'other reasons' category, the non-willingness of the parents for the continuation of their girl child is important. For some the pressure of marriage is intense by kins and relatives and this obstructing their urge of education. Likewise during interaction some respondents said that there is no school of the secondary level in their locality and they were not supposed to travel far, due to security reasons. So, there are different kinds of factors which are creating problem in girl education in universe of study in particular and in India in general.

Discrimination between boys and girls education is very common feature in the patriarchal society like India. Boy's education in most of the families is considered as indispensable matter while education of the girls are second in the priority list and a matter of plenty. During the study it was found that still the social norms carrying the imprints of the patriarchal society where educational preferences to the girl child is still a matter of secondary importance and this tendency is more among the family of the muslim respondents.

Regarding the social values and norms it is found in the study that the predominant social values and norms are still carrying the basic premises of the patriarchal society and these premises are well carried forward by the current generation. As the response reflects there is big gap in the perception in the average ideal age of marriage for the boys and girls. Also, if we see the difference on the socio-religious dimension we found that this difference is steeper in the Muslim community than the Hindus. Secondly, in both the socio-religious groups the average ideal age for the marriage for the girls is far less than the average ideal age for marriage for the boys. It reflects that in both the community social structure is predominantly patriarchal and preference for late marriage for the boys is comparatively more.

During the study it was found that respondents of both the socio-religious groups are of the opinion that boy's education up to higher level is relatively more important than the girl's education. The social construct of the patriarchal society is has its implications on the younger generation also.

The feeling of being less importance than the boys among the girls is found in many of the families. This is a kind of the social construct that emerges from the family and especially by the parents and other near relatives.

Conclusion

The aforesaid findings speaks that socio-cultural factors are an important determinants of the girls education in India. Since, many of the socio-cultural norms follow the religious line, educational status of the girls varies on the religious lines. Islam has a comparatively close value structure regarding women and a large chunk of the muslim population is still away from the mainstream developmental process (as evident from the Rangnath Mishra Committee, Sachar Committee, NSSO, 61st round report) which results in comparatively low educational level and low level of urge and awareness among the girls of the muslim community.

Notes

1. Indian Council of Social Science Research, Status of Women in India: A Synopsis of the Report of the National Committee in the Status of Women, Allied, New Delhi, 1975, p. 88.
2. Agrawal, S.P., Aggrawal, J.C., *Women's Education in India: Historical Review Present Status Perspective Plan*, Concept Publishing Company Pvt. Ltd., New Delhi, 1994, p. 113.

3. Desai Neera, *Women in Modern India*, Vora and Company, Bombay, 1957, p. 23.
4. Sinha, Niroj, *Women and Violence*,Vikas Publishing House, New Delhi, 1989, pp. 47-48.
5. Spear, P., *A History of India*, Vol. 2, UK, Penguin Book, 1956, p. 167.
6. Hasan Zoya, (ed.) *Forging Identities: Gender, Communities and the State, Kali for Women*, 1994, p. 12.
7. Jalal A., 'The Convenience of Subservience: Woman and the State of Pakistan, in D. Kandiyoti (ed.) *Woman, Islam and the State*, London MacMillan, 1991, p. 81.
8. Hunter, W.W., *The Indian Mausalmans*, 1871, quoted by Lateef, *ibid.*, p.38.
9. First Quinquennial Review of Education, cited in Lattef, *ibid.*, pp. 48-49.
10. First Quinquennial Review of Education, cited in Lattef, *ibid.*, pp. 48-49.
11. Ninth Quinquennial Review of Education, quoted in Lateef, *Muslim Women* in India, *op. cit.*
12. *Ibid.*, *op. cit.*, p. 51.
13. https://www.eastwestcenter.org/fileadmin/resources/education/asdp_pdfs/frontline-phoenix_1_.pdf
14. Sachar Committee Report, 2005.

PART II
Women Empowerment: Through Political Representation

3
Examining Women Empowerment through Representation in Pakistan
Who Gets to Represent Whom?

Muhammad Usman Amin Siddiqi

Introduction

Politics has been defined and understood in as many ways as the academic disciplines are; in its narrower sense to mean art of government or public affairs, and in its wider sense to mean as a game of power, irrespective of level (global, state, local, workplace, family etc.). In order to distinguish criminality from politics, the element of legitimacy is attached with power to mean politics. This legitimacy may come from Constitution, law, religion, morality, ethics, or social norms. Therefore, politics can be conceptualized as anything to attain, retain, or exercise of legitimate power offered by law of the land or norms embedded in economic and social configurations of society.

Power is normally defined as an ability to do or get things done. The word comes from Latin, *potere*, which refers to potentiality and means 'to be able'. However, the notion that power is an *ability* to do things is over simplifying, if not misleading. "In its emphasis on concerted agency, the Latin root obscures the significance of power's dispersion, circulation, and microphysical mechanics, its often automatic rather than intentional workings, and its detailed imbrication with knowledge, language, and thought."[1] Moreover, considering power a quality undermines its meanings as a relation, especially the one that makes and shapes social order and human subjects. Furthermore, the notion of power as ability is also oppugned by incommensurability between what holder of power intends and what power actually does.

Empowerment refers to conferring legality or sanctioning of legitimate power to an individual or a group. Women empowerment denotes empowering women—not necessarily in terms of achieving power to dominate others but in terms of gaining control over their own lives and securing equal rights to that of men in a given society. The aforementioned complexity attached with the concept of power entails multidimensionality of the concept of women empowerment as well. Women's empowerment, with its political, economic, social, religious, cultural, psychological, and personal elements, is a fluid and emerging concept; which has been catapulted in significance with feminism and development literature in last quarter of twentieth century. Like the concept of power, women empowerment is also context-specific and multiple actors, agencies, and determinants can create supportive or inauspicious environment for it.

Political empowerment is the highest level of women empowerment, which is a result of social and economic empowerment of women and, in turn, ensures continuity of their social and economic empowerment. Political empowerment is, *inter alia*, gauged by women representation in government in general and in national legislatures in particular. Women representation in Pakistan's national legislature is 19.3 per cent,[2] which is third highest in South Asia, higher than almost two-thirds of Muslim countries, and higher than the average of the Asia (18.3%). But unfortunately this ranking does not commensurate with the rank of Pakistan in terms of women status in society or women empowerment—approaching 150th in the world. This chapter analyses why political empowerment through representation of women has not brought fruits in terms of equal rights for women and their real empowerment in society. The chapter would examine available lines of arguments to explain the incommensurability between political representation and socio-economic empowerment of women in Pakistani society.

Women Empowerment: Unraveling the Conundrum

Women empowerment, as mentioned earlier, is a fluid concept, which has been defined in a variety of ways, but in general the concept is linked with gender equality and equity. Feminists believe in structured discrimination of women in society, as Kate Millett, an American feminist writer, defines politics as "power structured relationships—arrangements whereby one group of persons is controlled by another."[3] They are concerned with politics of everyday life, whereby women are subjugated by men against their will; and therefore, the ultimate goal of women empowerment is gender equality and equity in family, employment, and politics.

The fluid and multidimensional nature of the concept of women empowerment must be realized before measuring it in a given society and making any interventions to ensure it. In general, the concept of women empowerment is related to changes in social structures and human relations and to individual power to change to make women more and more equal to men.[4] Different scholars and institutions weigh these aspects differently and add different elements to define women empowerment: fundamental human rights, access to basic necessitates of life,[5] land rights, food security, employment in formal and informal sectors,[6] control over sexuality and reproductive choices,[7] control over one's life through mobilization and participation,[8] access to information, economic and social resources, and autonomy in decision-making.[9]

There are as many varying views regarding the sources of women empowerment as its definition: state policies and laws, social norms, and individual efforts and initiatives. The most popular view about the sources of women empowerment holds that empowerment is context-specific and social norms and traditions are the most important determinants of women empowerment. A similar view is held by the post-structuralist writers who do not understand power in explicit scene of domination or rule-giving, but embedded in a variety of domains and discourses, including those normally considered to be free of power (sexual desire or arts, for example). They equate power with knowledge and consider it dispersed everywhere in the form of norms and traditions, in the knowledge about one's own identity and about the law of truth that dictates him to recognize himself and others in a particular way and act in a desirable manner of that knowledge.[10] While state policies and laws allocate authoritative values to social norms and traditions, individual initiatives and efforts have also been emphasized as a source of women empowerment.

The Gender-related Development Index (GDI), Gender Empowerment Measure (GEM), Gender Gap Index (GGI) used as measurement indices were replaced by Gender Inequality Index (GII) in 2010.[11] Though measuring women empowerment using these quantitative indices is useful for policy-makers, these indices lack subjective and lived experiences and do not take into consideration the context-specificity of the concept of women empowerment. Furthermore, empowerment is not a point at which a woman may one day arrive, but is a lifelong process; which may be reversed at time because of some change in political or social environment. A single legislation or judicial decision may reverse the process.

Representation: A Mean or a Goal of Women Empowerment

Women empowerment has political, economic, and social spheres. Empowerment in one sphere does not necessarily lead to empowerment in others, but they are definitely interlinked-creating conducive or impending context for one another. Political empowerment of women in a society portrays social and economic empowerment of women. It is because in order to achieve political empowerment in real sense, women should be empowered socially and economically, whereas politically empowered women, in turn, should strive to institutionalize social and economic empowerment of women through state intervention by laws and policies.

Women's access to the sphere of political decision-making is an important measure of women empowerment. Women constitute half of the world's population, and they must have their say in political decision-making, for which they must have representation in governments. No democratic system can justify its legitimacy or can successfully work with just half of its population. Like any employment, access to economic and social resources, or access to knowledge and options, access to political decision-making is also a right women must have just like men; but politics is considered something 'alien' to their nature.[12]

In modern representative democracy, the legitimate power to govern is linked with representation. Democracy works on the principle that representatives of people decide on their behalf and make authoritative allocation of resources and values in society. Representation is the central 'rule of the game' determining who governs. Therefore, in order to empower women, representation must be an ultimate goal.

There are different theories or models of representation: Trustee Model of representation holds that a representative is a trustee of his constituents' authority; and once elected, he would act on his own judgment and not on the whims of the constituents. Delegate Model, on the other hand, views representative as conduit conveying the opinions of his constituents. Mandate Model, developed after the emergence of modern party system, declares that people give mandate to party manifestos they outline before elections. Resemblance Model suggests that the legislature should mirror the population it is representing. In the words of John Adams, "a legislature should be an exact portrait, in miniature, of the people at large, as it should feel, reason, and act like them."[13] The model holds that only people belonging to a particular group, sharing the experiences of that group, can completely identify with the interests of that particular group. It is because putting oneself in the shoes of somebody else and having experienced what other people actually go through are two different things. Therefore, women in a given society should be represented by women.

Women representation is a prerequisite not only to justify legitimacy of political system or on the grounds of social justice, but is also indispensible because higher level of women's political representation will strike at the roots of gender hierarchy in public life and challenge the socio-cultural contexts impeding women empowerment by seen to be wielding power and articulating women's interests. It is because unless a group is not sufficiently visible in political arena and seem to wield political power, its ability to influence policy-making or political culture that forms the contours of representative system cannot be effective. Therefore, in order to make women related issues important in public policy calculus and to put them on political agenda, there must be sufficient number of women in legislatures and higher echelons of governmental machinery.

The idea is that a woman can understand the needs of her fellow women—women she is representing in legislature. A woman should understand the demands by other women and would strive to get them converted into decisions. Women representatives would make laws and policies aimed at developing and strengthening institutions of women empowerment on the principle of equality of women. Women representatives can have better access to their women constituents, can better understand their demands, and can better suggest befitting remedies. Critical mass of women in law and policy-making bodies can effectively assert their views to shape and prioritize women related policies of government to ensure socio-cultural and economic changes that may yield positive impact on women's access and control over social and economic resources, access to education and healthcare, and their control over their bodies, sexuality, and reproductive choices. Therefore, representation of women in political system of a country is not only a goal of women empowerment in itself but in turn also a mean to ensure and enhance women empowerment.

Regional Context of Women Representation and Leadership (South Asia)

A number of studies have presented and tried to theorize about the paradox of women leadership and women empowerment in South Asia. South Asia has more powerful women politicians than any other set of countries in the world. Women in South Asian countries have held positions of Presidents, Prime Ministers, leaders of major political parties, speaker/chair of the legislative assemblies, governors or chief ministers, and cabinet ministers. Yet, overall situation of women political participation in the region portrays a gloomy picture. The average membership of women in popular houses of parliaments is still around 8 per cent.[14] This phenomenon poses two important questions: (a) Despite being patriarchal societies and having paternalistic socio-cultural and political structures institutionalizing subordination of women, how have these countries produced so many politically prominent women? (b) Why there seems to be no implication of this predominance of women political leadership for women in their respective societies who normally send these women leaders to the echelons of the government. Why the overall condition of women in these societies has not been improved despite having been ruled by women? Why have they not done something to improve the plight of their gender, or why their leadership has not shown trickledown effect?

Apart from Presidents and Prime Ministers, South Asian countries have seen a number of other prominent women leaders holding key positions in government; for example, Speaker or Chair of Legislative Assemblies like Shirin Sharmin Chaudhury (Bangladesh) and Fahmida Mirza (Pakistan); Governors like Begum Dr. Habiba Sarobi (Bamyan, Afghanistan) Ra'ana Liaquat Ali Khan (Sindh, Pakistan), Sharada Mukherjee (Gujarat and Andhra Pradesh, India), Sheila Kaul

Table 3.1: Women Presidents and Prime Ministers in South Asia

Sr. No.	*Position*	*Country*	*Name*	*Tenure*
1.	President	India	Pratibha Devisingh Patil	2007-2012
		Sri Lanka	Chandrika Bandaranaike Kumaratunga	1994-2005
2.	Prime Minister	Bangladesh	Begum Khaleda Zia	1991-96 2001-06
		India	Indira Priyadarshini Gandhi	1966-77 1980-84
		Pakistan	Benazir Bhutto	1988-90 1993-96
		Sri Lanka	Sirimavo Bandaranaike	1960-65 1970-77 1994-2000
			Chandrika Bandaranaike Kumaratunga	Aug.-Nov. 1994

(Himachal Pradesh, India), V.S. Ramadevi (Karnataka, India), Jothi Venkatachalam (Kerala, India), Vijayalakshmi Pandit (Maharashtra, India), Pratibha Patil (Rajasthan, India), Fatima Beevi (Tamil Nadu, India), Margaret Alva (Uttarakhand, India), Sarojini Naidu (Uttar Pradesh, India), Padmaja Naidu (West Bengal, India); Chief Ministers like Anwara Taimur (Assam, India), Rabri Devi (Bihar, India), Uma Bharati (Madhya Pradesh, India), Nandini Satpathy (Orissa, India), Rajinder Kaur Bhattal (Punjab, India), Vasundhara Raje (Rajasthan, India), Janaki Ramachandran (Tamil Nadu, India), Sucheta Kriplani (Uttar Pradesh, India), and Mamata Banerjee (West Bengal, India); and important Cabinet Ministers like Dipu Moni (Foreign Minister, Bangladesh), Sahara Khatun (Home Minister, Bangladesh), Mariyam Shakeela (Foreign Minister, Maldives), and Hina Rabbani Khar (Foreign Minister, Pakistan).

Despite the fact that women have served in such high governmental positions, the overall representation of women in the countries of the region is not up to the mark. Following Table 3.2 shows women representation in South Asia:

Countries like Nepal, Afghanistan, Pakistan and Bangladesh, where percentage of women in national legislatures is comparatively high is because of quota system, and more importantly does not translate into real empowerment of women. For example, Afghanistan, traditionally not included in South Asian region before its membership of SAARC Countries, has second highest women representation in

Table 3.2: Percentage of Women in National Legislatures in South Asia

World Rank	*Country*	*Lower or Single House*				*Upper House*			
		Elections	*Seats*	*Women*	*% W*	*Elections*	*Seats*	*Women*	*% W*
36	Nepal	11 2013	575	172	29.9%	—	—	—	—
41	Afghanistan	9 2010	249	69	27.7%	1 2011	102	28	27.5%
73	Pakistan	5 2013	323	67	20.7%	3 2012	104	17	16.3%
77	Bangladesh	1 2014	348	69	19.8%	—	—	—	—
117	India	4 2014	543	62	11.4%	2 2014	243	29	11.9%
132	Bhutan	7 2013	47	4	8.5%	4 2013	25	2	8.0%
139	Maldives	3 2014	85	5	5.9%	—	—	—	—
140	Sri Lanka	4 2010	225	13	5.8%	—	—	—	—

Source: "Women in National Parliaments," Inter-Parliamentary Union website, accessed September 20, 2014, http://www.ipu.org/wmn-e/classif.htm.

national legislature in South Asia–27.7 per cent in lower house, Wolesi Jirga (House of the People) in September 2010 elections, and 27.5 per cent in upper house, Mesherano Jirga (House of Elders) in January 2011 elections.[15] Afghanistan is important *vis-à-vis* Pakistan's regional context for women representation because of cross-border ties of Pashtun community residing on both side of Durand Line. Although, women representation in Afghanistan is quite high (higher than the US),[16] this has not translated into real power, or even fair treatment of women in Afghanistan. "Noor Zia Atmar, a former parliamentarian, ended up in a battered women's shelter, and eventually fled the country after repeated beatings by her husband."[17] The high level of representation is because of the quota law enacted in 2004 reserving at least 27 per cent of seats for women. Recently, the women reserved quota has been reduced to 20 per cent, following a trend of regressing women's rights.[18] No wonder, Afghanistan along with Pakistan, and India constitute three out of five most dangerous countries for women.

India, though having witnessed highest number of women leaders on key governmental positions, still stands at 117th number in the world *vis-à-vis* percentage of women representation in national legislatures. A proposed bill, passed by Rajya Sabha in 2010 and awaiting clearance from Lok Sabha, stipulates 33 per cent seats for women in all legislative assemblies. It is hoped that proposed quota for women representation would help empower women in India, where gender-based violence keep claiming headlines time and again.[19] The

Source: Thomson Reuters Foundation.

Fig. 3.1: The World's Five Most Dangerous Countries for Women

good thing about women's political representation in India is that the current 11.7 per cent is without quota; but 632 women running for national legislature in recent general elections compared to 7527 men depicts lack of women empowerment owing to socio-cultural context of society. Socio-cultural context of women empowerment in India can be assessed by UNICEF's report that asserts that "50 million women are 'missing' in India as a result of female foeticide and infanticide,"[20] despite prenatal sex determination being banned since 1996. Women's access to education is distinctly limited compared to men. Literacy rate among men is 76 per cent, whereas, that among women stands at 54 per cent, which further limits their chances of entry in politics—an example of how lack of socio-cultural empowerment of women impedes their political participation.

Representation and Women Empowerment in Pakistan

Pakistan, as mentioned earlier, has quite satisfactory representation of women compared to its regional and religious context–3rd highest in South Asia and higher than almost two-thirds of Muslim countries. Table 3.3 shows percentage of women representation in lower houses, upper houses, and combined in both houses of national legislatures of the Muslim countries in descending order. The table would also help in analyzing the religious context of Pakistan.

Table 3.3: Percentage of Women in National Legislatures of Muslim Countries

Sr. No.	Country	Single / Lower House		Upper House		Total
		Election	%	Election	%	%
1.	Senegal	7 2012	43.3			43.3
2.	Mozambique	10 2009	39.2			39.2
3.	Uganda	2 2011	35.0			35.0
4.	Guyana	11 2011	31.3			31.3
5.	Tunisia	10 2011	28.1			28.1
6.	Afghanistan	9 2010	27.7	1 2011	27	27.6
7.	Cameroon	9 2013	31.1	4 2013	20	27.1
8.	Turkmenistan	12 2013	26.4			26.4
9.	Algeria	5 2012	31.6	12 2012	7	25.7
10.	Iraq	4 2014	25.3			25.3
11.	Sudan	4 2010	24.3	5 2010	17	23.8
12.	Kyrgyzstan	10 2010	23.3			23.3
13.	Mauritania	11 2013	25.2	11 2009	14	22.2
14.	Guinea	9 2013	21.9			21.9
15.	Albania	6 2013	20.0			20.0
16.	Saudi Arabia	1 2013	19.9			19.9
17.	Bangladesh	1 2014	19.8			19.8
18.	Kazakhstan	1 2012	25.2	8 2011	6	19.8
19.	Pakistan	5 2013	20.3	3 2012	16	19.4
20.	Uzbekistan	12 2009	22.0	1 2010	15	19.2
21.	Burkina Faso	12 2012	18.9			18.9
22.	Bahrain	10 2010	10.0	11 2010	28	18.8
23.	Togo	7 2013	17.6			17.6
24.	UAE	9 2011	17.5			17.5
25.	Indonesia	4 2014	16.8			16.8
26.	Libya	6 2014	16.0			16.0
27.	Gabon	12 2011	15.0	1 2009	17	15.8
28.	Azerbaijan	11 2010	15.6			15.6
29.	Chad	2 2011	14.9			14.9
30.	Tajikistan	2 2010	15.9	3 2010	12	14.4
31.	Turkey	6 2011	14.4			14.4
32.	Malaysia	5 2013	10.4	N.A.	29	14.2
33.	Somalia	8 2012	13.8			13.8
34.	Guinea-Bissau	4 2014	13.7			13.7
35.	Niger	1 2011	13.3			13.3
36.	Djibouti	2 2013	12.7			12.7
37.	Sierra Leone	11 2012	12.1			12.1
38.	Jordan	1 2013	12.0	10 2013	12	12.0
39.	Syria	5 2012	12.0			12.0
40.	Suriname	5 2010	11.8			11.8

(Contd.)

Table 3.3: (*Contd.*)

Sr. No.	Country	Single / Lower House		Upper House		Total
		Election	%	Election	%	%
41.	Morocco	11 2011	17.0	10 2009	2	11.0
42.	Oman	10 2011	1.2	10 2011	18	9.6
43.	Mali	11 2013	9.5			9.5
44.	Gambia	3 2012	9.4			9.4
45.	Benin	4 2011	8.4			8.4
46.	Nigeria	4 2011	6.7	4 2011	6	6.6
47.	Maldives	3 2014	5.9			5.9
48.	Lebanon	6 2009	3.1			3.1
49.	Iran	5 2012	3.1			3.1
50.	Comoros	12 2009	3.0			3.0
51.	Kuwait	7 2013	1.5			1.5
52.	Yemen	4 2003	0.3	4 2001	2	0.7
53.	Qatar	7 2013	0.0			0.0

Source: Based on data from Inter-Parliamentary Union as of September 1, 2014.

Pakistan has also witnessed women leaders of national stature before and after partition. Begum Shah Nawaz, an active Muslim women leader in United India, represented Muslim women in Round Table Conferences, Geneva session of League of Nations in 1931, and ILO in 1935.[21] She is famous for her demand of women quota in legislative assembly of United India, efforts for recognition of women's right to inheritance of property in Muslim Personal Law of Sharia in 1948, and representing women in first constituent assembly of Pakistan along with Begum Shaista Ikramullah. Begum Ra'ana Liaqat Ali Khan, a prominent figure of freedom movement and Pakistan's first lady, struggled for women's socio-cultural uplift throughout her political career, and founded All Pakistan Women's Association (APWA). Likewise Miss Fatima Jinnah, Begum Muhammad Ali Jauhar, Begum Salma Tassaduq Hussain, Abadi Begum, popularly known as 'Bi Amma', Lady Sughra Hidayatullah, Geti Ara Bashir Ahmed, Begum Viqarunnisa Noon, Lady Nusrat Haroon, and Begum Nawab Muhammad Ismail are some of the worth mentioning women leaders of freedom movement who continued to participate in politics after 1947.

Benazir Bhutto (Two-time Prime Minister of Pakistan), Nusrat Bhutto (Chairperson of Pakistan People's Party), Fahmida Mirza (Speaker National Assembly), and Hina Rabbani Khar (Foreign Minister) are the prominent women who served on key positions in Pakistan's post-independence politics. Although Pakistan was the first

Muslim country to elect a women as head of national government, the overall picture of women representation in national legislature has been gloomy since 1947. Table 3.4 shows women representation in lower house (popularly elected) of parliaments in Pakistan.

Table 3.4: Women Representation in Parliaments in Pakistan

Sr. No.	*Legislatures*	*Total Seats*	*Women Elected Directly*	*Women Reserved Seats*	*Seats Held by Women*	
					Number	*Percentage*
1.	1st Legislature (10-08-1947 to 24-10-1954)	30	—	—	2	6.7%
2.	2nd Legislature (02-05-1955 to 07-10-1958)	80	—	—	0	0%
3.	3rd Legislature (08-06-1962 to 12-06-1965)	156	6	—	6	3.8%
4.	4th Legislature (12-06-1965 to 25-03-1969)	156	6	—	6	3.8%
5.	5th Legislature (14-04-1972 to 10-01-1977)	144	6	—	6	4.2%
6.	6th Legislature (26-03-1977 to 05-07-1977)	210	1	10	11	5.2%
7.	7th Legislature (20-03-1985 to 29-05-1988)	217	1	21	22	10.1%
8.	8th Legislature (30-11-1988 to 06-08-1990)	217	4	20	24	11.1%
9.	9th Legislature (03-11-1990 to 17-07-1993)	217	2	—	2	0.9%
10.	10th Legislature (15-10-1993 to 05-11-1996)	217	4	—	4	1.8%
11.	11th Legislature (15-02-1997 to 12-10-1999)	217	6	—	6	2.8%
12.	12th Legislature (16-11-2002 to 15-11-2007)	342	13	61*	74	21.64%
13.	13th Legislature (17-03-2008 to 16-03-2013)	342	16	61*	77	22.51%
14.	14th Legislature (01-06-2013 to date)	342	8	61*	69	20.18%

Source: Pildat, Women Representation in Pakistan's Parliament.

In the first two Constitutions of Pakistan, 6 seats were reserved for women in National Assembly. The current Constitution of Pakistan stipulated that there would be 10 seats reserved for women for next 10 years or for next three general elections, whichever occurred later. The number was raised to 20 in 1985 by General Zia ul Haq, but then these seats lapsed after three general elections of 1977, 1985, and

1988; and therefore, there were no women reserved seats in elections of 1990, 1993, and 1997. Then General Pervaiz Musharraf increased the number of women reserved seats to 60 in 2002.

Currently women representation in Pakistan's National Assembly and Senate combined stands at 19.3 per cent. The number of women members of National Assembly is 69 out of 340 filled seats, out of which 8 women have been elected in general elections, 60 women have been elected on women reserved seats, and one woman member has been elected on minority reserved seat. The number of women in Senate currently stands at 17 out of 104 total seats, all of which are reserved seats (4 seats are reserved for women to be elected by each provincial assembly and one from federal capital). Moreover, 137 seats are reserved for women in provincial assemblies – 61 seats in Punjab Assembly, 37 in Sindh, 25 in Khyber-Pakhtunkhwa, and 14 seats in Balochistan Assembly. Seats reserved for women are allocated to political parties as per their general seats in National Assembly on the basis of list system.

The participation of women members of parliament is satisfactory, to say the least, in terms of parliamentary business. Following excerpt of a report by FAFEN (Free and Fair Election Network)[22] on women parliamentarian's performance fourth parliamentary year of 13th National Assembly of Pakistan gives an idea about the level of their participation:

> "The fourth parliamentary year was marked by passage of four pro-women bills... [including] Prevention of Anti-Women Practices (Criminal Law Amendment) Act 2011... Acid Control and Acid Crime Prevention Bill 2010... National Commission on the Status of Women Bill 2012... Women in Distress and Detention Fund (Amendment) Bill 2010... Single Female Members [authored] 20 out of the 53 Private Members' bills that appeared on the Orders of the Day in the fourth parliamentary year. Similarly, during the third parliamentary year, 17 out of 34 were authored by single female Members... [T]heir legislative interests encompass a variety of important national issues. They moved two bills each on criminal law, employment, elections and NADRA and one each on the Capital Development Authority (CDA), banking, child rights, food security, foreign affairs, health, housing and works, citizenship, and right to information.

> [They] contributed exceptionally to oversight of executive by putting up questions. Out of 2,365 questions raised during the fourth parliamentary year, more than half (1,196 or 51%) were put forward by female Members. On average, 16 questions were submitted by each female MNA, almost four times more than their male counterparts who raised 1,169 questions... [W]omen legislators were part of 75 of the total 97 Calling Attention Notices either individually or jointly with their male and female colleagues… Out of 1764 Points of Order raised in the House, the women parliamentarians' share was 252 or 14 per cent… The female representatives moved 42 Resolutions."[23]

Situational Analysis

The abovementioned facts and figures are impressive, and portray quite optimistic picture of women participation in parliamentary role in Pakistan. In fact women role in parliamentary business makes us believe that women are far more active and empowered than their male counterparts in legislature. But one cannot keep his eyes from looking back to the ground realities. Pakistan has been ranked 145th in Gender-related Development Index (GDI), 127th in Gender Inequality Index of 187 countries of the world. Pakistan has been ranked among top five most countries of the world by Thomson Reuters Foundation Survey from 213 experts from all over the world on the basis of sexual and non-sexual violence, health threats, tradition and/or religion, harmful practices rooted in culture, lack of access to economic resources and overall perception of danger.[24]

Socio-cultural practices in Pakistan pose serious threats to women empowerment in Pakistan. Forced or early age marriages, so-called honour killings (Karo Kari), dowry killings, *Purdah*, *Watta Satta*, *Swara* and *Wani*, and 'Marriage to *Quran*,' perpetuate subjugation of women in Pakistani society. Their right and liberties are constrained in the name of protection, modesty, and prevention of immoral activities. Women's access to education, healthcare, and gainful employment is limited because of socio-cultural and economic constraints.

Socio-cultural and economic indicators of political empowerment draw a deplorable image of Pakistani society. The most important parameter of women empowerment is ownership of land, which is systematically denied to women in Pakistan in general. In spite of the fact that Islam and the state laws allow women to inherit and have property, women in Pakistan normally do not own land; most of the cultural practices like Marriages to *Quran*, or to the boys of very young age, or to the brothers of deceased husband are aimed at depriving women of their inherited land. Even in cases where women do have property, they seldom exercise decision-making power *vis-à-vis* use, rent, or sale of that property, which is done by male members of the family. Access to other economic resources and employment is also very limited. They normally do not have access to formal sectors of employment; even when they do, they do not get equal pays to that of men. Women constitute major chunk of informal sector employment, where they are more vulnerable to exploitation. Where they are self-employed, there are very limited credit and extension services available to them, and because of limited access to markets, they have to rely on middlemen and sell their products cheaply.

The access to education is very limited for women in Pakistan. Parents normally do not send their girls to school in rural areas, and even when they do, they dropout early on account of financial limitations, early marriages, traditional beliefs. The condition of health sector in Pakistan is not up to the mark in general, but for women it is miserable to say the least. Women do not normally exercise reproductive choices either in terms of number or spacing of children, due to which they often face serious health issues. Frequent pregnancies in pursuit of male off springs lead, domestic violence, malnourishments, and treatment by pseudo doctors, quacks and *peers* often cause physical and psychological disorders.

This incommensurability between political representation of women in Pakistan and socio-cultural and economic indicators of women empowerment puts a question mark to the quota system of women representation adopted in Pakistan, or elsewhere in the world. The principle of reserved women seats is in place in around 40 countries on the premise that equal or proportional representation of women—no matter how it is accomplished–is the first step towards women empowerment and establishment of a more balanced system of governance. It is, no doubt, a very plausible argument, especially considering the performance of women in Pakistan's parliament. But the why this performance of women on reserved seats has not transformed into socio-economic empowerment of women at the grassroots level? Why women political leaders at the highest level of the government machinery and women in parliament on reserved seats don't seem to have any implication for the women whom they supposedly represent.

There can be two lines of arguments in response to this question: the first challenges the representation criteria or process through which these women elites come to power, whereas, the other argument challenges the whole idea of bringing change through legislation and state policies. Let's apply both of them to analyze the relation between political empowerment through representation and socio-economic empowerment of women.

The first explanation for incommensurability between representation and women empowerment at grassroots level challenges the criteria and the processes for the election of these women representatives on reserved seats. As mentioned earlier, the reserved seats are allocated to political parties as per their general seats in National Assembly on the basis of list system. But who gets to represent on reserved seats? The answer is kith and kin of top political leaders get to be elected on these reserved seats. The major chunk of the women on these reserved seats comprises of daughters, wives, sisters, sisters-in-law, and close relatives of the top leadership of different political parties. In 14th National Assembly of Pakistan elected in May 2013 general elections, the relatives of male political leaders have "have once again grabbed a lion's share of the reserved seats for women in both the National Assembly and provincial assemblies."[25] These reserved seats are also used by the political parties to get those women of their party elected who have otherwise lost in the general elections. "Some of the lucky women, who lost on May 11, are now members of the assemblies via the reserved seats route."[26]

What adds to the problem of women representation is the fact that the women who have been elected in general elections are also relatives of the top political leadership and belong to influential political families. Furthermore, most of them have been elected on the seats of their relatives after death, removal, or disqualification of male members of their family. Let's take the example of current national assembly. Total 8 women have been elected in general elections and all of them belong to influential political families with a history of male members of their family being former or current office holders.

Shazia Mubashir, elected from NA-129 (Lahore) on PML(N) ticket, got elected against the seat left vacated by Chief Minister Mian

Shehbaz Sharif, who kept his seat of provincial assembly. Ms. Shazia Mubashir contested the election after his husband Rana Mubashir was disqualified by Lahore High Court on account of fake degree. Ghulam Bibi Bharwana, elected from NA-88 (Jhang-Cum-Chiniot) on PML(N) ticket, is the grand-daughter of Mehr Ghulam Haider Bharwana, who became member of parliament several times from the same area. Saira Afzal Tarar, elected from NA-102 (Hafizabad) on PML(N) ticket, is daughter in law of Rafiq Tarar former President of Pakistan.

Faryal Talpur and Dr. Azra Fazal Pechuho, both elected on PPP ticket from NA-207 (Larkana) and NA-213 (Nawabshah) respectively, are sisters of former President of Pakistan, Asif Ali Zardari. Dr. Fehmida Mirza, elected from NA-225 (Badin) on PPP ticket, is daughter of Qazi Abdul Majeed Abid, who has served as minister in federal and provincial (Sindh) cabinets in 1980s. Her husband, Dr. Zulfiqar Mirza, remained Home Minister Sindh and a close friend of Former President Asif Ali Zardari. Her brother, Qazi Asad Abid has also remained member of National Assembly; her son, Hasnain Mirza, is member Sindh Provincial Assembly. Shazia Mari, elected from NA-235 (Sanghar) on PPP ticket, is daughter of Atta Muhammad Marri, who was member of National Assembly and also served as Deputy Speaker Sindh Provincial Assembly. Shamas-un-Nisa, elected from NA-237 (Thatta) on PPP ticket, is wife of Abdul Hameed Memon, a parliamentarian, and daughter-in-law of Sadiq Memon, founding members of PPP. She got party ticket after her son, Jalil Memon, the then Sindh minister, died in a road accident, and her younger son, Sadiq Ali Memon, who won the same seat, got disqualified by the court.

So all of them belong to influential political families with a history of male members being elected traditionally from the constituencies they have been elected in recent elections. What is wrong with belonging to influential political families? First and the foremost is that most of them do not contest elections as long as male members of family 'eligible' to contest are available, which means they are not contesting elections as 'women' candidates but as substitute of their 'ineligible' male family members. Otherwise most of them belong to the families that are traditionally conservative feudal in nature, and do not allow women to go out of their homes, let alone contest elections. For example, when abovementioned Ghulam Bibi Bharwana the then a PML(Q)[27] candidate in NA-87, along with another Bharwana woman, Saima

Akhtar, an independent candidate in NA-90, decided to contest in 2002 general elections, a leading newspaper of the country, *Dawn*, published the news under heading, "Bharwana women set to create history."[28] Furthermore, they are elected because of the influence of their families, whose male members are the source of their strength in their respective constituencies but are not eligible to contest elections or have influence in more than one constituency therefore need another candidate. So how can they act independently? How do they represent women of Pakistan?

Therefore, the first line of argument, the one challenging the modus operandi of the election on reserved seats that ends up sending female relatives of top leadership to parliament, does not hold water; because women who do not come on reserved seats do not also represent the common women of Pakistan. Let's analyze the second line of argument that challenges the whole idea of bringing change through legislation and state policies.

Second explanation of the lack of women empowerment despite women representation in legislative assemblies and cabinets is close to Foucauldian discourse, which equates power with knowledge, norms, and values and with laws and force. It understands power to flow along discourses and move through populations and does not accept power as a property of individuals or institutions. In the words of Wendy Brown, "If power operates through norms, and not only through law and force, and if norms are borne by words, images, and the built environment, then popular discourses, market interpellations, and spatial organization are as much a vehicle for power as are troops, bosses, prime ministers, or police."[29] Applying this explanation of power to the problem of incommensurability between women representation and women's socio-economic empowerment leads us to conclude that no matter how many women are present in national legislatures and no matter how much legislation is done to empower women, women would not be empowered practically unless the society is not structurally transformed.

Laws and state policies cannot change the fate of women in any society unless the norms and values do not equate them with their male counterparts and favour their real empowerment. There is a popular saying in Pakistan that before we make laws, we decide how to break it without being punished. State policies and laws declaring women equal to men would not have any practical value unless there's acceptance of the fact in general masses. What is the point in making offences against women more and more severely punishable, if they are not reported because the norms and values of Pakistani society dictates to keep matters related to female members of family undisclosed in the name of 'family honour'? What benefit would it yield to fix minimum wages for women workers, when they are not employed in formal sectors of economy and informal sectors are not regulated by law? What purpose would it serve to reserve seats for women in legislative assemblies, if only women from influential political families can get elected on those seats and common women of society cannot afford to contest in general elections and do not have influence to get elected on reserved seats?

This phenomenon can be substantiated by the difference of male and female literacy rate in rural and urban areas of the four provinces. In rural areas, the difference between male and female literacy rates is more than that in urban areas. The difference between urban and rural area literacy rates can be attributed to availability of schools, infrastructure, and economic status of parents, but the difference between male and female literacy rates is, inter alia, linked with willingness of parents to send their girls to schools.

As mentioned earlier, women representation in South Asia and Muslim countries, providing regional and religious context for Pakistan respectively, exhibit the same pattern where increase in the number of women representatives has not transformed in socio-economic empowerment of women. Afghanistan for example has highest women representation in women and still is the most dangerous country to be a woman, Saudi Arabia has more women representation than that of the US and women are not allowed to drive vehicles there.

Another interesting fact is that while members of 13th national assemble asked almost four times more questions than their male counterparts during 4th parliamentary year, women representations from traditionally conservative parties—ANP, PMLF, and MMAP—did not ask any question on the floor of the House. So women would be empowered with increasing their number in legislative assemblies but by changing the laws of truth (embedded in norms, values, and knowledge) about their status and capabilities.

Conclusion

Political empowerment must not be understood in terms of quantitative measurement of women representation in legislative assemblies, but in terms of quality socio-political participation of women in political system of the country through indigenous acceptance of society rooted and expressed through norms and values. Musai, Alehashem, and Abhari present a model of socio-political participation of women, which outlines a hierarchy of women political participation.

Table 3.5: Hierarchy of women political participation

Having formal political position (governmental)
Active membership in organization or political party
Participation in public societies, demonstrations etc
Passive membership in organization or political party
Participation in informal political discussions
Voting
Non-involvement in politics

Source: Maysam Musai, Berad Razavi Alehashem, and Seyede Marzieh Fatemi Abhari, "Participation of Women in Socio-political Development in Iran," *International Journal of Academic Research in Business and Social Sciences* 4, No. 3 (March, 2014): 574-75.

An indigenous movement for political empowerment of women would be the one achieved as a result of these steps of political participation. In Pakistan, women have right to vote and they do vote as well, but that is the lowest level of political participation as voting is not necessarily based on rational choice. Rather in most of the cases women vote because the male members of the family or even of locality take them to polling stations and ask them to vote for someone. Even if they cast vote on their own will, they are supposedly not familiar with the political system and its realities, because of the level of their awareness and access to education, and therefore, not able to make a learned choice. The next level is participation in informal political discussions, which is generally not observed in Pakistan. It is because the norms and values impose the 'law of truth' that politics and activities and discussions related to it belong to the 'public sphere' and women by nature belong to the 'private sphere'. The social norm set in this regard is that politics is alien to women nature and is not their 'sphere'.

The higher levels of political participation of women are actually alien to common women of Pakistani society. The higher levels are 'assumed' to belong to upper class—either activists from ultramodern cadre of society or women from influential political families. Social norms—set to impose the laws of truth—make these activities undesirable for women, who are supposed to do household activities, give birth and take care of their children, and remain within the four walls of their homes. Likewise membership of political parties is not common in Pakistan. Political parties in Pakistan do have women workers, but they normally belong to political families. The women, who do not hail from political families and still take part in political parties or activities like demonstrations, are considered indecorous and shameless as the social norms expect women to observe modesty and protect the honour of their families.

Reserved seats for women in Legislative Assemblies of Pakistan provided an opportunity for highest level of women's political participation. The absence of intermediary stages between voting and having formal political position creates a gap between electors and their representatives. The women in Pakistan have right to vote (lowest level) and they have representation in parliament (highest level), but intermediary levels of political participation of women are missing in Pakistan. Women do not take part in political discussions, women membership of political parties is very rare, and they do not take part in political demonstrations. So, the women representatives on reserved seats do not follow the stepwise route of political participation to the highest level, and therefore, remain alien to the system. Electors, on the other hand, do not make learned choices as the system is alien to them.

A recent phenomenon of political mobilization triggered by Imran Khan and his political party Pakistan Tehreek-e-Insaf (PTI) is an example of this gap. Pakistan Tehreek-e-Insaf, founded in 1996 by former cricketer and philanthropist, Imran Khan, is centrist political party and claims to be the only non-family party in Pakistan. The anti-status quo movement of PTI got momentum and popular support on the eve of 2013 general elections, in which the party got second highest popular votes and third highest seats in National Assembly of Pakistan. The unique feature of PTI movement was the support of a very large number of urban women families. PTI attracted the middle class families, which are highly educated but hitherto were indifferent to political activities in Pakistan—the common women of Pakistan, not typical segment that has an acceptance in society as 'political'.

So when they started coming out to express their political views, started taking part in discussions, and started to join rallies and demonstrations, they were and are still being labelled as vulgar, immodest, indiscreet, unscrupulous, and pseudo 'ultra-modern' (as if ultra-modern are allowed to participate in political parties, but they are pseudo ultra-modern and therefore are not acceptable). Recently, PTI has launched a massive campaign against alleged rigging in 2013 general elections, which ended up in a sit-in in Islamabad near parliament house and is still on after 50 days. The supporters of PML(N), the party in power, responding to this phenomenon in discussions and social media declare these gatherings as concerts and accuse women of immoral activities with the men in those gatherings. It is because norms and values of the society do not expect women to participate in such gatherings and demonstrations as they are the domain of men only. Social norms in Pakistan do not question the voting right of women nor do they object political representation of women in parliament, but the intermediary stages of political participation of women do not have the social legitimacy or sanction of social norms and the law of truth imposed by those norms.

Where does this social legitimacy come from? Social norms, values, and traditions, borne by the language, symbols, and words. Who decides these norms? The answer is Knowledge. Our knowledge about the social realities makes our norms, and dictates us to behave accordingly. People accept or reject social realities on the criterion of norms and values dictated by law of truth which is imposed by the knowledge they have about those realities. So real empowerment of women would not come from higher representation of women in legislative assemblies or from women empowerment laws imposed through legislation but from laws imposed by the knowledge. Knowledge, that women are equal to men and should have equal rights, equal access to social and economic resources, and have equal capabilities to participate in politics. This knowledge would impose the law or truth embedded in social values empowering women in Pakistani society. This knowledge is not necessarily related to literacy or formal education, but about awareness in society about the equality of women to men.

Political empowerment is indeed highest level of women empowerment which results from socio-economic empowerment of women, but it does not work the other way around. Political empowerment of women can, however, ensure continuity of socio-economic empowerment of women in society, provided former is a result of latter. If political empowerment comes through socio-economic empowerment, it would definitely strengthen and perpetuate socio-economic empowerment of women.

Notes

1. Wendy Brown, "Power after Foucault," in *The Oxford Handbook of Political Theory*, eds. John S. Dryzek, Bonnie Honig, and Anne Phillips, New York: Oxford University Press, 2006, 65.
2. National Assembly of Pakistan currently have 69 women out of 340 sitting members (60 women reserved seats, one woman on minority reserved seat, and 8 elected in general elections), and Senate has 17 women senators out of total house of 104.
3. Kate Millett, *Sexual Politics*, Champaign: University of Illinois Press, 2000, 23.
4. CARE, "Women's Empowerment," quoted in Gender Equity Program (GEP), *Women's Empowerment in Pakistan: A Scoping Study*, Islamabad: Aurat Publication and Information Services Foundation, 2011, 2.
5. Augusto Lopez-Claros and Saadia Zahidi, Women's Empowerment: Measuring the Global Gender Gap, Switzerland: World Economic Forum, 2005.
6. Gender Equity Program (GEP), *Women's Empowerment*, 7-28.
7. Bushra Zulfiqar, *Women and Economy: The Politics of Empowerment*, Saarbrücken, Germany: Lambert Academic Publishing, 2010, quoted in *ibid.*, 4.
8. Azra Asghar Ali, "Empowerment and Political Mobilization of Women in Pakistan," *Pakistan Vision* 13, No. 2 (2012): 96-108.
9. Naila Kabeer, "Gender Equality and Women's Empowerment: A Critical Analysis of the Third Millennium Development Goal," *Gender and Development*, 13, No. 1 (2005): 13-24.
10. For detailed analysis, see Brown, "Power after Foucault," 65-84.
11. Gender Equity Program (GEP), *Women's Empowerment*, 4.
12. Ali, "*Women in Pakistan*," 96.
13. John Adams, Letter to John Penn (1776), quoted in Robert E. Goodin, *Innovating Democracy: Democratic Theory and Practice after the Deliberative Turn*, New York: Oxford University Press, 2008, 233.
14. Pildat, *Women Representation in Pakistan's Parliament*, Background Paper, Islamabad: Pildat Publications, 2004.
15. "Women in National Parliaments," Inter-Parliamentary Union website, accessed September 20, 2014, http://www.ipu.org/wmn-e/classif.htm.
16. *Priceconomics Blog*; "Afghanistan Has More Women in National Parliament Seats than the U.S.," blog entry by Zachary Crockett, January 30, 2014.
17. *Ibid.*
18. *Ibid.*
19. Neeta Lal, "Women's Political Representation Lagging in India," Inter Press Service, New Delhi, June 29, 2014, accessed September 20, 2014, http://www.ipsnews.net/2014/06/womens-political-representation-lagging-in-india/.

20. UNICEF, cited in *ibid.* Neeta Lal further alleges, "Those girl children who survive this mindset tend to be given poorer care than boys. The patriarchal attitude is so deeply entrenched across the country that, according to the 2011 census, India now has 37 million fewer women than men (586.5 million women to 623.7 million men)."
21. Ali, "*Women in Pakistan*", 98-99.
22. FAFEN is a coalition of forty two leading organizations of civil society, aimed at strengthening all forms of democratic accountabilities, primarily by scrutinizing elections and parliamentary proceedings in Pakistan.
23. FAFEN, Women Legislators Assert Lawmaking, Oversight Roles.
24. "The world's five most dangerous countries for women: A Thomson Reuters Foundation global poll of experts," *Thomson Reuters*, June 15, 2011, accessed August 12, 2014, http://www.trust.org/documents/2011-women-poll-results.pdf.
25. Zahid Gishkori, "Women's Reserved Seats: Top Politicians' Spouses, Kin Strike It Lucky," *The Express Tribune*, May 30, 2013.
26. *Ibid.*
27. Pakistan Muslim League (Quaid-e-Azam), a king's party assembled by General Pervaiz Musharraf by gathering 'electables' from all over Pakistan formerly associated with PML(N), PPP, and other parties.
28. *Dawn* (Lahore), October 10, 2002. The newspaper outlined a detailed history of Bharwanas and went on to describe the family traditions: "Bharwanas are traditionally very strict about their women. They are kept under strict *purdah* within the four walls of their havelis. They have to wear old-fashioned shuttlecock burqa when they are allowed to go out on very rare occasions. They are seldom sent to school and literacy rate among Bharwana women is negligible."
29. Brown, "Power after Foucault," 66.

4

Parliamentary Representation of Women in India

Problems, Pitfalls and Areas of Reform

Chanchal Kumar Sharma

Introduction

The parliamentary representation of women has been hailed for various reasons. First of all, the presence of women in parliament can make a difference to the quality of parliamentary debates and discussions, as they can easily empathize with issues of daily life and hence can introduce new perspectives to the debates. Indeed, a perceptible presence of women representatives in the Parliament would lead to better decision-making and political priorities that more closely reflect concerns women voters. For instance, this can make the matters of importance to women, to move up the political agenda. These include, inter alia, childcare, sanitation, domestic violence, rape crisis centres, anti-rape legislations, etc. Thus the increased political empowerment of women will help them overcome deprivation and fight the abuse and discrimination.

Furthermore, the presence of women in parliament creates a 'role model effect' whereby the visible presence of women in public life inspires and motivates other women to come forward. Finally, it has a great symbolic value too as it serves to increase respect for women in the society. Thus, many benefits can accrue to the women community by virtue of there being a provision for the parliamentary representation of women. Besides, the presence of women in the parliament increases the legitimacy of the Parliament itself as a truly representative institution.

73rd Constitutional Amendment Act 1992 provided for reservations for women in PRIs in two ways; for the office of the members and for that of the chairpersons. As per the clause (2) and (3) of Article 243 (d), not less than one third of the seats meant for direct election of members at each tier of the Panchayats are to be reserved for the women. In 2011, the Cabinet approved the proposal for enhancing reservation for women in Panchayats from the present 33 to 50 per cent. However, the Constitution (110th Amendment) Bill for reserving half the seats in Panchayats for women is still pending. Similarly, the Constitution (112th Amendment) Bill reserving one-third of elected seats in municipalities for women is also pending. The experience of women's reservation at the Panchayat level has been very encouraging. A million women are being elected to the Panchayats in the country every five years. This is the largest mobilisation of women in public life in the world. Although, the percentages of women in various levels of political activity have risen considerably, women are still under-represented in governance and decision-making positions.

In view of the significance of women representation, a bill was drafted by the H.D. Deve Gowda-led United Front Government and introduced in the Lok Sabha (as 81st Amendment Bill) on September 12, 1996. However, the Bill could not be passed because of lack of political consensus. The Women's Reservation Bill provides for reservation of 33 per cent of all seats in the Lok Sabha (the lower house) and in all state legislative assemblies for women. The seats to be reserved in rotation will be determined by draw of lots in such a way that a seat shall be reserved only once in three consecutive general elections. Rajya Sabha (the upper house) passed the Bill on 9 March, 2010. The Bill is pending for approval in the Lok Sabha. In 2010, the UPA government couldn't pass the Women's Reservation Bill due to the opposition from allies. Note that the highest opposition to the Bill came from SP and BSP who had higher per cent of Women MPs (in 15th Lok Sabha) in their parties in comparison to the Congress and the BJP (Fig. 4.1). In terms of actual numbers however, the Congress and the BJP, had the largest number of women MPs in the 15th Lok Sabha. The BJP had 13 female MPs and the Congress party had 25. With the dissolution of the 15th Lok Sabha, the Constitution

(108th Amendment) Bill has lapsed. Now, it will be reintroduced by the 16th Lok Sabha.

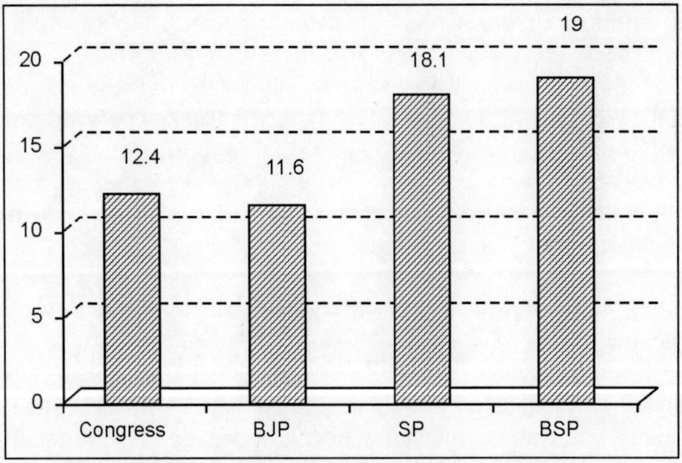

Source: Election Commission of India (eci.nic.in)

Fig. 4.1: Percentage of Women MPs by Party (15th Lok Sabha)

However, the present Modi government (The BJP led-NDA Government) has the requisite majority. Given the BJP's commitment to 33 per cent representation of women in Parliament and state assemblies the Bill may not encounter much opposition in the Lok Sabha this time around. However, being a Constitution Amendment Bill, the Bill would have to be passed by half of India's state legislatures, after it is passed by the Parliament.

Given the overwhelming benefits of increased representation of women in the Parliament, the question that perplexes an observer is the successful opposition of Women's Reservation Bill in Lok Sabha?

The question becomes more intractable given the relative ease with which the political class has accepted reservation of women in Panchayati Raj Institutions (PRIs). It seems, Panchayat system does not threaten Patriarcy even with provision for women's reservation because it is easy for influential *patis* (husbands) to get their reluctant *patnis* (wives) elected (on their behalf) and drive from backseat at the Panchayat level. The story may be entirely different as far as reservation in the Lok Sabha is concerned, because the bill could challenge the general election scenario to utter disadvantage of the male leaders.

This chapter attempts to address the puzzle of Parliamentary opposition to Women's Reservation Bill by highlighting the causes from two perspectives: The first group highlights technical, historical and cultural reasons which we categorize under the section on 'Problems'. The second group of causes is more serious in nature and is appropriately captioned 'Pitfalls', as it alerts us to the possibility that the women who are already enjoying the fruits of political power as MPs or ministers may behave like *partisan politicians* rather than as advocates for women rights. Thus, the final section reflects on the reforms that can address the problems and pitfalls of Parliamentary representation of women in India.

Women Representation in Indian Parliament: A Comparative Overview

While the percentage of women representatives in the 16th Lok Sabha is 11.23 per cent, the highest number recorded so far (Fig. 4.2), it still lags behind other countries. Figure 4.3 shows that many other countries have been much more successful in increasing women's representation in their national legislatures. Research shows that the key factor that is responsible for rise of women's representation is the adoption of representation quotas for women in the legislatures. Fig. 4.4 shows that the global figure has nearly doubled since 1997.

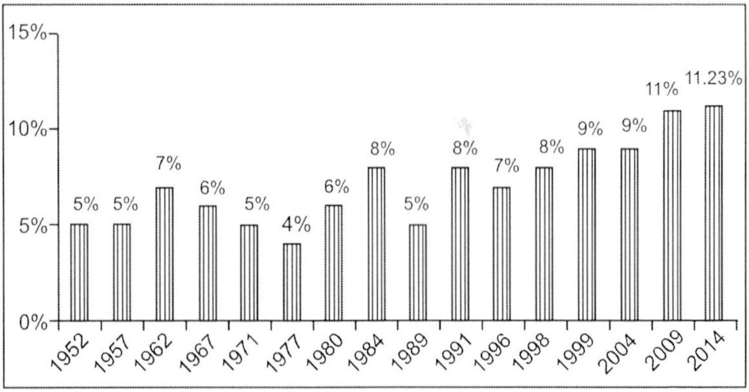

Source: Election Commission of India (eci.nic.in)

Fig. 4.2: Women MPs in Lok Sabha: 1952-2014

India is placed at 111th position out of 189 countries in a list prepared by the Inter-Parliamentary Union (IPU), an international organization that ranks nations on the number of women representatives in parliament. Rwanda leads the list of 189 countries surveyed, with its lower house recording more than 60 per cent women followed by Andorra and Cuba. India ranks lower than even her immediate neighbours. For instance, Nepal is ranked at 24, China at 55 and Pakistan is placed at 66. All the high performing countries reserve seats for women in national legislatures.

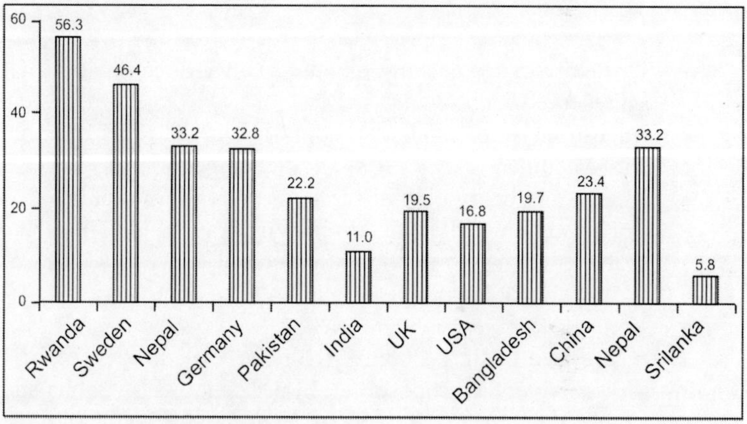

Source: Inter-Parliamentary Union.

Fig. 4.3: Global Comparison of Women in the Lower House (or single representative house)

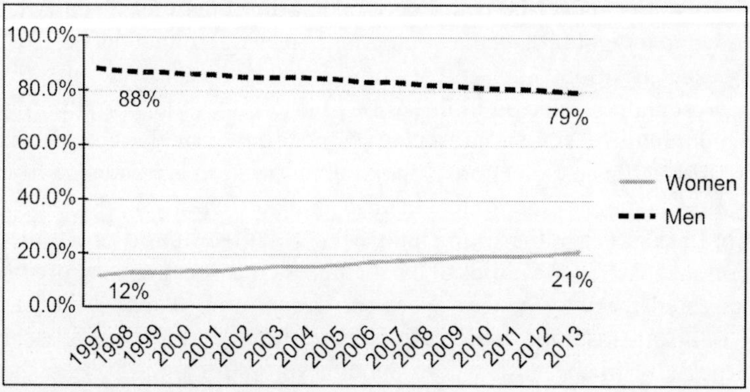

Source: Inter-Parliamentary Union.

Fig. 4.4: Global Average of Men and Women in Parliaments 1997-2013

Parliamentary Representation of Women: Identifying the Problems

There are a few hurdles that have made it difficult for the parliamentarians to arrive at a consensus. Some of the issues are technical, some are purely political. Four Problems can be identified:

Technical Aspects: Problems with the Bill Itself

The Constitutional Amendment Bill includes the following key provisions:

- One-third of all seats in Lok Sabha and Vidhan Sabhas shall be reserved for women.
- Such reservation shall also apply in case of seats reserved for Scheduled Castes (SCs) and Scheduled Tribes (STs).
- There shall be rotation of seats so reserved for women.
- Such rotation shall be determined by draw of lots, in such a manner that a seat shall be reserved only once in a block of three general elections.

There are two basic problems with the Bill. Firstly, from a feminist perspective, the proposal for 33 per cent of Lok Sabha and state assembly seats to be reserved for women will encourage the ghettoization of women representatives. This is because, as the argument goes, the condition of running only women candidates in the reserved constituencies will encourage pitting women against women. Secondly, the Bill proposes that the constituencies allotted to women would rotate every election. From a feminist perspective, the seat rotation requirement could impede career continuity for representatives elected in this way. Further, it would also diminish accountability, since representatives need not fear the electorate's verdict at the next election. Rotational reservation is a bad idea from male perspective as well, because it would spoil the long-term political career of the sitting male MPs. It will definitely erode their political base as two-thirds of the incumbent members will be forcibly unseated in every general election. Reservation of constituencies will also restrict the choice of voters in the reserved constituencies especially in the case where enough suitable candidates are not available.

Sociological Dimension: Caste based Opposition

The OBC leaders oppose the Bill as a bid by parties dominated by upper castes to increase representation of already privileged, urban, educated, upper caste women, what, Sharad Yadav (an OBC leader), called the "bobbed hair brigade" (Randall, 2006). Mulayam Singh Yadav, described the Bill as a "conspiracy to eliminate smaller parties" based on lower castes and minorities. According to Nitish Kumar, another OBC leader, the Bill will change the social composition of the Lok Sabha that has been achieved after a long struggle from the backdoors." (Lok Sabah debates, September 13,1996, Col 336). Similarly, a Muslim MP argued the Bill would mean that "representation of Muslim population in the country will get a set back." (Eleventh Lok Sabha Debates, May 16, 1997, 476).

Political-Cultural Dimension: Vested Interests of the National Male Politicians

Atal Bihari Vajpayee, himself once referred to the "general insecurity of menfolk" and their vested interest in "perpetuating male supremacy" (Randall, 2006). SP leader Mulayam Singh had said, "The Women Reservation Bill, if passed in present format, would provoke young men to whistle in Parliament." The general argument that betrays lack of faith in women parliamentarians on one hand and male insecurity on the other is that women are politically inexperienced and that the country's security would be jeopardized if they constituted more than 10 per cent of Lok Sabha members. The much easier adoption, in 1993, of seat reservations for women at the local level confirms the fact that reservations in Lok Sabha could also have materialized but for the imaginary perception of threat to the vested interests of national politicians.

Historical Dimension: Absence of a Political Conjuncture

In order to explain why parties in Latin America and Africa have implemented gender quotas, but a democratic and politically progressive like India did not, it is necessary to take account of the broader political conjuncture (Randall, 2006). In developing countries in recent years demands for gender quotas have regularly emerged during periods of democratic transition. Quotas for women are included in broader packages of political reform. Such a political conjuncture is absent in contemporary India. Before a deliberate attempt to create a new set of democratic institutions to increase women's parliamentary representation could be established, was already a thing of past. Thus, gender quotas may have been the victims of India's "exceptional" pattern of political development. A possible parallel can be found in Jamaica, another former British colony which, like India, on independence adopted and has since maintained a parliamentary system of government together with a first-past-the-post electoral system. In these countries there was no pressure for democratic reform (as a part of the era of democracy building) that more recently provided an opening for the advocacy of gender quotas elsewhere.

Ideological Dimension: Fear of Femocracy

There is another important dimension that is acting a powerful 'inertia' factor. It is the ideology which has found its expression in those countries where women do not suffer the kind of disadvantages they suffer in India. The trend, as the argument goes, has a beginning but has no end. In some countries the dawn of the so called age of Misandry—which means, the age of hating men, has led to the formation of "Men's Activist Groups" who are busy preparing ground for a political crusade to defend Men's rights. They believe that a time will come when it will be considered a matter for shame for a political party to have more male candidates, for a department/organization/institute to have more male employees.

The advocates of so called "Men's voice" smitten by femophobia argue that the time is not far away when this worldwide trend towards women favouratism through reservation would leave men jobless and bankrupt. The Phenomena of social power always swings from one extreme to another; there may be a semblance of balance (parity) for a while, but that is more often than not a temporary phase and the culmination always takes shape in the form of imbalance and disparity.

Forcing women to participate in politics appears strange (especially in the context of developed countries) as there is nothing that prevents them from contesting elections. The reality, according to the advocates of this counter-movement, is that many more men than women are interested in participating in politics. This lack of interest is the key reason for their under representation, if any. Quotas in one area will lead to more quotas in other walks of life. Higher quota for women in government jobs and private companies will be the next step. This despite the fact that research in human behaviour has shown that if a male and a female appear for an interview and both get equal marks; the female is more likely to be favoured with appointment.

Many more arguments and debates can be found on the Web site launched by a radical group called Mens' Rights Movement. The title of the website is: A Voice for Men: Humanist Counter—Theory in the Age of Misandry.

Parliamentary Representation of Women for Sake of It: The Pitfalls

There are various pitfalls of women reservation in the parliament. Presence of these pitfalls alerts us to various possibilities that may defeat the very purpose of women's representation in the Parliament. The pitfalls listed below must be overcome in order to make the Parliamentary representation of women effective and productive.

Tokenism

It has been feared that parliamentary representation of women would simply produce "tokenism," coopting women rather than providing meaningful change. Individual feminist academics also suggest that women MPs are unrepresentative of women as a whole (Campbell, Childs, & Lovenduski, 2010). There is a wide gulf between women MPs and disadvantaged Indian women. Indeed the presence of women may be used, as an alibi for policies with a disproportionate impact on women. This has happened in Australia where cuts to child care funding were implemented with explicit consent of women senators! (Sawer, 2000)

Political Career Approach of Women Parliamentarians

Women associations and academic departments often complain that women parliamentarians act more as a politician than as a women activist (Sawer, 2000). The desire to break out of the role of a feminist or a woman activist and gain access to the more prestigious masculine portfolios or committee assignments leads to the denial of gender ("I'm a politician not a woman"). Adopting politics as a professional career often means that party and factional discipline will take precedence over other affiliations. They start nurturing their political career at the cost of promoting women's cause. On the other hand the political activists are also found describing themselves as getting little help from women's studies departments.

Encouraging Groupism among Women Parliamentarians

International experience, for instance of Australian Senate, suggests that whenever a group of women begin to pose threat to the party hierarchy, the party bosses attempt to neutralize it by establishing a rival women groups under party control.

Making Women's Representation Effective: Areas of Reforms

Reforming Political Parties

The women's movement in India has been a victim of the nature of party politics in the country. Indian political parties are organizationally weak and dependent on local elites. This leads to the marginalization of issue-based politics as well as the resistance to gender-sensitive initiatives (Bjorkman, 1987). (Caul, 1999) found that four party-level factors have some explanatory power: organizational structure, ideology, women party activists and gender-related candidate rules.

According to Lovenduski and Norris (1993) political parties are the greatest barriers to the parliamentary representation of women (Also see: Lovenduski, 2005). It has been observed that with the increase in the international and national pressure for granting parliamentary representation to women, the left parties tend to adopt quotas, whereas, the rightist parties favour strategies such as training and mentoring programmes. More effective participation of women in political sphere can be ensured by providing more opportunities for women's advancement within a party. For instance, if internal party procedures are relatively democratic and explicit, it may be easier for women to plan an effective campaign. However, if there is a sympathetic party leadership, it may be easier to secure a favourable outcome even in a more centralized party organization.

It has been suggested that a better option, in comparison to the reservation of seats in the Parliament, is to make a provision for the reservation for women candidates within political parties, as some countries do (see Table 4.1).

Table 4.1: Country data on political representation of women

	% of elected women	*Quota in Parliament*	*Quota in political parties**
Sweden	47 (2006)	No	Yes
Argentina	40 (2007)	Yes	Yes
Norway	36 (2005)	No	Yes
Canada	24 (2006)	No	Yes
Pakistan	21 (2008)	Yes	No
United Kingdom	20 (2005)	No	Yes
France	18 (2007)	No	Yes
USA	17 (2006)	No	No
Sri Lanka	6 (2004)	No	No

Sources: Global Database of Quotas for Women. International IDEA and Stockholm University and Inter Parliamentary Union (http://www.ipu.org/wmn-e/classif.htm).

Reforming the Electoral System

Adoption of gender quotas is positively associated with proportional representation systems. Of the five countries in the world who have 30 per cent or more female parliamentarians in their single or lower house (Sweden, Norway, Finland, Denmark and the Netherlands), three have a proportional electoral system, and two have a mixed electoral system (with none having a majoritarian system). However, as Table 4.1 shows, PR is the electoral system of the countries with the highest (Sweden) and lowest (Greece) levels of female political representation. Therefore, proportional representation alone is not responsible for the strength of women parliamentarians in other European Union countries. An important factor within PR is the placement of female candidates in eligible positions on party lists.

Matland (1998) estimated that switching over to PR can cause women's representation to rise by at least 15.6 per cent. Indeed in New Zealand the replacement of an electoral system based purely on single-member constituencies by the Mixed Member Proportional (MMP) system in 1996 saw a significant increase in the representation of women (Sawer, 1997). It is noteworthy that all twelve Latin

Table 4.2: Women Representation in the Lower or Single Houses of National Parliaments of 15 European Countries and the Type of Electoral System

Order	*Country*	*%W*	*Electoral System*
1.	Sweden	40.4	Mixed (Closed lists)
2.	Finland	33.5	Mixed (Preferential)
3.	Denmark	33.0	Proportional (Preferential)
4.	Netherlands	31.3	Proportional (Preferential)
5.	Austria	26.8	Proportional (Closed lists)
6.	Germany	26.2	Mixed/Two (Closed lists)
7.	Spain	24.6	Proportional (Closed lists)
8.	Luxembourg	20.0	Proportional (Preferential)
9.	Ireland	13.9	Proportional (Multi seat)
10.	Portugal	13.0	Proportional (Closed list)
11.	Belgium	12.0	Proportional (Preferential)
12.	Italy	11.1	Mixed (Weak PR)
13.	United Kingdom	9.5	Majoritarian (Plurality)
14.	France	6.4	Majoritarian (Two ballot)
15.	Greece	6.3	Mixed (Weak PR)

Source: Figures from Inter-Parliamentary Union (1997:90-92, 136) and Inter-Parliamentary Union "Electoral Systems: A Worldwide Comparative Study" (1993).

American countries that have adopted gender quotas elect their national legislatures from multi-member districts using a party-list form of proportional representation. In Australia, the upper house that has adopted a proportional representation (PR) system has a higher proportion of women as compare to the lower house that adopts a single-member electorate system with preferential voting.

The desirability of the PR system can be estimated form the fact that whenever countries adopt new electoral systems or modify existing ones, change is almost always away from first-past-the-post systems towards some form of proportional representation or mixed system. In India, however, the existing system is so deeply entrenched that a serious discussion about changing it is rare outside academic circles.

Institution Building

The question here is who will hold parliamentarians, whether male or female, accountable for their contribution to advancing the status of women? It is the lack of accountability mechanisms which has been one of the major criticisms of identity politics. For this purpose separate institutions can be established that will provide a framework for woman-centred debate and for the crystallization of claims on the broader political system. These institutions will assist the women into the parliament, support them and hold them accountable. The view here is that it is not sufficient to assist women into parliament. There have to be strategies to support feminists operating within political institutions where the institutional culture is antithetical to feminism. Such support involves monitoring the women who have entered parliament and accountability is the other side of this coin.

Conclusion

This article has argued that parliamentary representation of women is the first step that can begin the process of democratization of women's political engagement and empowerment and also feminization of the democratic institutions and the policy making process. However, mere presence of a few women in the parliament will not automatically serve the goal of representation of women as a collectivity. For political representation of women to serve the purpose it is intended to, requires two key prerequisites. One of them is education. In fact, education and empowerment are in a constant loop. On one hand, education can lead to women empowerment and at the same time, women empowerment also leads to a rise in female literacy. However, the institutions of higher education in India have not been able to make a dent in the plight of Indian women, who continue to be a victim of manifold discriminations and attitudinal barriers created by the male dominated, patriarchal society. The reason for this is to be found in the socialization that happens outside the formal education system. The overall social milieu renders them economically and educationally vulnerable. Thus, systemic reforms must take place in the form of more awareness and a change at the ideational level. Second prerequisite is putting robust accountability mechanisms in place. A more representative legislature does not guarantee more effective representation of women's interests because "standing for women" is not always the same as "acting for them" (Childs, 2002; Pitkin, 1972). Thus, representation in itself is not sufficient unless it is accompanied with accountability mechanisms. We need women representatives who will *act for* rather than just stand for women. Thus, what we need is a democrary where women have a voice in the policy process and participation in policy advice and evaluation. Let us not call it femocracy in the sense in which it has been used by the Men's Rights Activists.

References

Achen, C. (1978). Measuring Representation. *American Journal of Political Science*, 22, 475-510.

Bjorkman, J.W. (1987). India: Party, Personality and Dynasty. In A. Ware (Ed.), *Political Parties*. Oxford: Blackwell.

Campbell, R., Childs, S., and Lovenduski, J. (2010). Do Women Need Women representatives? *British Journal of Political Science*, 40(1), 171-94.

Caul, M. (1999). Women's Representation in Parliament. *Party Politics*, 5(1), 79-98.

Childs, S. (2002). Hitting the Target: Are Labour Women MPs "Acting For" Women? *Parliamentary Affairs*, 55, 143-53.

Chin, M. (2004). Reflections on Women's Empowerment through Local Representation in South Korea. *Asian Survey*, 44(2), 295-315.

Converse, P. (1964). The Nature of Belief Systems in Mass Publics. In D. Apter (Ed.), *Ideology and Discontent* (pp. 206-61). New York: The Free Press.

Jayal, N.G. (2001). Introduction: Situating Indian democracy. In N.G. Jayal (Ed.), *Themes in Politics: Democracy in India*. New Delhi: Oxford University Press.

Lovenduski, J. (2005). *Feminizing Politics*. Cambridge: Polity Press.

Lovenduski, J., and Norris, P. (1993). *Gender and Party Politics*. London: SAGE.

Matland, R.E. (1998). Women's Representation in National Legislatures: Developed and Developing Countries. *Legislative Studies Quarterly*, 23, 109-25.

Pitkin, H. (1972). *The Concepto of Representation*. Berkeley: University of California Press.

Randall, V. (2006). Legislative Gender Quotas and Indian Exceptionalism: The Travails of the Women's Reservation Bill. *Comparative Politics*, 39(1), 63-82.

Sawer, M. (1997). Mirroring the Nation? Electoral Systems and the Representation of Women. *Current Affairs Bulletin*, 73(5), 8-12.

Sawer, M. (2000). Parliamentary Representation of Women: From Discourses of Justice to Strategies of Accountability. *International Political Science Review*, 21(4), 361-80.

Tolleson-Rinehart, S. (1992). *Gender Consciousness and Politics*. London: Routledge.

PART III
Legal Dimensions of Women Empowerment

5

Women Empowerment

Role of Legislature and Judiciary in India

Samiksha Godara

"I measure the progress of a community by the degree of progress which women have achieved".

—Dr. B.R. Ambedkar

Introduction

In ancient India, women enjoyed a very high position but gradually their position degenerated into merely objects of pleasure meant to serve certain purposes. They lost their individual identity and even their basic human right. Since long, the position of women in our society was miserable. In Hindu *Shastras*, she has been branded just like animals. The deep rooted gender bias is evident from the verses of *Ramcharit Manas* written by Tulsi Das which says that *"Dhol, ganwar, shudra, pashu aur naari, Yeh sab tadan ke adhikari"*. It literally means that, "the drums, the illiterate, the lower caste, the animals and the women are meant for being beaten up." Even in *'Manusmriti'* the status granted to women is quite visible and she was put to the lowest rug of humanity as she was treated at par with the animals and slave by the proprietors of Hindu *Dharma*. Such was the placement earmarked to our sisters, mothers and even great grandmothers that humanity was ashamed of.

In the present era, women have worked very hard to improve their position in the society. As a result of which the debates and discussion relating to women empowerment and gender parity are heard all over. Empowerment is a multi-faceted, multi-dimensional and multi-layered concept. Women's empowerment is a process in which women gain greater share of control over the resources and a participation in the decision-making process. According to the *Country Report of Government of India*, "Empowerment means moving from a position of enforced powerlessness to one, of power". Empowerment essentially means giving voice to the voiceless. Women empowerment can influence not only their own lives but also the lives of men, children and the society at large.

Laws Enacted by Legislature for the Empowerment of Women

In India, there are numerous laws aimed at empowerment of women in social, economic, political, civil, criminal personal, labour and service matters. Some of these legislations are briefly discussed as under:

The Constitution of India 1950

The Fundamental Law of the land namely the Constitution of India not only guarantees equality to women but also empowers the State to adopt measures for positive discrimination in favour of women. The principle of gender equality is enshrined in the Indian Constitution in its Preamble, Fundamental Rights, Fundamental Duties and Directive Principles of State Policy. Following salient features of Indian Constitution directly or indirectly refers to the idea of women empowerment:

(i) Article 14 guarantees that the State shall not deny equality before the law and equal protection of the laws;
(ii) Article 15 prohibits discrimination against any citizen on the ground of sex;
(iii) Article 15(3) empowers the State to make positive discrimination in favour of women and children;
(iv) Article 16 provides for Equality of Opportunity in matters of public employment;
(v) Article 23 prohibits trafficking in human beings and forced labour;
(vi) Article 39(a) and (d) enjoins the State to provide equal means of livelihood and equal pay for equal work;
(vii) Article 42 enjoins upon the State to make provisions for

securing just and humane conditions of work, and for maternity relief;

(viii) Article 51A(e) imposes a Fundamental Duty on every citizen to renounce the practices derogatory to the dignity of women;

(ix) Article 243D(3) provides that not less than 1/3rd of the total number of seats to be filled by direct election in every Panchayat to be reserved for women, and such seats to be allotted by rotation to different constituencies in a Panchayat;

(x) Article 243T(3) provides that not less than 1/3rd of the total number of seats to be filled by direct election in every Municipality shall be reserved for women and such seats may be allotted by rotation to different constituencies in a Municipality;

(xi) Article 243T(4) provides reservation of offices of Chairperson in Municipalities for SC, ST, Women in such manner as the legislature of a State, may by law provide;

In pursuance of the above Constitutional provisions, various legislative enactments have been framed to protect, safeguard and promote the interests of women.

The Indian Penal Code 1860

Sections 292, 293 and 294 provide for punishment for sale and exhibition of obscene books objects and obscene acts in the public place. Section 304(b) deals with murder of women in connection with demand for dowry. Sections 312 to 318 deals with punishment for causing miscarriage. Section 354 provides punishment for outraging the modesty of any women. Section 366 deals with kidnapping for marriage against her will. Section 366A deals with procuring minor girls for sexual purpose. Section 376 deals with punishment for rape. Section 494 protects women from bigamy. Section 497 deals about protection of married women from adultery. Section 498A deals about subjecting women to cruelty by her husband or relatives of her husband. Section 509 provides punishment for uttering words and gesture or acts intended to insult the modesty of a woman.

The Code of Criminal Procedure 1973

Under Section 125, a woman has right to claim maintenance from her father, brother, husband, son and even the father-in-law under certain circumstances.

The Indian Evidence Act 1872

Sections 113(a), 113(b) and 114(c) provide for presumptions as to abetment of suicide by a married woman within 7 years of marriage, as dowry death of a woman and as to absence of consent of woman for sexual intercourse.

The Hindu Adoption and Maintenance Act 1956

Section 7 says that a married Hindu male cannot adopt a child except with the consent of his wife. Section 18A provides for obligations of husband to maintain his wife. Section 18(2) provides right of wife to live separately and Section 19 provides for maintenance of widow by her father-in-law.

The Hindu Succession Act 1956

Section 14 provides that the property of female Hindu should be treated as her absolute property. Section 23 provides right of female legal heirs in the dwelling house.

The Hindu Minority and Guardianship Act 1956

Section 6 provides that the mother is a natural guardian for minors below 5 years.

The Hindu Marriage Act 1955

Section 13(2) provides empowers a wife to present a petition for divorce. Section 13(b) provides equal right of wife for getting divorce by mutual consent. Section 24 provides for relief for interim maintenance and expenses. Section 25 provides for right of wife to seek permanent alimony and maintenance and Section 26 provides right to claim custody of children.

The Dowry Prohibition Act 1961

Section 3 and 4 declares that giving, or taking, or demanding dowry either before marriage, or during marriage, or after the marriage is an offence.

The Muslim Women (Protection of Right on Divorce) Act 1986

Section 4 says that if the Magistrate is satisfied that a divorced woman has not re-married and is not able to maintain herself after the *iddat* period, he may make an order directing such of her relatives as would be entitled to inherit her property on her death according to Muslim law to pay such reasonable and fair maintenance to her as he may determine fit and proper, having regard to the needs of the divorced woman, the standard of life enjoyed by her during her marriage and the means of such relatives and such maintenance shall be payable by such relatives in the proportions in which they would inherit her property and at such periods as he may specify in his order.

The Factories Act 1948

In order to ameliorate the working conditions of women labour, Section 66 provides that 'no woman shall be required or allowed to work in any factory except between the hours of 6 a.m. and 7 p.m. Section 27 deals with prohibition of employment of women near cotton-openers. It provides that "No woman shall be employed in any part of a factory for pressing cotton in which a cotton-opener is at work."

The Equal Remuneration Act 1976

Section 4 provides for payment of equal wages to both men and women workers for the same work or work of similar nature. Section 5 prohibits discrimination against women in the matter of recruitment.

The Employees State Insurance Act 1948

Section 46 deals with periodical payments to an insured woman in case of confinement or miscarriage or sickness arising out of pregnancy, confinement, premature birth of child or miscarriage. Section 50 prescribes the qualification of an insured woman to claim maternity benefit.

The Maternity Benefit Act 1961

Section 4 says that "No employer shall knowingly employ a woman in any establishment during the six weeks immediately following the day of her delivery or her miscarriage." Section 13 provides for maternity benefit with full wages for women workers.

The Medical Termination of Pregnancy Act 1971

Section 3 safeguards women from unnecessary and compulsory abortions by providing that where the length of the pregnancy does not exceeds twenty weeks, and the registered medical practitioners is of opinion that the continuance of the pregnancy would involve a risk to the life of the pregnant woman or of grave injury physical or mental health, then such pregnancy can be legally terminated.

The Immoral Trafficking (Prevention) Act 1986

This law acts as a safeguard to protect women from prostitution. Section 3 provides that "any person who keeps or manages, or acts or assists in the keeping or management of, a brothel shall be punishable on first conviction with rigorous imprisonment for a term of not less than one year and not more than three years and also with fine which may extend to two thousand rupees and in the event of a second or subsequent conviction, with rigorous imprisonment for a term of not less than two years and not more than five years and also with fine which may extend to two thousand rupees". Section 4 deals with punishment for living on the earnings of prostitution by providing that "any person over the age of eighteen years who knowingly lives, wholly or in part, on the earnings of the prostitution of shall be punishable with imprisonment for a term which may extend to two years, or with fine which may extend to one thousand rupees, or with both.

The Prenatal Diagnostic Technique (Regulation and Prevention of Measure) Act 1994

Section 3 and 4 prohibits diagnosis of pregnant women for the purposes of identification of sex of foetus in the womb which helps in reducing the incidents of female foeticide.

The Indecent Representation of Women (Prohibition) Act 1986

Section 3 and 4 prohibits advertisements containing the indecent representation of women. Section 6 says that any person who contravenes the provisions of Section 3 or Section 4 shall be punishable on first conviction with imprisonment of either description for a term which may extend to two years, and with fine which may extend to two thousand rupees, and in the event of a second or subsequent conviction with imprisonment for term of not less than six months but which may extend to five years and also with a fine not less than ten thousand rupees but which may extend to one lakh rupees.

The Commission of Sati (Prevention) Act 1987

Section 3 says that whoever attempts to commit *sati* and does any act towards such commission shall be punishable with imprisonment for a term which may extend to one year or with fine or with both. Section 4 provides that if any person commits *sati*, whoever abets the commission of such *sati*, either directly or indirectly, shall be punishable with death or imprisonment for life and shall also be liable to fine. Further, if any person attempts to commit *sati*, whoever abets such attempt, either directly or indirectly, shall be punishable with imprisonment for life and shall also be liable to fine. Section 5 says that whoever does any act for the glorification of *sati* shall be punishable with imprisonment for a term which shall not be less than one year but which may extend to seven years and with fine which shall not be less than five thousand rupees but which may extend to thirty thousand rupees.

The National Commission for Women Act 1990

Section 3 provides for a setting up a statutory body namely the National Commission for Women to take up remedial measures, and facilitate redressal of grievances and advise the Government on all policy matters relating to women. Section 10 enumerates various functions of the Commission like:

(i) investigate and examine all matters relating to the safeguard provided for women under the Constitution and other laws;
(ii) review the existing provisions of the Constitution and other

laws affecting women and recommend amendments thereto so as to suggest remedial legislative measures to meet any lacunae, inadequacies or shortcomings in such legislations;

(iii) take up the cases of violation of the provisions of the Constitution and of other laws relating to women with the appropriate authorities;

(iv) look into complaints and take *suo moto* notice of matters relating to:

  (a) deprivation of women's rights;

  (b) non-implementation of laws enacted to provide protection to women and also to achieve the objective of equality and development;

  (c) non-compliance of policy decisions, guidelines or instructions aimed at mitigating hardships and ensuring welfare and providing relief to women;

(v) call for special studies or investigations into specific problems or situations arising out of discrimination and atrocities against women and identify the constraints so as to recommend strategies for their removal;

(vi) undertake promotional and educational research so as to suggest ways of ensuring due representation of women in all spheres and identify factors responsible for impeding their advancement, such as, lack of access to housing and basic services, inadequate support services and technologies for reducing drudgery and occupational health hazards and for increasing their productivity;

(vii) participate and advise on the planning process of socio-economic development of women;

(viii) evaluate the progress of the development of women under the Union and any State;

(ix) inspect or cause to be inspected a jail, remand home, women's institution or other place of custody where women are kept as prisoners or otherwise, and take up with the concerned authorities for remedial action;

(x) fund legislation involving issues affecting a large body of women; and

(xi) make periodical reports to the Government on any matter pertaining to women and in particular various difficulties under which women toil.

The Protection of Women from Domestic Violence Act 2005

It provides for punishment for domestic violence committed by husband and his relatives and also provides legal assistance for women suffering from domestic violence. Section 17 provides that every woman in a domestic relationship shall have the right to reside in the shared household, whether or not she has any right, title or beneficial interest in the same. Similarly, Section 22 and 23 deal with provisions for compensation and interim maintenance respectively.

The Sexual Harassment of Women at Workplace (Prevention, Prohibition and Redressal) Act 2013

Section 3 says that "no woman shall be subjected to sexual harassment at any work place." Further, Section 4 enjoins a duty upon the employer to constitute an internal complaints committee to deal with the complaints of sexual harassment at workplace. Section 19 casts a responsibility upon the employer to provide a safe working environment to women employees. Section 26 provides for penalty on the employer for non-compliance with the provisions of said Act.

Judicial Initiative Towards Empowerment of Women

Though hundreds of women welfare legislations are enacted by the Indian parliament but the stark reality is that due to their ineffective enforcement they have not been able to achieve the goal of gender parity and women empowerment. Male dominated society has found ways to circumvent the provisions of the legislations and to act as a blockade against women empowerment. Due to illiteracy, backwardness, unawareness and various socio-economic-political factors of the Indian women, we can say that the legislations, to a certain extent, have failed to protect women. Therefore, apart from performing its traditional role of interpreting the laws, the judiciary has come forward to protect women through its pro-active role. In protecting the women, the Indian Judiciary has removed all the procedural shackles and has completely revolutionised the idea of women empowerment. The judiciary has encouraged widest possible coverage of the legislations by liberally interpreting the terms. The judiciary, by its landmark judgments, had tried to fill up the gap created by the legislative machinery. In order to understand the role played by Indian judiciary in protecting the dignity of women, we can analyse certain case laws at this juncture.

In *Municipal Corporation of Delhi* vs. *Female Workers (Muster Roll)* [AIR 2000 SC 1274, 1281], the Supreme Court extended the benefits of the Maternity Benefit Act, 1961 to the Muster Roll (Daily Wagers) female employees of Delhi Municipal Corporation. In this case, the Court directly incorporated the provisions of Article 11 of the Convention on Elimination of All forms of Discrimination Against Women (CEDAW), 1979 into the Indian Law. Further, the Supreme Court held that a just social order could be achieved only when inequalities are obliterated and women, which constitute almost half of the segment of our society, are honoured and treated with dignity.

In *Chairman, Railway Board* vs. *Chandrima Doss* [AIR 2000 SC 988], it was a case of gang-rape of a Bangladeshi national by the employees of the Indian Railway in a room at *Yatriniwas* at Howrah station. The government contended that it could not be held liable under the law of torts as the offence was not committed during the course of official duty. However, Hon'ble Court didn't accepted this argument and stated that the employees of Government of India, who are deputed to run the railways and to manage the establishment, including the Railways station and *Yatrinivas* are essential components of the government machinery which carries on the commercial activity. If any such employee commits an act of tort, the Central Government of which they are the employees can be held vicariously liable in damages to the person wronged by those employees. The Supreme Court awarded a compensation of Rs. 10 lakhs to that victim of gang rape on the grounds of violation of her right to life and personal liberty guaranteed under Article 21 of the Constitution of India.

In *Githa Hari Haran* vs. *Reserve Bank of India* [AIR 1999 SC 1149], the Supreme Court interpreted Section 6(a) of the Hindu Minority and Guardianship Act, 1956 and Section 19(b) of the Guardians and Wards Act, 1890 in such a way that father and mother get equal status as guardians of a minor.

In *Mohammed Ahmed Khan* vs. *Shah Bano* [AIR 1985 SC 945], the judgment of this case created uproar in the Muslim Community. A five Judges Bench of the Supreme Court declared that a Muslim husband having sufficient means must provide maintenance to his divorced wife who is unable to maintain herself. Such a wife is entitled to the maintenance even if she refuses to live with Muslim husband because he has contracted another marriage within the limits of four wives allowed to him by *Quran*. The Bench declared that a Muslim divorced woman who cannot maintain herself is entitled to get maintenance from her former husband till the time she gets remarried. The Court rejected the plea that maintenance is payable for the *iddat* period only. Pointing to the *aiyats* of the *Quran*, the Judges declared that the *Quran* imposes an obligation to provide maintenance to the divorced wife. The judges also rejected the contention that deferred *Mahr* (dower) is a payment to the wife on divorce and hence such payment under the personal law excludes the payment of any maintenance by the husband in consideration of marriage. It was observed that according to *Quran*, the dower is a consideration and mark of respect for the Muslim woman instead of being a consideration for divorce. Further, it was stated that the religion professed by spouse has no place in the scheme of Section 125 Cr. P.C. which is measure of social justice to prevent vagrancy and destitution. The court held that if there is any conflict between personal law and Section 125 Cr.P.C. then it is clear from the language of the Section that it over-rules the personal law. Thus, the Supreme Court granted equal right of maintenance under Section 125 of the Cr.P.C., 1973 to a divorced Muslim woman notwithstanding the personal law. This judgment created a storm and priests of Islam started agitation.

In *Charan Singh* vs. *Union of India* [ILR 1979 Del 422], the Delhi High Court expressed that women are a backward class as compared to men.

In *Government of Andhra Pradesh* vs. *P.B. Vijay Kumar* [AIR 1995 SC 1648], the Supreme Court has held that the issue of reservation for women in State services was upheld under Article 15(3) of the Indian Constitution.

In *Air India* vs. *Nargesh Mirza* [AIR 1981 SC 1829], the Air India Regulation 46 was challenged as violative of Article 14 of the Constitution as it provided that an air hostess was to retire from service upon attaining the age of 35 years, or on marriage if it took place within four years of her joining service, or on first pregnancy, whichever occurred earlier. The Supreme Court struck down the Regulation providing for retirement of the Air Hostess on her first pregnancy, as unconstitutional under Article 14. The Court explained that the Regulation did not prohibit marriage after four years of joining service and if an Air Hostess after having fulfilled the first condition became pregnant, there was no reason why pregnancy should stand in the way of her continuing in service. After utilizing her service for four years, to terminate her service if she became pregnant, amounted to compelling the poor Air Hostess not to have any child. Thus, it amounted to an interference with the ordinary course of human nature. It is not only a callous and cruel act but an open insult to Indian Womanhood and therefore, it is manifestly unreasonable and arbitrary.

In *Bodhisathwa Gowtham* vs. *Ms. Subhra Chakaraborty* [AIR 1996 SC 922], the complainant was a student of the Baptist College, Kohima and the accused Sri Bodhisathwa was a lecturer in that college. The complainant alleged that the accused cohabited with her, giving her a false assurance of marriage. He fraudulently went through a certain marriage ceremony and thereby dishonestly made the complainant to believe that she was lawfully married wife of the accused by putting vermilion on her forehead in a temple. But later he refused to recognise her as his life partner. The Supreme Court ordered the accused to pay Rs. 1000 per month as an interim compensation to the victim of rape during the pendency of the criminal case. Further, referring to the pitiable condition of women in society *Mr. Justice Saghir Ahmad* observed that "unfortunately, the women in our country, belongs to class or group of society who are in disadvantaged position on account of several social barriers and impediments and have therefore, been victims of tyranny at the hands of men with whom they, unfortunately, under the Constitution enjoy 'equal status'. Women also have the right to life and liberty; they also have the right to be respected and treated as equal citizens. Their honour and dignity cannot be touched or violated. They also have the right to lead an honourable and peaceful life." The Supreme Court observed that rape is not only an offence under the criminal law, but it is a violation of the fundamental right to life and liberty guaranteed by Article 21 of Indian Constitution and is a crime against basic human rights.

In *Vishakha* vs. *State of Rajasthan* [AIR 1997 SC 3011], Vishakha, a non-governmental organization working for gender equality, had filed a writ petition seeking the protection of the fundamental rights of working women under Article 21 of the Constitution of India. The immediate reason for the petition was the gang rape of a saathin (a social worker involved in women's development programmes) of Rajasthan in 1992. The assault was an act of revenge as the saathin had intervened to prevent a child marriage. The Supreme Court took a serious note of the increasing menace of sexual harassment of women at workplace and elsewhere. Considering the inadequacy of legislation on the point, the Court even assumed the role of legislature and defined sexual harassment and laid down certain guidelines to be followed by the employers for providing safe working conditions to the women employees.

In *Apparel Export Promotion Council* vs. *A.K. Chopra* [AIR 1999 SC 625], the accused (Secretary to chairman of a Delhi based Apparel Export Promotion Council) tried to molest a women employee Miss X (a clerk cum typist) at Taj Hotel, Delhi. He persuaded her to accompany him while taking dictation from the Chairman. While she was waiting in the room, he taking advantage of the isolated place tried to sit too close to her and touch her despite her objections and tried to molest her physically in the lift also, but she saved herself by pressing emergency button which made the door of lift open. The Supreme Court held that "in a case involving charge of sexual harassment or attempt to sexually molest, the courts are required to examine the broader probabilities of case and not swayed away by insignificant discrepancies or narrow technicalities or dictionary meaning of the expression 'molestation' or 'physical assault'.... The sexual harassment of a female employee at workplace is incompatible with the dignity and honour of a female and need to be eliminated and there can be no compromise with such violation".

In *C.B. Muthamma* vs. *Union of India* [AIR 1979 SC 1868], a service rule whereby marriage was a disability for appointment to Foreign Service was declared unconstitutional by the Supreme Court.

In *Shobha Rani* vs. *Madhukar* [AIR 1988 SC 121], the Supreme Court held that dowry demand was enough to amount to cruelty.

In *Prathibha Rani* vs. *Suraj Kumar* [AIR 1985 SC 628], the Supreme Court upheld women's right to the *Stridhana*.

In *State of Punjab* vs. *Gurmit Singh* [AIR 1996 SC 1393], the Supreme Court held that rape is violative of the right of privacy.

In *Savita Samvedi* vs. *Union of India* [1996 SCC (2) 380], the Supreme Court held that a married daughter was allowed accommodation in parental house.

In *Delhi Domestic Working Women's Forum* vs. *Union of India* [1995 SCC (1) 14], the Supreme Court suggested the formulation of a segment for awarding compensation to rape victims at the time of convicting the person found guilty of rape. The Court suggested that the Criminal Injuries Compensation Board or the Court should award compensation to the victims by taking into account, the pain, suffering and shock as well as loss of earnings due to pregnancy and the expenses of child birth if this occurs as a result of rape.

In *Gaurav Jain* vs. *Union of India* [AIR 1997 SC 3021], the Supreme Court laid down guidelines including the necessity of counselling, cajoling, and coercing the women to retrieve from prostitution and rehabilitate them.

In *Deelip Singh* vs. *State of Bihar* [AIR 2005 SC 203], the Court held that consent given by a women believing the man's promise to marry her would fall within the expression 'without her consent' for the offence of rape under Section 375(ii) of the I.P.C., 1860 if it is established that from the very inception the man never really intended to marry her and the promise was a mere hoax.

In *State of Maharashtra* vs. *Madhukar Narayan Mardikar* [AIR 1991 SC 207], the Court observed that even a woman of easy virtue is entitled to privacy and no one can invade her privacy as and when he likes. She is entitled to protect her person if there is an attempt to violate it against her wish. She is equally entitled to the protection of law. Therefore, merely because she is a woman of easy virtue, her evidence cannot be thrown overboard.

Conclusion

The Indian legislature as well as the judiciary is trying hard to empower women, protect their dignity and enable them to attain the equality of status at par with men in the society. In fact, as a result of such efforts the position of women has undergone a sea change in the recent past. But, we must understand that only enacting laws in favour of women or delivering women-centric judgements will not suffice the purpose of women empowerment. For this, the mindset of the people has to be changed. No doubt, the legislative and judicial initiatives have placed women at a better place in the society, yet women in India has to go miles for transforming the equality on paper into the real equality.

References

Agarwal B.D., "Curing Gender Bias", *AIR 2000 Jour* 85.
Air India vs. *Nargesh Mirza* [AIR 1981 SC 1829].
Apparel Export Promotion Council vs. *A.K. Chopra* [AIR 1999 SC 625].

Bhatt D.K., "Human Rights and Status of Women: A Socio-Legal Analysis", *AIR 2000 Jour* 79.

Bodhisathwa Gowtham vs. *Ms. Subhra Chakaraborty* [AIR 1996 SC 922].

C.B. Muthamma vs. *Union of India* [AIR 1979 SC 1868].

Chairman, Railway Board vs. *Chandrima Doss* [AIR 2000 SC 988].

Champa Limaye, *Women Power and Progress*, B.R. Publishing Corporation, New Delhi, 1999.

Charan Singh vs. *Union of India* [ILR 1979 Del 422].

Deelip Singh vs. *State of Bihar* [AIR 2005 SC 203].

Delhi Domestic Working Women's Forum vs. *Union of India* [1995 SCC (1) 14].

Gaurav Jain vs. *Union of India* [AIR 1997 SC 3021].

Githa Hari Haran vs. *Reserve Bank of India* [AIR 1999 SC 1149].

Government of Andhra Pradesh vs. *P.B. Vijay Kumar* [AIR 1995 SC 1648].

Josli, K.C., "Universalization of Human Rights of Women: Supreme Court Sets the Pace", *AIR 2001 Jour* 59.

Krushna Chandra Sena, "Violence against Women: A Human Right Violation", *AIR 2003 Jour* 312.

Mohammed Ahmed Khan vs. *Shah Bano* [AIR 1985 SC 945].

Municipal Corporation of Delhi vs. *Female Workers (Muster Roll)* [AIR 2000 SC 1274, 1281].

Nandita Haksar, (1986), *Demystification of Law for Women*, Lancer Press, New Delhi.

Pandey, J.N., *Constitutional Law of India*, Central Law Agency; 41st ed. 2004, p. 259.

Prathibha Rani vs. *Suraj Kumar* [AIR 1985 SC 628].

Preeti Mishra, "Gender Justice: Some Issues", *AIR 2001 Jour* 149.

Prof. Narender Kumar, (2006), *Constitutional Law of India*, Allahabad Law Agency, 5th ed., p. 590.

R. Revathi, (2004), *Laws Relating to Domestic Violence*, Asia Law House, Hyderabad.

Reddy G.B., "Women and Law in India—Issues and Challenges", *AIR 2003 Jour* 331.

S.R. Myeni, (2003), *Women and Law*, Asia Law House, Hyderabad.

Savita Samvedi vs. *Union of India* [1996 SCC (2) 380].

Shobha Rani vs. *Madhukar* [AIR 1988 SC 121].

Siddhartha Dash, (2004), "Women Empowerment in India", *Orissa Review*, December, p. 56.

State of Maharashtra vs. *Madhukar Narayan Mardikar* [AIR 1991 SC 207].

State of Punjab vs. *Gurmit Singh* [AIR 1996 SC 1393].

The Commission of Sati (Prevention) Act 1987.

The Constitution of India, 1950.

The Criminal Procedure Code, 1973.

The Dowry Prohibition Act 1961.

The Equal Remuneration Act 1976.
The Factories Act 1948.
The Hindu Adoption and Maintenance Act 1956.
The Hindu Marriage Act 1956.
The Hindu Minority and Guardianship Act 1956.
The Hindu Succession Act 1956.
The Immoral Trafficking (Prevention) Act 1986.
The Indecent Representation of Women (Prohibition) Act 1986.
The Indian Evidence Act 1872.
The Indian Penal Code, 1860.
The Maternity Benefit Act 1961.
The Medical Termination of Pregnancy Act 1971.
The National Commission for Women Act 1990.
The National Policy for the Empowerment of Women, 2001, Government of India, Department of Women and Child Development, Ministry of Human Resource Development, New Delhi.
The Pre-Natal Diagnostic Technique (Regulation and Prevention) Act 1994.
The Sexual Harassment of Women at Workplace (Prevention, Prohibition and Redressal) Act 2013.
Vishakha vs. *State of Rajasthan* [AIR 1997 SC 3011].

6

Addressing Socio-Legal Problems Concerning Women

An Imperative for Inclusive Growth

Pardeep Singh

Building Dialogue

In the post-independence India, number of legislative measures, policies and schemes aiming at ameliorating women's condition have been promised. In spite of all these seemingly robust policy initiatives *Nirbhaya, Gudia* and many other ghastly inhuman episodes transpire and traumatize the whole society. Though *Nirbhaya* incident received exceptional attention and led to a country-wide protest particularly amongst '*youngistan*' resulting into a new set of initiatives including certain amendments in the Criminal Law, emergence of *Nirbhaya Fund*, creation of women banks etc. But the real question before the society is whether these promises are sufficient for making a change in the society or we need to adopt an action-based approach to mete out gender discrimination. The present goal of Twelfth Five Year Plan *viz*. faster and sustainable inclusive growth can only be realized by giving women their due by addressing their socio-legal problems. The sympathetic approaches of politicians, writers and social workers need to be deconstructed and a constructive paradigm with self-realization is required to be built.

Position of Women Globally

"Women constitute half the world's population, perform nearly two-third of its work hours, receive one-tenth of the world's income, and less than one-hundredth of the world's property."[1] A recent report by the World Health Organization (WHO) says that more than one third of women world-wide are victims of physically or sexual violence. A vast majority of women are attacked or abused by their husbands (through whom perhaps they are being recognized in society) or boyfriends. Also, almost 38 per cent of all women murder victims were killed by intimate partners.[2] Prof. Martha Nussbaum pointed out that these are not rare cases of unusual crime but are common realities.[3] According to the Human Development Report (1999) of the United Nations Development Programme (UNDP), there is no country that treats its women as well as its men, according to a complex measure that includes life expectancy, wealth, and education (United Nations Development Programme, 1999).

Prof. Martha Nussbaum also pointed out that if we turn to the very basic area of health and nutrition, there is pervasive evidence of discrimination against females in many nations of the developing world. It is generally believed that, where equal nutrition and health care are present, women live, on average, slightly longer than men: thus, we would expect a sex ratio of something like 102.2 women to 100 men (the actual sex ratio of Sub-Saharan Africa). Contrary to this, India is having a far lower sex ratio of 92.7 women to 100 men, the lowest sex ratio since the census began early in this century.

Women in India: Riddled with Agony

Women form a unique class of minority who has low standing as compared to men in Indian society and are considered generally political minority. As per the provisional figure of 2011 census population of Women in India was nearly 58.64 crore[4], out of which 40.51 crore lives in rural areas and only 33.42 crore women are literate. They have little control on the resources and on important decisions related to their lives. Women face double discrimination being members of specific caste, class, or ethnic group apart from experiencing gendered vulnerabilities which includes infanticide, sexual violence, forced abortion, etc. In India, early marriage and childbearing affects women's health adversely. As per UNICEF, more than 40 per cent of the world's child marriages take place in India. Throughout infancy and growing years a girl child faces different forms of violence like—infanticide, neglect of nutrition needs, education, and healthcare. As adults they face violence due to unwanted pregnancies, domestic violence, sexual abuse at the workplace and sexual violence including marital rape and honour killings.

India ranked poorly at global level in Gender Inequality Index (GII) having 129th position out of 145 countries surveyed. A G-20 survey has ranked India as the worst place for a woman. The National Crime Records Bureau shows that a crime is committed against a woman every third minute, a woman is raped every 29th minute, a dowry death occurs every 77th minute and one case of cruelty, committed by either the husband or relative of the victim, every ninth minute.[5]

Adding fuel to these pathetic conditions, the UNICEF's Global Report Card on Adolescents 2012, shows that 57 per cent of boys and 53 per cent of girls in India think that a husband is justified in hitting or beating his wife.

Furthermore, as per the data issued by the National Crime Records Bureau, Ministry of Home Affairs, Government of India in the name of SNAPSHOTS–2012, incidences of crime against women have increased from 2,28,650 in 2011 to 2,44,270 in 2012.[6] The State of West Bengal alone reported 12.7 per cent of total such cases in the country (30,942 out of 2,44, 270).[7] The proportion of IPC[8] crimes committed against women has increased during last 5 years from 8.9 per cent in the year 2008 to 9.4 per cent during the year 2012.[9] Madhya Pradesh has reported the highest number of Rape cases (3,425), Assault on Women with intent to outrage her modesty (6,655) and Importation of Girls from foreign country (59) accounting for 13.7 per cent, 14.6 per cent and 10.1 per cent respectively of total such cases reported in the country.[10] Andhra Pradesh has reported 40.5 per cent (3,714) of Insult to the modesty of Women cases.[11] Highest cases of Kidnapping and Abduction 20.7 per cent (7,910) and Dowry Deaths 27.3 per cent (2,244) were reported in Uttar Pradesh.[12] Offenders were known to the victims in 98.2 per cent of Rape cases (24,470 out of 24,915).[13] A total of 36,622 cases of crime against women were reported from 53 mega cities out of 2, 44, 270 cases reported in the country during 2012. The rate of crime in these cities at 47.76 was comparatively higher as compared to national rate at 41.74.[14] Among

53 mega cities, Delhi (City) accounted for 14.2 per cent (5,194) of such crimes followed by Bengaluru 6.2 per cent (2,263) and Kolkata 5.7 per cent (2,073). An increase of 1.1 per cent in human trafficking incidence was observed (3,554 cases in 2012 as compared to 3,517 in 2011).

Out of total 2.5 million people who are in forced labour (including sexual exploitation) at any given time as a result of trafficking, 56 per cent are in Asia and the Pacific.[15] Cases under Immoral Traffic (Prevention) Act increased by 5.2 per cent (from 2,435 in 2011 to 2,563 in 2012). Tamil Nadu (500 cases) followed by Andhra Pradesh (472 cases) reported the highest incidence of 19.5 per cent and 18.4 per cent respectively of total cases (2,563) under Immoral Traffic (Prevention) Act.[16] In spite of having a number of promises for human rights and human dignity-based rights and laws,[17] the ailment of human trafficking has been alarming, which poses a serious threat towards realizing the constitutional objective of prohibiting trafficking in human beings. India is one of the worst countries which have significantly failed in tackling human trafficking,[18] affecting on the most disadvantaged socio-economic strata such as Scheduled Tribes, Scheduled Castes, Other Backward Castes, ethnic minorities, tribal communities, undocumented migrant workers, stateless people or refugees.

Moreover, post-crime investigation and delay in trial proceeding also adding fuel to these mounting crimes in India as Prof. Amartya Sen too rightly pointed out that high frequency of rape[19] [or other offences] may not be the real issue in India, but all the evidence suggests that India has a huge problem in seriously monitoring rape and taking steps to reduce it. Prof. Sen opined that failure of the police to help rape victims and to ensure the safety of women is particularly lamentable.[20]

The shocking fact, that has come to light in a survey by the Mathura District Legal Services Authority (DLSA) on the "Plight of Forsaken/Forlorn Women—Old and Widows Living in the religious place like Vrindavan in the State of UP"[21] that the bodies of widows who die in government-run shelter homes in Vrindavan are taken away by sweepers at night, cut into pieces, put into jute bags and disposed of as the institutions do not have any provision for a decent funeral. This, too, is done only after the inmates give money to the sweeper! Taking cognizance of a report published in *The Hindu* on August 11, 2011 on the plight of the widows living in Vrindavan in

Mathura district of Uttar Pradesh, Mr. Justice Altamash Kabir, the then Executive Chairperson of the National Legal Services Authority, had asked the U.P. State Legal Services Authority to survey the conditions of the women. In that survey it was found that in most cases widows are denied remarriage after the death of their husband even in childhood or young age. While some are forced to leave the marital home and native place by the family members just to division of share in the family property or to avoid maintenance in old age and bearing the burden of a non-productive family member, many others leave their homes due to physical and mental torture. This kind of sorry state makes us realize about the pathetic conditions of a single woman particularly after the death of her husband.

Women from Minorities in Particular

The conditions of women of minorities in particular are more deteriorated socially, economically and politically. In India still, there exists a provision of four marriages by one person in Muslim community, which is the largest minority community in the India, though it is not mandatory as per their personal law. Further the interpretations of personal law of some minorities are being construed wrongly in number of instances, which sometimes create a problem in cases like—divorce, maintenance, etc.

Furthermore, there is no provision of claiming maintenance from the husband by a Muslim woman under Sections 125-128 of Criminal Procedure Code 1973, unless and until an affidavit in writing is given by husband and wife both to the court that they are ready to get their suit of maintenance be heard by the respective court.[22] Husbands will rarely give his consent to this kind of suit; hence it is very much seems to be a paper tiger. To overcome these kinds of problems, the concept of *Uniform Civil Code*[23] may be implemented which is a directive for the government by Constitution of India itself under Part-IV.

In the present context, the pathetic conditions prevailing all around poses a challenge to be mete out. Though the Justice Verma Committee set out an objective for reducing the annual growth rate of crime against women and children by at least 25 per cent per annum, but it seems not to be a cakewalk and definitely requires greater role to be played by policy-makers, civil society and other agencies and instruments of the government.

Scrutiny of Legal Policies framed for the Women Empowerment

By inserting the various legal provisions we have probably won the battle but, still we need to fight the war against gender discrimination in our day to day life. In any patriarchal society, women are second class citizens and widows third class. She has equal legal rights but, still unawareness, customary practices and other social construction prevent their full expression. Very often daughters are persuaded by the family and by the mother herself to relinquish her share so that she can continue her association with the natal home. The arguments given are that the natal family had acquired huge expense at the time of the marriage in solemnizing the same or on dowry. Further, the day today expenses on customary practices like: *Bhaat, Teez, Bhai dooz*[24] etc. after the marriage, are to be borne by the parental family. Most women do require the emotional support from the parental family. But this support comes in lieu of willing away her property right. Ironically, by making the legal provisions like— Amendments of 2005 in the Hindu Succession Act, 1956, which have created the legal rights as far as ownership of property by woman is concerned the women issues seems to be addressed on papers but the existing social constructions, prevailing customary practices have hijack these rights and left this segment of the society in a situation of helplessness.

At the same time 73rd and 74th Amendment of our Constitution may have inserted the provisions regarding the participatory role of the of women in the Panchayati Raj Institutions at the grassroots level, but the ground reality whereby they are being governed by their counterpart is not hidden to anyone in the present society.

Further the Protection of Women from Domestic Violence Act 2005 is also seems to be a paper tiger in reality. As per the 5th monitoring report of the PWDWA brought out by the Lawyer's Collective and International Centre for Research on Women, the Protection officers are discouraging women from seeking justice and are pushing them in to "settlement." On the question raised by this body while survey that is Domestic Violence a family affair? 57.1 per cent of Delhi's protection officers said 'yes,' which indicate that they still don't see it as a social problem.[25]

Furthermore Representation of Indian Women in Indian Legislature is marginal and is not according to their population. The present 16th Lok Sabha of Parliament has 11.3 per cent (61 in total, though highest ever) MPs as women. For more inclusion of women in policy-making bodies the only light seems to be seen at the end of this dark black tunnel is the Bill of 33 per cent reservation for women in Lok Sabha, which is to be discussed in the Parliament.

Post *Nirbhaya* India

The ghastly incident of *Nirbhaya* waked up India with a country-wide protest demanding the stringent law pertaining to the violence against women. The Constitution of Justice J.S. Verma Committee; which acted so rapidly and came with its report favouring some amendments in the existing set up of criminal law, was definitely a stride toward curbing such crimes. The insertion of new criminal offences such as causing grievous hurt through acid attacks, sexual harassment, use of criminal force on a woman with intent to disrobe, stalking, voyeurism etc. undoubtedly expanded the horizon of definition of sexual assault. Perhaps this was for the first time in the history of India that policy-makers came with the Act in the form of Criminal Law (Amendment) Act 2013 so expeditiously which was never seen before. The spark generated through this horrific incident, though with a heavy cost of compromising the life of a brave daughter of India, ignited the young minds and which consequently contributed in the amendment of criminal law. After a nine-month-long trial, a fast track court in Delhi handed down death penalty to all the four convicts in the *Nirbhaya* gang rape and murder case. The court while pronouncing the judgment opined that, "in these times when crime against women are on rise, judiciary cannot turn a blind eye towards such gruesome crime and certainly a need arise to send a message that it will not be tolerated." On the another hand in the same case the decision of Juvenile Justice Board, Delhi on August 30, 2013, added to cynicism by convicting the minor accused only for 3 years and it is a sobering reminder that the Criminal Law (Amendment) Act, 2013 is insufficient reform[26] as far as the accused being a minor, although the matter pertaining to the culpability of a minor in exceptionally horrified crimes is to be decided by the Apex Court.

Notably after the *Nirbhaya* episode India has witnessed the barbaric events even in 2013 such as the rape of five year old girl child in NCR, acid attack on number of women, the horrific cases of honour killings, the gang rape of a photo journalist in Mumbai, Badaun rape and murder case and as well as countless other similar incidents which are alarming with an uncontrolled speed.

Conclusion and Suggestions

In spites of all the legal protections given to the women, which seem to be a paper tiger, this segment of the society is still marginalized and requires more attention. There is no dearth, as such, of the Legal provisions as far as the protection of the interest of women are concerned but the evil resides in the way of proper implementation of the statutory laws. Women being minorities continue to live in miserable conditions like—malnutrition, harassment, ignorance, denied ownership of means of production and property, etc. It is the high time to have such social movement, whereby we can deconstruct all our social constructs of gender discrimination and to achieve in particular the shorter mission in the form of more faster, sustainable and inclusive growth and in general the Constitutional goals of justice, liberty, equality and fraternity by awareness, sensitization, imparting skills and building capacities with in this vulnerable segment of the society. Policy-makers should promote the concept of gender budgeting for making an access to mainstream for this vulnerable segment of the society. Problems being faced by the women in the present society are of such kind that the entire idea of Inclusive Growth seems to be unrealistic unless we devise a mechanism for the upliftment of this segment of society.

The creation of certain rights or defining something as an offence in black and white is not going to serve the purpose rather time has come now for the society to deconstruct our societal behaviour and to replace it with more humane approach. It is high time to devote more time in building the capacity and developing the skills of women for their real empowerment in tune with the Nussbaum's capabilities approach who talk about 'bodily integrity'[27] as one of the parameters of the standard that should be adopted by any just political society. In this background, Malala Yousafzai,[28] a girl from Pakistan emerged as a trendsetter before the world today, when she set an example of her capability while addressing the world in the UN General Assembly for Youth in New York. She gave a stress buster caption of women empowerment when she said: "one child, one teacher, one pen and one book can change the world."

The insertion of new criminal offences such as causing grievous hurt through acid attacks, sexual harassment, use of criminal force on a woman with intent to disrobe, stalking, voyeurism, etc. undoubtedly expanded the horizon of definition of sexual assault. Perhaps this was for the first time in the history of India that policy-makers came with the Act in the form of Criminal Law (Amendment) Act 2013 so expeditiously which was never seen before. The spark generated through this horrific incident, though with a heavy cost of compromising the life of a brave daughter of India, ignited the young minds and subsequently contributed in the amendment of criminal law.

The Constitution (108th Amendment) Bill, 2008 and Constitution (110th Amendment) Bill, 2009, which provide for reservation for women in Parliament and State Legislative Assemblies and for reservation for women from one-third to 50 per cent of total number of seats and offices of Chairpersons in Panchayats at each level, respectively may prove potent weapons, if passed by Parliament, for addressing the pathetic conditions of women and for sharing the equal pie by women in policy making process of country.

In India, the present five-year-goal of faster, sustainable and more inclusive growth can only be feasible by addressing women's plight which inter alia demands bringing changes in societal mental attitudes. Recently the Supreme Court of India has rightly shown its intolerance towards the crimes against the women and held that a compromise entered into between a rape victim and the accused/convict not to prosecute the complaint further cannot be a leading factor in lesser punishment. The Apex Court reiterates its earlier judgments by recognizing these kinds of cases under the category of non-compoundable ones and by adopting a zero tolerance approach towards these kinds of heinous crimes against women. While upholding the right of livelihood of female dancers of dance bars of Maharashtra, the Supreme Court held that instead of generating unemployment, it may be wiser for the State to look into ways and means in which reasonable restrictions may be imposed on bar dancing, but without completely prohibiting or stopping the same.[29] These kinds of pro-women judicial pronouncements will certainly set a tone for the women empowerment. Augmentation of funds for women under gender budgeting may also prove a remarkable stride and can rightly be said as dire need of the present day India. Also, there is a need to have normative approach to deal with sexual offenders. For example registration of sexual offenders as is the practice prevailing in many countries of the west. We have to create a well-defined protocol for police and police stations to deal with incidences and complainant of sexual offences. This may include defining time limits and targets without which even establishing of fast track courts may not be very effective as is so often argued. In the present world of ICT there is a need for creating possibilities of using technologies and providing access for filing online complaints involving sexual offences.

Rajasthan Model in the form of *'Bhamashah Scheme'* which got inaugurated in Udaipur recently happens to be a unique initiative for uplifting the status of women. The basic difference between the *'Aadhaar'* and the State government plan is that the Rajasthan scheme will come to beneficiaries with a bank account. While *'Aadhaar'* is later linked to beneficiaries' bank accounts, the *'Bhamashah Scheme'* is a card that comes with a bank account number registered in the name of the female head of the family. Her biometrics is being recorded and only she can withdraw money. Such kinds of initiatives will certainly deconstruct the long rooted social construction of the society which uses to treat man; as the only suitable choice for heading the family in the capacity of '*Karta.*'

No denial to say that constitutional goal of justice—social, economic and political, equality and liberty which have been devised for assuring the dignity of individual, unity and integrity of nation and for promotion of fraternity, can only be achieved by shunning the practices derogatory to the dignity of women (as promised under Article 51A(e) of Constitution of India) like violence against women, child marriage, all kinds of discrimination against women. Let's pledge together that without developing only sympathetic approaches towards these sensitive issues we will adopt a pragmatic approach in order to have a holistic development of the society; which can only be possible by giving women their due. India with a robust demographic dividend is very much capable of playing a greater global participatory role in the World economy. India is having the largest chain of working professional qualified women in the world as per UN, which can contribute a lot in the Nation's growth. At the same time no one can deny the wording of legal luminary Prof. Mool Chand Sharma,[30] when he said:

Whatever whiff of emancipation has blown during this period has been enjoyed largely by urban women whereas women belonging to the rural areas are still totally untouched by the wind of change.[31]

At end, really it needs to be understood that sex is biological thing but gender is a 'social construction' which definitely requires deconstruction.

Notes

1 United Nations Report, Programme of Action for the Second Half of the UN Decade for Women, 1980.
2. Atiya Anis, "Better Half But in Bad Shape," *The Hindu,* July 21, 2013.
3. Martha Nussbaum, "Women's Capabilities and Social Justice," *Journal of Human Development,* Vol. 1, No. 2, 2000.
4. As per provisional figures of 2011 census, total population of India was 1210,193,422 and women constitute 48.4 per cent of total population.
5. Atiya Anis, "Better Half But in Bad Shape," *The Hindu,* July 21, 2013.
6. See also, National Crime Records Bureau (2013), "Crime in India 2012 Statistics," Ministry of Home Affairs, Government of India. Notably in 2012 the incidences of cognizable crimes under IPC have been multiplied 296 times as compare to 1953. (From 6,01,964 incidences in 1953 to 23,87,188 in 2012).
7. *Ibid.*
8. Indian Penal Code.
9. *Supra* note 7.
10. *Ibid.*
11. *Ibid.*
12. *Ibid.*
13. *Ibid*
14. *Ibid.*
15. International Labour Organization, *Forced Labour Statistics Factsheet* (2007).
16. *Supra* note 14.
17. Despite having the Constitutional mandate in form of a fundamental right for prohibiting human trafficking (Article 23) and ratifying the *UN Protocol to Prevent, Suppress and Punish Trafficking in Persons, Especially Women and Children* (Trafficking Protocol), India is still to bring its law in conformity with international standards against trafficking.
18. "India among worst ranked countries in tackling human trafficking," *The Hindu,* June 16, 2010, available online at: http://www.thehindu.com/news/article.
19. The United Nations Office on Drugs and Crime found the incidence of rape in India for 2010 to be 1.8 per 100,000 people, compared with, for example, 27.3 in the US, 28.8 in the UK, 63.5 in Sweden, and 120.0 in South Africa. (though this does not include the unreported cases of rape which are huge in number in India).

20. Professor Amartya Sen, "*India's Women: The Mixed Truth—An Exchange,*" December 19, 2013.
21. "Dignity denied even in death for Vrindavan widows," *The Hindu,* 08-1-2012.
22. Section 5 in The Muslim Women (Protection of Rights On Divorce) Act 1986 provides that—If on the date of the first hearing of the application under sub-section (2) of section 3, a divorced woman and her former husband declare, by affidavit or any other declaration in writing in such form as may be prescribed, either jointly or separately, that they would prefer to be governed by the provisions of sections 125 to 128 of the Code of Criminal Procedure, 1973 (2 of 1974), and file such affidavit or declaration in the court hearing the application, the Magistrate shall dispose of such application accordingly.
23. Article-44, Part-IV of Indian Constitution requires the State to secure for the citizens a Uniform Civil Code throughout the territory of India.
24. These are some customary practices wherein, on some particular occasions gifts are to be given to girl by her natal family.
25. "Protection officers hardly of any help to victims: survey", *The Tribune,* 31-01-2012.
26. Aparna Viswanathan, "A task only half finished," *The Hindu,* August 28, 2013.
27. As per Martha Nussbaum's capabilities approach, 'bodily health' as one of the capabilities out of ten covers—being able to move freely from place to place; to be secure against violent assault, including sexual assault and domestic violence...
28. A victim of a murderous Taliban assault in Swat.
29. State of Maharashtra & Ors. *vs.* Indian Hotel and Restaurants Assn. & Ors., Civil Appeal No. 2705 of 2006. (decided on July 16, 2013).
30. Presently Member (full time) Law Commission of India.
31. See *Women Empowerment: A New Dawn, a Monograph Launched by Central University*, Haryana, Feb. 2012.

7

From Suppressed to Acknowledged

A Paradigm Shift from Legal Perspective

Anju Beniwal

Prologue

> "Women will work out their destinies – much better too than men can ever do for them. All the mischief to women has come because men undertook to shape the destiny of women."
>
> — Swami Vivekanand

Women are put on high pedestal of goddess calling her "*shaktirupa*" on one hand, but in reality treated as a less human even. Women want and deserve a life with dignity, equality and freedom and not just being a maimed animal to be tamed and instructed for every dos and don'ts. What is required is to give women regard as an equal human being, who is having all rights to decide about herself. On the name of security women are devoid of their most precious and important virtue i.e. Freedom. As well said by Swami Vivekanand, "*The idea of perfect womanhood is perfect independence.*"[1] He believed in the self-respect and self-dignity of women and wanted no man to trample upon it, be it in the guise of protection or in the guise of reformation.[2] Irrespective of religion, culture and economic system, women suffer deprivation, humiliation and denial of basic human rights in almost all walks of life, everywhere, at every stage in varying degrees.

Due to excessive rise in crime against women now days Indian capital is being called as 'rape capital' in the media. Rape cultures are nourished by norms, attitudes, and practices that trivialize, tolerate, or even condone violence against women. They are further normalized if there is impunity for perpetrators either due to a lack of effective legal mechanisms or apathy to prosecuting crimes against women. Crime or violence against women are on a rise unabated in one form or another, despite various laws and legislations to curb it. There are innumerable reasons for this, just taking one aspect is not going to help since total overhauling of the system is required to control crime against women. According to a study, within the span of three generations India has systematically targeted and annihilated more than 50 million women from its population. One illustration of this is the skewed sex ratio as evident from the 2014 data according to that there are 940 women for every 1000 men, which is much below the world average of 990 females, and this national figure hides significant regional discrepancies.[3]

Being a Woman in India: The Statistics

According to a Report, there are reported cases of one rape every 54 minutes, a molestation every 26 minutes; and an act of cruelty every 33 minutes. National Crime Records Bureau (NCRB) statistic says—every 20 minutes, a woman is raped somewhere in India, not to mention the countless number of cases of molestations or rapes going unreported. Rape has increased by 1255.3 per cent (from 2,487 cases in 1971 to 33,707 cases in 2013).[4] Child rape cases have increased by 336 per cent in the last 10 years. Government data shows crimes by juveniles—especially rape and abduction of women—has seen exponential rise in the past decade—from 48.7 per cent in 2002 to 66.5 per cent in 2012. There is dire need to address the issue of rape in a more powerful manner. Number of dowry-deaths is quite alarming in the country—a dowry death every one hour forty two minutes.

Secondary Status to Whom

Apartheid of gender exist in almost all societies. In our society women have always been provided a secondary status. A woman is not treated as a human being with her own identity but as a property of the family she belongs to and so through ages she has been confined on the name of honour. Credit of her contributions goes to society, nation or to their male counter-parts, who have retained power, prestige and pleasures of the world leaving women remain ignorant, illiterate and ill-informed, invisible and unrewarded. Moreover, perpetrators of heinous crimes are mostly known or related to victim women.

Women in one form or other has been given back seat in our male chauvinistic society. The status of women in modern India is a sort of a paradox. If on one hand she is at the peak of ladder of success, on the other hand she is mutely suffering the violence afflicted on her by her own family members. At various high positions we have women as officers, prominent leaders' etc. but in a population like ours these are just an exception to rule and exceptions can't change the rule. As compared with past women in modern times have achieved a lot but in reality they have to still travel a long way. Their path is full of roadblocks. The women have left the secured domain of their home and are now in the battlefield of life, fully armored with their talent. They had proven themselves. But in India they are yet to get their dues. The sex ratio of India shows that the Indian society is still prejudiced against female.

Systematic Subjugation of Women

In our country women seems to be in situations worse than cattle. This is not just restricted to the rural area but extends to the so-called urban civilized world. Even here the so-called educated, well-fed, well-dressed, highly paid white collar job holders behave with gruesome savagery and unbelievable ruthlessness when it comes to matters related to women in their families. At that time, they cannot accept the equality of man and women. They cling on to the 18th century dogmas and beliefs of subjugation of women. They are not prepared to give women the basic safety, security and respect that is needed to normal sustenance. They want the women to earn those things by serving them and pleasing them through her sacrifies. If the woman fails to comply to those rotten norms she can be shown the door without assigning any reason. Though there are laws that protect women's rights, but the efficiency of Indian's judicial system is not hidden.

All these glory stories of real life situations make a strong case for building a discourse for addressing the socio-legal problems concerning women. Unfortunately a significant section of men belonging to today's generation believe in this kind of subjugation of women. They along with their parents create havoc in women's lives. And ironically women often themselves are a party to it. Mothers instigating their sons to beat up the wife are a common sight. Numbers of studies say that a boy-child is treated with more care than a girl-child. Women often feel that giving birth to a boy-child will enhance their status in the society. They even look down upon women with girl child. These people think that since they have a son they are a privileged class and they naturally have the right to inflict pains on the family of the girl to whom their son is married to.[5]

Women Role is Undervalued or Unrecognized

Women's role is undervalued or unrecognized in our societies. Gender inequality is still very evident in this respect, as indicated by the following United Nations Statistics: Women perform 2/3 of the world's work, earn 1/10 of the world's income. Women are 2/3 of the world's illiterates; Women own less than 1/100 of the world's property.[6] The tasks women usually perform in carrying out their different roles do not generally earn them an income. Women are often defined exclusively in terms of their reproductive roles and these reproductive roles, together with their community management roles, are perceived as natural. But because these roles do not earn income, they are not recognized and valued as economically productive. Women's contributions to national economic development are, therefore, often not quantified and invisible. A laudable step in this direction has been taken by an American court which has made it mandatory for a husband to be present at time of his child's birth to sensitize them to the pain and suffering undertook by a women for the sake of their child. Moreover, the concept of gender budgeting has to be implemented to recognize the role and labour of women in monetary terms.

Pragmatic Judicial Approach

Judiciary in India has always played a laudable role in eradicating social evils, and to bring social justice to masses. Supreme Court of India has devised various ways like epistolary jurisdiction, relaxing *locus standi* criteria, allowing Public Interest Litigation (PIL) and has played a pro-active role to bring justice to every doorstep. Through various cases several guidelines has been provided by the Apex Court to eradicate social evils and specially to curb crimes against women. Following are some recent judgments of Apex Court with some strict guidelines with a view to minimize crime against women.

Time and again judiciary has taken a pro-active approach in identifying and tackling crime against women. The focus of judiciary has been mainly towards identifying, punishing and the most important about rehabilitation of the victims e.g. from *Vishaka* vs. *State of Rajasthan*[7] to *Medha Kotwal Lele* vs. *Union of India*[8] till the passing of Sexual Harassment Act. Supreme Court constantly through providing guidelines from time to time provide for effective tackling of crime of sexual harassment. Again the decision of Supreme Court in *Laxmi* vs. *Union of India*[9], regarding rehabilitation and providing compensation is laudable as for acid attack. *In Delhi Domestic Working Women's Forum* vs. *Union of India and Others*.[10] The SC pointed out the defects of the criminal justice system that, complaints are handled roughly and not given warranted attention. SC indicated the broad parameters for assisting the victims of rape and asked for effective implementation of these schemes. The Supreme Court has issued notice to all States and Union of India on the issue of Rehabilitation. The Apex Court pointed out that this is the right time we thought seriously about rehabilitation of victims of human trafficking. We don't need to think about ifs and buts—it is time for action.[11] Apex Court took a strong view regarding heinous crime against women and called for a "complete overhaul" of the system for curbing the spurt in crime against women, including rape and sexual harassment, saying only deterrent punishment will be effective.[12] The Supreme Court said that honour killings fell in the category of rarest of rare crimes and those committing them deserved capital punishment.[13] The Apex Court further direct all trial Courts in India to ordinarily add Section 302 to the charge of section 304B, so that death sentences can be imposed in such heinous and barbaric crimes against women.[14]

Legislative Measures

As Dr. Ambedkar has said: "Indians today are governed by two different ideologies. Their political ideal set in the preamble of the

Constitution affirms a life of liberty, equality and fraternity. Their social ideal embodied in their religion denies them."[15]

Despite the constitutional mandate of equal legal status for men and women, the same is yet to be realized. The *dejure* laws have not been translated into *de facto* situation for various reasons such as illiteracy, social practices, prejudices, cultural norms based on chauvinistic values, poor representation of women in policy-making, poverty, regional disparity in development, lack of access and opportunity to information and resources, etc. The ground situation more or less remains the same. The situation of law and order has been deteriorating day by day and crime against women is increasing unabated. But the view after "*Nirbhya* case" and its strong reaction in Delhi make government strictly think in this matter and accordingly amendment 2013[16] in criminal law has been brought. The insertion of new criminal offences such as causing grievous hurt through acid attacks, sexual harassment, use of criminal force on a woman with intent to disrobe, stalking, voyeurism, etc. undoubtedly expanded the horizon of definition of sexual assault undoubtedly expanded the horizon of definition of sexual assault. Also various other laws has also been brought, changed or amended to take stock of the situation. Such some enactment by legislature is The Protection of Children from Sexual Offences [POCSO] Act 2012[17], The Pre-Natal Diagnostic Techniques (Prohibition of Sex-Selction) Act 1994[18], Sexual Harassment of Women at Workplace (Prevention, Prohibition and Redressal) Act 2013.[19]

Social Perception

> "A society that is unable to respect, protect and nurture its women and children loses its moral moorings and runs adrift."[20]

Crime against women are never seen in a straight manner as a crime. In our patriarchal society we always seek sides on any such kind of crimes, instead of fixing liability on the perpetrators of such crime; we try to fix liability on the victim. The common perception is that if the women have been violated, then they must have done something to deserve it. The end result is that many victims refuse to speak out about their abuse to avoid being humiliated the second time. This makes them easy prey for attackers and exposes them to even greater violence, completing a vicious cycle.[21]

The welfare of women is taken in hand by patriarchs with a typical mentality that women are born to serve, so the result is in front of us. Now, it is a high time and we can't just put a blind eye towards the problem of crime against women.

Moreover, we don't identify with the culprits and think them different from us. It is like that the thief is only one who is caught. We fight only for the immediate cause and ignore the larger perspective altogether, that's why the problem of crime against women is far from being solved as individually taking of problems can't help. Crime against women has to be solved as a whole taking all dimension like: economic, political, social, educational and working women related.

Changing Perception

Younger generation is quite responsive towards crime against women. Literacy and increasing participation of women in both public and private sectors has made people aware towards the need for good environment for their co-workers since they relate them with all women, which can be from their own families also.

The ghastly incident of *Nirbhaya* waked up India with a country-wide protest demanding the stringent law pertaining to the violence against women, which finally lead to the passing of Criminal Law (Amendment) Act 2013 so expeditiously which was never seen before. The tens of thousands of protestors who marched in several cities and signed online petitions were acting not just in response to this incident but also to express their anger at the way women in India are treated more generally, criticizing in particular state apathy in the face of rape, and the severe deficiencies in law and order. There is a widespread perception within and outside of India that the country has 'a woman problem.'

Women Empowerment: A Double Dividend

If women are being empowered it help directly in betterment of children and a productive approach towards a more progressive and egalitarian society. So with women empowerment we can expect a better society and an improved culture.

Need for Gender Justice

Viewing the sex ratio as an individual or medical issue and suggesting medical or legal interventions to end the practice reflect poor understanding. While women are guaranteed equality under the Constitution, legal protection has little effect in the face of the prevailing patriarchal culture. India needs to confront its gender bias openly. It would appear that nothing short of a social revolution would bring about an improvement in the health and status of women in the country. Irony and hypocrisy are the two words that come to mind when patriarchal societies talk about justice for their women. Surely, the disappearance of millions of girls in India is reason enough to question the acceptance of patriarchy and search for an egalitarian social order.[22]

What is Required to be Done?

As the Apex Court has said "lip service, hollow statements and inert and inadequate laws with sloppy enforcement are not enough for true and genuine upliftment of our half most precious population– the women".[23] Now its time for action, the researcher is strongly of opinion that we Indians don't believe in solving problem but only in absolving ourselves from the responsibility. Whenever, we confront with any issue, some agitation and protest what we finally do is enactment of a heavy law to silence the protestors. But how far these laws are effective in stopping crime against women, the increasing crime rate decreasing conviction rate and delay in judgment is a sobering reminder that Criminal Law Amendment Act 2013 is insufficient reform.[24]

What is required is implementation of law and finally curbing of crime against women and establishing a position of dignity in the society. An overhauling of system is required and that can't be done by just bringing new laws since we already have hundreds, the real efforts has to be from within society in various steps, first equality is gender neutral and every human deserve it. Secondly, this feeling has to be inculcated within us and our coming generations, and finally a strong public opinion against tolerance of such crimes has to be made to provide a harassment free environment in our society for future development of our country. Following steps can be helpful to improve overall condition of women in the society.

Internalization of Conceptions of Freedom and Dignity

The whole thing could be resolved if people internalise the concept of freedom. Freedom means each person in every role respects the other's liberty and dignity. This respect is accorded both at work and at home. Unfortunately, conceptions of freedom and dignity are not yet known, leave alone internalized, in India. The idea that women should choose their life, their career, their gods, their husbands, and their future: this idea is anathema to many Indians.

True, India does have a faint tradition of freedom. As the religious leader Vivekananda said, "Liberty is the first condition of growth. Just as man must have liberty to think and speak, so he must have liberty in food, dress, and marriage, and in every other thing, so long as he does not injure others."[25] I don't believe Vivekananda restricted his concept of freedom only to men. But his ideas (110 years ago) were too advanced even for today's India. India doesn't have even the rudimentary understanding of liberty.

What is Required is 'Equality'

What is required is to give women regard as an equal human, who is having all rights to decide about herself. Women today excelled in every field. With her talent she has proved herself in every walk of life. Against all odds women have been working very well. But women are yet to get their proper dues. They have to face hurdles and tests at every step. With progress it was intended that we are heading towards a civilized world, but increasing rate of crime against women is pointing otherwise. Now despite being an equal being in every sense in reality women have been provided with only two options that are submit herself at the mercy of male either in the name of security or submit your economic freedom. Women form almost half of population, but still is fit to be put in list of endangered species, since she is safe nowhere. As Swami Vivekananda has rightly said, "the progress of a society can be rightly judged only by condition of its women." The progress of a society is impossible till the condition of its women got better. The alarming increase in crime rate very clearly shows the extreme price women have to pay for her respect, independence and pride.

Gender Sensitization

"Gender" refers to the socially constructed roles and responsibilities of women and men, in a given culture or location. Different roles are played by male and female in the society according to their culture etc. gender sensitization is to provide equal respect to the all the roles in the society since all these roles are basic and equally important for the existence of society. Women work more than men in terms of daily labour but still she is kept at the lower footing than men. The researcher propose that there is requirement of equal recognition of work of male and female for overall development of country, since women form ½ the labour force. The informal slogan of the Decade of Women became "Women do two-thirds of the world's work, receive 10 per cent of the world's income and own 1 per cent of the means of production".[26]

Gender Budgeting

There is a need to acknowledge the role of women in the development of country and this can be possible by concept like gender budgeting, etc., where role of women is provided recognition in monetary sense which is really necessary for the growth and development of women community as a whole. If role of women is recognized in terms of money, then definitely her condition is going to improve, so gender budgeting can prove to be an important instrument in women empowerment.[27]

Effective Implementation of Laws

The study has found that though we have implemented plenty of laws, with big promises of women security but still the ground reality points otherwise. Actually in form of various laws we are only creating 'Paper Tigers' with no effective consequence. The perpetrators use these papers to make boat and make victim sit in those which drown in the sea of tiring long judicial procedure as unable to stand for long time, waiting for justice and with this die the hope of betterment of women. So effective implementation of all these laws is the foremost requirement of the hour.

Sensitization of Youth

As Kiran Bedi, a well known IPS (retd.) puts it: "now it's time for reversal of role, now we need to sensitize boys and make girls bold." This is the utmost requirement now to bring balancing in society and to create a safe environment for women in society. From the very inception there is a requirement that children should be brought up in a positive environment not only telling and teaching equality but actually being treated equal.

The main cause for it lies in the very roots of our upbringing of our children. From the very beginning male child is taught that he is superior than his female counterpart, and this superiority feeling grows with him and when in future he has to compete with female counterparts he look down upon them but when they prove superior to him, the feeling of revenge is vent out in various forms, or often anger is released on female as they are considered as physically weak and under their right and control by male. So, before anything else this mentality is required to be changed. First of all we will have to acknowledge that women also equal human beings, only after that we can bring change to the existing situation.

Renounce Social Ostracism Towards the Victim of Sexual Offences

Where we are talking about change at macro level to prosecute perpetrators of sexual crime, ground reality for victims is entirely stunning and shocking. Young victims find themselves moving from well-meaning anonymity to be turned in to non-entities at the behest of social ostracism. Societies do not accept them and due to the deep engrained chauvinism victim of sexual crimes are the worst sufferers.[28] A 13 year old girl who was raped by a 60 years old fruit vendor was expelled from school with her two younger sisters, in a similar incident the mother of a 16 year old gang rape victim was murdered for lodging F.I.R. against the accused. So along with the brunt of crime victim also face non-cooperation and repellence from the society as if they are criminals. This social abhorrence towards victim is required to be removed from the society and instead victim friendly atmosphere is required for rehabilitation of victims.

Proper Channelization of Young Asset

More than 50 per cent of India's population is below the age of 25 and over 65 per cent below the age of 35.[29] This way we have big human resource which can take our country to great heights, but if this asset is not channelized in the right direction, it can prove to be the biggest source of destruction. Since the people of this age group are most venerable and prone to vices. Recently we have received a very disturbing data showing that Over 33,000 juveniles, mostly between the age-group of 16 to 18, have been arrested for crimes like rape and murder across the country in 2011, the highest in last decade.[30] In an article for *the Hindu* newspaper written in January 2013, Praveen Swami makes a similar point. India's economic transformation is producing "a mass of young, prospect-less men", under enormous pressure to succeed in an economic sense but finding few opportunities to do so.[31]

Economic Independence

The bottom-line to women's status in India (or elsewhere in the world) is the level of economic independence. The differences in the work patterns of men and women, and the 'invisibility' of work that is not included in national accounts, lead to lower entitlements to women than to men. Women's lower access to resources and the lack of attention to gender in macroeconomic policy adds to the inequity, which, in turn, perpetuates gender gaps. Only through increased economic independence have women in the West found a relatively level playing field.

Women Participation in Judiciary

Women are considered partner in the democracy but still in judiciary her participation is not equal, till date we are having only a few percentage share of women in higher judiciary. The number of practicing women advocates is almost negligible; the highest body of justice is having only 2 women judges. On the other hand crime against women is rising at an unprecedented pace. So, it is high time now that more and more women should enter the judicial field.

Fixing Accountability of Judiciary and Police

The author sincerely believes in the need to sensitize the judiciary and police and to fix their accountability. It will be an important step towards affirming faith of women victims in judiciary. Lack of sensitivity is clear from the data of underreporting of cases of violence by women and even out of reported cases very less conviction rate i.e. only 19 per cent due to lack of evidence. There is rise of about 120 per cent in crime against women in past three years and the conviction rate is constantly falling. Investigation into crimes against women continues to be shoddy and slow and, at times are deliberately botched.[32] This is so because a very large number of officers and men in the police force share with the backwoodsmen of the country stupid views that by coming out after dark in western clothes women provoke men to rape them.

Women Participation in Decision-Making Bodies

The empowerment of women is possible only when they take decision for themselves. This is the first and foremost solution for the problem women are facing today. The current economic and socio-political maladies along with increasing violence against women and children are attributed to the failure of male oriented polity. Representation of women in higher bodies of political authority has been considered a prerequisite for the success of democracy at the grassroot level. For this the passing of women reservation bill providing 33 per cent reservation to women in Parliament and state legislatures is a pre-requisite. Now, it is high time that women oriented policies has to be made by women for the women, since rights are never given but has to be taken.

The double standards that are being adopted by our society towards female are quite evident. Since boys are carefree in our society and Girls at a very young age are asked to take precaution and told to be submissive. This kind of limitations at every step blocks their overall development. The deep entrenched patriarchal mentality that lies in the root of our society has systematically kept women as a second grader or to be very specific as a free of cost slave.

Epilogue

To sum up we can say that though we have entered twenty-first century and proudly talk of a civilized society yet the ground reality is shocking. Despite stringent laws and new guidelines from judiciary Crime against women are increasing at tremendous rate. The prejudice that women face is still present. Only, it has learnt to hide itself better.[33] The situation is really grim and need urgent attention and solution. After the above long discussion we find that solution of problem lies in the combined efforts by both the sexes. "We hold these truths to be self-evident, that all men are created equal, that they are endowed by their creator by certain inalienable rights, that among these are life, liberty, and the pursuit of happiness".[34] As Swami Vivekananda had repeatedly told that India's downfall was largely due to her negligence to women and there is no chance of the welfare of the world unless the condition of women is improved. It is impossible for a bird to fly on one wing.[35]

Now a days we need to usher in gender partnership. The relationship between the sexes should be based on mutual respect for each other's role, capabilities and sensibilities.[36] So, in our society children should be brought up in such an environment of equality that makes responsible future citizens. Women's perseverance, patience and devotion to duty, attitude to accept challenges unhesitatingly and nature to bear everything silently should not be taken for granted. They are the symbols of inner strength, not of their weakness. Violence against women is not inevitable. We can eliminate it. We just have to have the courage to take on that challenge.

> "Our deepest fear is not that we are inadequate. Our deepest fear is that we are powerful beyond measure. It is our light, not our darkness, that most frightens us. We ask ourselves, who am I to be brilliant, gorgeous, talented and fabulous?"
>
> — Marianne Williamson

Notes

1. http://www.womensweb.in/2013/01/a-feminist-from-the-19th-century-vivekananda/(visited on Nov. 12, 2013)
2. http://www.thehindu.com/news/national/other-states/swami-vivekananda-

promoted-selfrespect-of-women/article4297997.ece (visited on Jan.11, 2014).
3. http://www.indiaonlinepages.com/population/india-current-population.html (Visited on Aug. 12, 2014).
4. http://ncrb.gov.in/ (visited on Feb. 12, 2014).
5. file:///C:/Users/sahara/Desktop/Steps%20to%20radically%20improve%20women%E2%80%99s%20status%20in%20India.htm (Visited on July 1, 2011).
6. http://timesfoundation.indiatimes.com/articleshow/1254836.cms (Visited on Dec.11, 2013).
7. 1997 (6) SCC 241.
8. (2013) 1 SCC 297.
9. Criminal Writ Petition 129 of 2006.
10. 1995 SCC (1) 14, JT 1994 (7) 183 / Supreme Court of India.
11. *Available at*: shaktivahini.wordpress.com (visited on July 12, 2014)
12. http://zeenews.india.com/news/delhi/deterrent-punishment-required-to-curb-crime-against-women-sc_820825.html (last visited on Jan. 3, 2014).
13. *Bhagwan Dass v. State (NCT) of Delhi*, (2006) 5 SCC 47.
14. *Rajbir @Raju v. State of Haryana*, Petition(s) for Special Leave to Appeal (Crl)... 2010 CRLMP.NO(s). 23051, dated 22/11/2010.
15. http://aamjanata.com/babasaheb-ambedkar-quotes-democracy/ (visited on February 12, 2014).
16. Substituted by the Criminal Law (Amendment) Act 2013 (Act No. 13 of 2013) w.e.f. 3.2.2013 in Indian Penal Code, 1860 (45 of 1860).
17. (Act No. 32 of 2012).
18. Act No. 57 of 1994 w.e.f. (20th September, 1994).
19. (Act No. 14 of 2013) w.e.f. (22nd April, 2013).
20. *The Hindu*—Opinion September, 15, 2012 .
21. http://www.ips.org/mdg3/the-alarming-violence-against-northeasterners-and-women-in-india/ (visited on October 2, 2013).
22. Professor K.S. Jacob, "India's unwanted girls–female infanticide and reversed sex ratio", *available at:* http://www.hindu.com/2011/04/29/stories/2011042956001200.htm (Visited on February 6, 2012).
23. *Medha Kotwal Lele* v. *Union of India* (2013) 1 SCC 297.
24. Aparna Viswanathan, a task only half finished, *The Hindu (Delhi)*, August 28, 2013.
25. file:///C:/Users/sahara/Desktop/Thoughts%20on%20Women%20-0Swami%20Vivekananda%20%E2%80%94.htm (Visited on June 29, 2013).
26. Richard H. Robbins, *Global Problems and the Culture of Capitalism*, (Allyn and Bacon, 1999), p. 354.
27. http://timesfoundation.indiatimes.com/articleshow/1254836.cms (Visited on August 15, 2014).

28. Vandana Shukla, Rape Victims—from anonymity to non-entity, *The Tribune*, September 4, 2013.
29. http://www.indiaonlinepages.com/population/india-current-population.html (Visited on August 12, 2014).
30. Juvenile delinquency on rise, 33,887 minors arrested in 2011, PTI: New Delhi, Sun Jan 13 2013, 14:57 hrs available at http://archive.indianexpress.com/news/juvenile-delinquency-on-rise-33887-minors-arrested-in-2011/1058760/ (Visited on August 12, 2014).
31. http://www.theinternational.org/articles/467-violence-against-women-in-india-culture (Visited on August 11, 2014).
32. Inder Malhotra, Unending Scourage of Rape, *The Tribune*, March 20, 2014.
33. Charulata Venkateswaran, "Hey, its still a man's world," *The Hindu (Delhi)*, August 29, 2010.
34. American Declaration of Independence, 1776, *available at*: http://nlrd.org/resources-womens-rights/honour-killing-crimes/honour-killing-latest-judgements-of-supreme-courthigh-courts/arumugam-sevai-case-honour-killing-banning-of-khap-panchayats-judgement-2011-6-scc-405 (visited on 12-10-2013).
35. Refer to http:// www.businesseconomics.in (Visited on May 29, 2013).
36. V.N. Mukundarajan , "Gender equality is passé, let us usher in gender partnership", *The Hindu (Delhi)*, September 26, 2010.

PART IV
Women in the Corporate World

8
Myriad of Colours
From Household to Corporatism in India

Divya and Richa Mishra

India, a country where the most powerful political figures, two billionaires, three of the most dominant regional politicians, several prominent CEO's, and half of the local government representatives are women. Now imagine that, in the same country, one-third of adult women are illiterate, spousal rape is not illegal, sex-selective abortion and female infanticide are still widely practiced.

It may be hard to reconcile these two realities, but modern India somehow manages to be, at the same time, the land of Indira Gandhi and Mother Teresa and of child brides and dowry deaths.

The reality of women's lives remains invisible to men and women alike and this invisibility persists at all levels beginning with the family to the nation. Although geographically men and women share the same space, they live in different worlds. The mere fact that "*Women hold up half the sky*" but it does not appear to give them a position of dignity and equality. Over the years women have made great strides in many areas with notable progress.

As a girl grows up to become a woman, she is taught to take up 'light' jobs, jobs that would let devote time to her family, no adventurous outing, nothing that may infuse the feeling of being independent. And that's how she is blamed for being raped, "what, you were trying to fly like bird, go out for late night parties, movies, having fun; now you get this for being a free spirited woman" and "you were ought to face this". That's what we get to hear from the country's political leaders and self-styled gods when the nation burns in the fire of rape against rage, molesting, sexual abuse, violent attacks and when some women stand to protest for their rights, they are called "dented and painted".

Women in Household

> *Sanjukta is a 45-year-old housewife living in a rural village of Chhattisgarh. She hails from a lower middle-class family. She was educated up to 5th grade and then got married while she was 15-years old. Her husband has a small goods shop at Raipur, and stays in the city 100 km away from home.
>
> They have three sons. Her sons are educated; the eldest son is settled in the city with his family. Her second son lookafter the farm while the youngest is studying. Sanjukta's day is always busy. Her daily routine involves getting up at five in the morning. After sweeping the house and straightening up, she sweeps the yard to keep out the dust. Early in the morning, Sanjukta milks the family's cows and sends the milk to the co-operative. She takes her bath and starts preparing the morning breakfast.
>
> After preparing breakfast, she washes the dishes, cleans the kitchen, prepares food for the cattle, and then cleans the cattle shed. By this time it is almost late morning. She starts preparing for lunch by cleaning, cutting, and washing vegetables, then prepares the meal. Sanjukta has to ensure that her family gets lunch at the right time, as her son needs to get back to his work in the field. Sanjukta also works on the farm with her son.
>
> Sanjukta is fortunate that the family has a bore well, which makes it easier for her to collect water. Previously, they did not have one and she had to queue for hours in order to get water. Sanjukta alone takes care of the family kitchen garden. She is responsible for the planting, weeding, and watering. Her garden has potato, banana, and green vegetables, all of which are used to feed her family. In the afternoons, she takes the cows out, sometimes with the help of her two sons. She also prepares cow dung cakes for fuel, which is used during the winter. Before evening, she finishes her cooking.
>
> The family eats and goes to bed early as their day starts before sunrise. Sanjukta does the cooking and serves the family herself, though sometimes her second son helps her. She says that she very rarely has any free time; all day she is occupied with work. She prefers to rest or sleep whenever she has some time off from her work. Sometimes she visits her husband in the city.

*Name has been changed to maintain the privacy.

The above case is taken just to make an image of the role of Household contribution of woman. Traditional family structures have a disproportionate effect on Indian women, even those who are urban, college-educated professionals, and especially for those who are the first generation in their families to have a career. Indian women are pulled by demands from relatives as they attempt to conform to the paradigm of "ideal daughter," "ideal wife," and "ideal daughter-in-law." Among the many interviews conducted, it wasn't at all rare to hear of successful professionals who woke up at 4:30 am to make breakfast and lunch for children and parents-in-law, put in a full day at work, then returned home to clean up after the extended family and prepare dinner.

Traditionalists argue that India has survived for millennia with this patriarchal system, so what is the need for changes which are counter to Indian culture? Others would point to the problems of sex-selective abortions, millions of missing girls, dowry murder, low educational status and high illiteracy in girls and women, gender disparities in employment opportunities and wages, the glass ceiling, etc. to suggest that India cannot enter the modern age without learning to respect the rights of women and girls and addressing these disastrous aspects of traditional culture. They may also point out that those defending traditional patriarchal culture have no trouble embracing other non-traditional cultural changes such as cars, mobile phones, computers, and so on.

Work, whether paid or unpaid, is the foundation of a nation's economy. Yet, while paid jobs are counted as part of the economy, unpaid work is neglected. Unpaid workers are not considered part of the labour force and unpaid work is not counted as national income. Unpaid workers, therefore, fail to get the attention they deserve from the government and are inevitably left out of pension schemes and other programmes to support workers.

Around the world, most unpaid work is performed by women. The invisibility of, and low value given to, the work done by a vast majority of the women across the globe, particularly in countries like India, is an issue which is seldom addressed by policy-makers. In addition to their work in the formal sector, women spend countless hours in the unpaid sector of domestic work, yet such work is never counted. As most women give much of their time to the unpaid sector, the majority of them have limited access to higher education, health care, jobs outside the home, or even recreation.

There is no question that women are involved in a tremendous amount of work that has significant value to family, society, and the nation. If women were ever to go on strike, we would understand more fully the full worth and importance of their work. In fact, families would cease to function if women did not work. Men are able to engage in paid labour because of all the work that women do in the home: cleaning the home, washing clothes, preparing food, washing dishes, and engaging in all the tasks involved in bearing and raising children.

Policy-makers and others may be proud to see more and more women entering the formal economy, but they tend to forget that women who are coming out of their house for a paid job (or performing one in the home) are actually required to do a double day's duty, as they regularly remain the sole responsible person for domestic chores. While society recognizes women's role in the economy when they participate in the paid labour force, they remain hidden and unacknowledged when they do not, and thus the double burden on women is often not addressed.

According to Census of India 2012, over 687 million women in India—or 32 per cent of the entire population and 65 per cent of all females—have been classified by the Census of India as non-workers, placed in the same category as beggars, prostitutes, and prisoners. Of the total of those listed as non-workers in India, 74.3 per cent are women. Such a categorization of the majority of women cannot fail to have consequences in policies and programmes aimed at women.

Ambitious women often feel they have to overcompensate at work, too, to counter ingrained preconceptions about their commitment or competence. "There's a sense that a woman is just working until she gets married, [that] she is not a long-term resource," said one senior finance professional. But proving their worth by putting in longer hours or volunteering for business trips—the conventional methods to further one's career—isn't always possible.

Women in Corporatism

During the past decade, the environment for multinational corporations has been quite volatile, with numerous challenges for the firms operating in this arena. However, throughout this period there have emerged a number of executive leaders who have been recognized for their contributions to organizational excellence and leadership despite the environmental fluctuations. But invariably even few years back women power was not so welcome to hold and glorify the top positions of different corporate houses. Several myths were there and so women employees used to face barriers while climbing up the corporate ladder. But time and again women power have proved them, succeeded over those imposed barriers and made major contribution towards organizational excellence.

The role of women worldwide is undergoing a dramatic change. Women today share the podium with men in almost all fields, be it kitchen or in defense. Working women are no longer a rarity and are now accepted as an integral part of the working force. Indian organization has experienced a steady increase in the number of women employees and this pattern is bound to continue in the future as well. Women recently began to join the ranks of managers in large numbers. But women at the top management positions are still a rare species. Globally, they comprise only 10 per cent of senior managers in Fortune 500 companies, less than 4 per cent are in the uppermost ranks of CEO, president, executive vice-president and COO and less than 3 per cent of them are top corporate earners. In India too, it is no different. May be the situation is worse.

Though statistics elude, if we look around, we will not find even a handful of companies headed by women or women at the helm of strategic departments. Major road blocks for women who aspire to achieve and succeed in organizations are the presence of social and role of constraints imposed upon them by society, the family and women themselves. These constraints are referred as myths fostered and sustained with preconceived ideas and unsupported evidence, which generate guilt in women.

Myths Applied to Women in Business

- Women put their heart above their head, so at time they become over emotional.
- Women switch jobs more frequently than men.
- Women would not work if economic reasons did not force them into the labour market.
- Women fall apart in a crisis.
- Women are too concerned with the social aspects of their jobs and cannot be trusted with important matters.
- Women are more concerned than men about working conditions.
- Women are not willing to travel extensively for the organization.

Although the number of women in the workforce has increased

and will continue to increase in the fields of governmental service and education, the advancement of women into management has not kept pace with increase of working women. The reasons are:

- Society has its own stereotypes and biases against women in executive positions. Women are viewed as fragile and lacking in the qualities that are considered beneficial to be effective managers. Traditional masculine traits have higher perceived value than feminine traits in management world.
- The position which the individual hold within the organization shapes the traits and the behaviour they develop or posses. Women often secure positions that have titles with little real power or supervisory authority.
- Mentoring plays an important role in the advancement of women into management positions. However, mentoring is often limited for women, which in turn results in a lack of access and training that aids in advancement within the organization.
- Women managers had to face the glass ceiling. Majority of women because of glass ceiling are unable to advance their career.
- To complicate matter worse, women often have to deal with the complexities of dual role as working women and mother. Women stereotypically take away from the time, which the women can spend on the job subsequently, which slow down their careers. Women managers with children are often looked on less favourable than those without children and they are viewed as being less committed.
- Lastly, women managers also have their own inner battles, which need to be fought and overcome. Women need to develop the confidence and appropriate skills and attitude which are needed to succeed in business. Women manager needs to establish their career goals and acquire determination to overcome the obstacles that exist to keep women from accomplishing their goals.

Nevertheless, women who are at the top are determined to stay there and more are aspiring to reach there, glass ceiling or no glass ceiling. The term "*glass ceiling*" refers to situations where the advancement of a person within the hierarchy of an organization is limited. This limitation is normally based upon some form of discrimination, most commonly being gender and race. This situation is referred to as a "ceiling" as there is a limitation blocking upward advancement, and "glass" (transparent) because the limitation is not immediately apparent and is normally an unwritten and unofficial policy. The "glass ceiling" is distinguished from formal barriers to advancement, such as education or experience requirements. The term is often credited as having been originally coined by Carol Hymowitz and Timothy Schellhardt in the March 24, 1986 edition of the *Wall Street Journal*. However, the term was used prior to that; for instance, it was utilized in a March 1984 *Adweek* article by Gay Bryant.

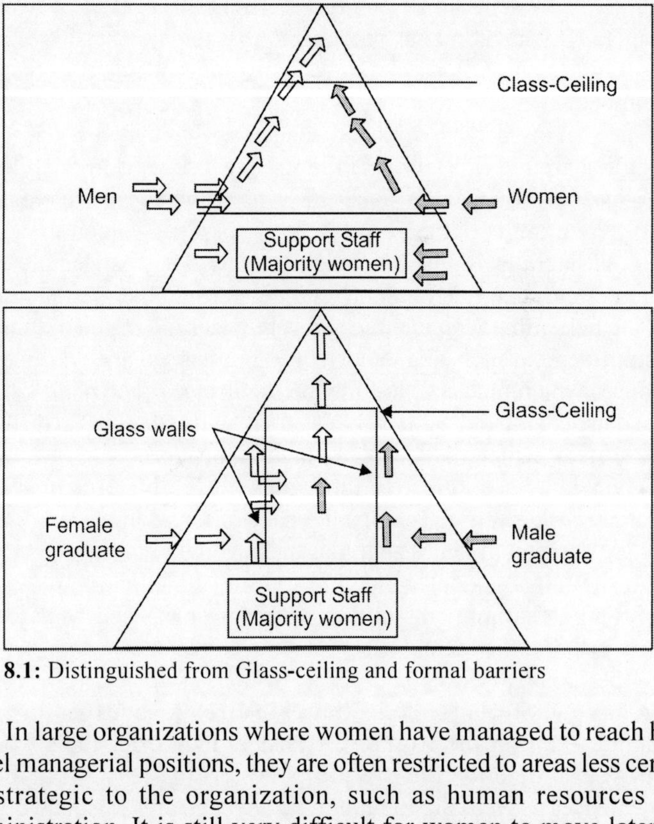

Fig. 8.1: Distinguished from Glass-ceiling and formal barriers

In large organizations where women have managed to reach high level managerial positions, they are often restricted to areas less central or strategic to the organization, such as human resources and administration. It is still very difficult for women to move laterally into strategic areas such as product development or finance, and then upwards through the central pathways to key executive positions in the pyramidal structures that is characteristic of large organizations. Sometimes these barriers are called "*Glass Walls*".

Apart from Glass Ceiling there is another term known as "Glass Elevator" (or glass escalator). This means the rapid promotion of men over women, especially into management, in female-dominated fields such as nursing.

However, in order to overcome such insurmountable obstacle, women need to seek support. Success today requires organizations to best utilize the talent available to them irrespective of the gender. To do these, barriers to upward mobility for women needs to be removed. Organizations need to redefine and restructure the organization systems to respond to the dilemmas faced by women managers. Organization has recognized that female executives offer a wealth of talent. Often women become 'super women' to respond to being equal.

The striking part of women managers is that they are very good at juggling around tasks. One of the strongest skills is their ability at multi-tasking. Also women managers bring with them a different style and different skills. Research also confirms that women managers see things laterally, intuitively and differently. They can handle more contradictions, can tolerate more and deliver much more than men.

The belief that women managers are uncertain of them, look for constant reassurance and tend to be aggressive are stereotyped responses which feed and multiply on themselves. The reality is that women in general and women managers in particular have a different value system, which they bring to the organization.

Management studies on the gender initiatives taken by the corporate world show that companies have followed three approaches: there are some companies that like their women employees to be a part of the 'boys', adopt masculine styles of functioning, play golf, take on tough assignments in factories or overseas and be assertive leaders just like the men.

Other companies recognise that women do the same work but they have different needs that require be addressing and accommodating at the workplace. Hence, they offer their women employees not only the statutory maternity leave, but other conveniences as well. So, inbuilt in their system are flexible working hours, working from home, allowing women transfers easily (when the husbands move) or even being amenable to women choosing alternate career tracks within the organisation itself.

The third set of companies goes the whole hog. They not only accommodate women employees, but recognise that women bring with them a difference in approach and attitude to the workplace. Hence, they also palce them appropriately, so that their skills and interactive style of leadership brings gains to the organization.

However, management studies on gender equity also recoognise that all the three approaches have their limitations. That being part of the boys' golf game or making use of flexi hours or even being praised for bringing in the 'feminine' approach to running an organisation do not change the essential gender inequity inherent in the system that would require a larger social change and more so, a drastic shift in perspective.

Therefore, women in corporate India are aware of the constraints they work under and obviously try to make the best of the bargain. They typically bear a disproportionate amount of responsibility for home and family and thus have more demands on their time outside the office. And when they do reach the managerial level, they bring with them both silver lining and dark clouds. But they flower, if they are allowed to flower, despite all the obstacles, which are mainly societal and perceptual.

According to a survey done by *Economic Times*, there are only 16 women on the board of directors of the 30 Sensex companies, or only 4.8 per cent of the 335 people who hold directorship positions. In the Bombay Stock Exchange (BSE) 100 companies, which throws up 923 directors, only 50 (or 5.4%) are women, while companies in the BSE 500 index have only 192 women (or 5.3%) out of 3650 persons holding directorship positions. According to Poonam Barua, founder chairperson of the Forum for Women in Leadership, India's 500 million strong female populations does not find representation in even 10 per cent of the managerial posts across companies.

Today it is about calibrating how many of women are in the key leadership roles. There it looks like India has still some way to go. An increasing number of companies are striving to enhance women representation in their workforce, but they may not be enough.

According to Catalyst India Benchmarking Report for 2010, only 17 per cent of Indian companies offered target leadership development programme for women. Another study for women in leadership (WILL) Forum shows that Indian companies have much lower women representation in senior position compared with Multinational Firms. While Indian companies such as Tata Consultancies Ltd., Zensar Technologies, Tata Steel and JSW Steel. Had 5-6 per cent women in senior positions, multinationals such as PepsiCo. KPMG, Citigroup, GE, and Pfizer had 15-20 per cent women at the same level in 2010, the WILL study shows.

The Catalyst study shows Fortune 500 companies with three or more women on the board, had significant performance advantage over those with fewer women on the board, which includes up to 73 per cent higher returns on sales, upto 83 per cent higher return on equity, and up to 112 per cent higher return on invested capital.

During 2010, Indian Banks like Axis Bank had 21 per cent women participation in its total workforce. In comparison American Express in India had 43 per cent women representation in its total staff strength of 5500. The study also shows that 84 per cent of Indian subsidiaries of multinationals have adopted women's advancement strategy, compared with only 37 per cent of India headquartered companies.

Women entrepreneurs are a vital source of growth that can power our economies for decades, yet they face tremendous challenges to their full economic participation. The GEM Women's Report provides important data which is critical to our understanding of women-run SMEs (Melanne Verveerin, 2010).

More than half (55%) of the Indian women interviewed have encountered workplace bias severe enough to make them consider scaling back their career goals, reducing their ambition and engagement, or quitting altogether, feeding into the very biases they grapple with and dealing a sharp blow to the country's demographic dividend, a key factor in India's growth which is experiencing its own stress.

Some Indian companies are taking steps to help these stressed women. For example, Infosys, the Bangalore-based info-tech powerhouse, offers the Infosys Women's Inclusivity Network (IWIN). IWIN makes Infosys a female-friendly environment by identifying the stress points at which women tend to leave the organization and creating policies that help them deal with those stresses. Surveys showed that many Infosys women dropped out after getting married; the numbers skyrocketed after the birth of their first child and were almost universal after the second. In response, Infosys introduced a one-year "child care sabbatical" with the option of working part-time for the next two years.

Women are critical contributors in finance, info-tech, pharmaceutical research, and other industries that are driving the growth of India Inc. Easing the stresses that prevent them from reaching their full potential at work is a smart way for companies to attract and retain key talent. Keeping women's careers on track may not guarantee ongoing economic success but not doing so will surely limit it.

Tapping its rich mine of educated female talent has been an important factor in allowing India to become one of the world's fastest-growing economies. But recently this particular dynamo has been showing signs of strain. According to "Women of Tomorrow," a recent Nielsen Survey of 6,500 women across 21 different nations, Indian women are the most stressed in the world today. An overwhelming 87 per cent of Indian women said they felt stressed most of the time, and 82 per cent reported that they had no time to relax.

The Nielsen survey's respondents blame the difficulty of juggling multiple roles at home and work. Career opportunities for women in "the New India" are rapidly expanding, but family expectations and social mores remain rooted in tradition.

Not surprisingly, the most stress is felt among women between 25 and 55 years of age, who are trying to balance demanding careers with obligations at home.

Conclusion

Women in India can broadly be categorized under the urban and the rural. While women's empowerment may mean a lot to the urban women of India, it may not even strike a chord for the countless women folk of rural India who by far outnumber women living in urban India.

While the women living in metropolitan cities as well as smaller cities can definitely identify themselves with any women linked programme or join a movement connected with women, and can hope to participate in that for their benefit, the rural-urban divide and disconnect in India prevents the same benefits from reaching the women folk living in our villages.

Another major drawback and difference between both the categories of women is that majority of women in rural India presently, in the age bracket of 35-65 years have been kept away from any form of formal education. The scene is changing rapidly for the better for the present younger generation where a large number of young girls from villages are seen to be attending schools and even colleges, but this was not so earlier.

Thus lack of basic education has indeed prevented the girls in rural India in comprehending what their basic civil liberties are. Their real empowerment is thus confined within the four walls of their homes, and there too they are a shadow of their own self and have to follow the wish of their men folk.

On the other hand, the urban woman is far more educated, sophisticated, demanding, and aware of her own rights and liberties and generally more well equipped to take care of her own self. Even among the urban women we have a divide; the rich and novae rich and the poor and the middle class. The rich and super rich class of women in India get the maximum advantage of women rights, civil liberties, the programmes beneficial to women and are generally in command of their situation both at home and at their workplace. This is generally the situation of urban women belonging to the upper strata in India across bigger metros as well as smaller cities.

However, the situation is not so rosy within the women comprising the upcoming growing middle class in India. This stratum of society generally forms the bulk of women in urban India spread across big and smaller cities as well as the metros. The women in this group are basically stuck between their homes and the office routine as most of them are in gainful employment either in the vast majority of Government offices or in private workplaces. They don't have sufficient time or freedom on their hands to put into practice the various benefits emanating from either schemes of social welfare or women oriented schemes announced by either Government or private sector.

The last affected in this category of urban women, which ultimately succeed in forming a bridge between the urban poor are the women who come looking for jobs in the city from a rural background. These urban women are from the poor stratum and fed up of the life of squalor and misery in their villages, take flight to the cities of urban India in the hope of getting a far more satisfactory lifestyle. In fact they are attracted by the alluring lifestyle and glamour promised sometimes by the touts and pimps of the city who are constantly roaming around villages scouting for their prey. Invariably they succeed in luring away to the city a large number of women who either end up as sex slaves in a sick brothel or get some menial jobs as maid servants in the bigger cities of India where household chores are generally looked down upon and frowned by the upper stratum of women.

When we talk about women's empowerment or movements like 'one billion rising' we have to keep in mind the status of women prevalent in all these above categories of both urban and rural India mentioned above.

If we feign ignorance about majority of the womenfolk in the villages of India, as well as those belonging to the poor and middle class working women in urban India, as and when we talk about women's empowerment, we could end up doing a great disservice to these women. It is in fact these women who remain mostly ignorant of their basic human rights, who need to be awakened from their stupor. It is in fact this class and stratum of society of women who need to unshackle themselves from the ignorance of backwardness and get acquainted with the promised life unfolding before them. These women both in the urban and rural sector, in fact account for at least 70 per cent of the total women force who are denied their basic rights available to them. It is this stratum of women in India who need to be really awakened, and made aware of what can unfold for them. These women if made to come up to their real potential can really redefine the meaning of women's empowerment in a developing Country like India. A Country where women are cherished and worshiped in the form of Goddesses' like Sita, Durga and Lakshmi is really struggling to make its women aware of their simple basic human rights.

A woman in most parts is looked upon more as an object of glamour or a mere sex object rather than somebody who can share and shoulder the equal and sometimes dominant responsibilities of decision-making in the home and at work place. Although things are slowly changing for most women in India, but the change is so slow and subtle that it is hardly noticeable. The core areas concerning women are still in the process of being discovered and opened up for them. Till that happens it is an uphill task for majority of the women in both rural and urban India.

The status of women in India has gone through the many great changes over the past few millennia. From equal status with men in ancient times through the low points of the medieval period, to the promotion of equal rights by many reformers, the history of women in India has been eventful. The Government of India declared 2001 as the Year of Women's Empowerment (*Swashakti*). The National Policy for the Empowerment of Women was also passed in the same year.

The Constitution of India guarantees to all Indian women equality (Article 14), no discrimination by the State [Article 15(1)], equality of opportunity (Article 16), and equal pay for equal work [Article 39(d)]. In addition, it allows special provisions to be made by the State in favour of women and children [Article 15(3)], renounces practices derogatory to the dignity of women [Article 51(A) (e)], and also allows for provisions to be made by the State for securing just and humane conditions of work and for maternity relief (Article 42).

The importance of women's organizations in bringing women in reach of the development process is widely recognized as vital for the advancement of women in India. However, there has been increased recognition that the role of such organizations has not always been clearly defined. In recent years, there has been increased recognition that such grassroots organizations with certain well defined objectives and roles can mobilize women to develop their economic activity in an organized manner-by ensuring access to key development inputs and to strengthen women's voices in development decisions and in the political process.

In fact it becomes the pious and solemn duty of those women who have understood the power of complete women's empowerment, to come forward and willingly educate and embolden the fortune of the less fortunate and under privileged section of Indian women. This would prove to be a real test of their character and magnanimity towards the less fortunate of their own. Till this happens, women in India will continue to suffer in silence. Time has come to break this chain, and free the women from their shackles and bondage from which society has constantly sought to bind them. Cheers for the awakening of all women!

References

Amarnath, Nischinta; Ghosh, Debashish. (2005), *The Voyage to Excellence: The Ascent of 21 Women Leaders of India Inc.*, Pustak Mahal.

Catalyst. (2009, March). Women CEOs of the Fortune 1000. Retrieved April 2, 2009, from www.catalyst.org, last accessed on 21/03/2011.

Manimala, J. Mathew. (2002), Founder Characteristics and Start-up Policies of

Entrepreneurial Ventures: A comparison between British and Indian Enterprises, *Journal of Entrepreneurship*, 11(2): 139-171.

Robbins, P. Stephens. (1999), *Organisational Behaviour—Concepts, Controversies, Applications*, Prentice Hall of India Private Limited, 8th Edition.

Sekharan, Uma. (2004), *Organisational Behaviour: Text and Cases*, Tata McGraw-Hill Publishing Company Limited, New Delhi, 2nd Edition.

The Census of India (2012), Haryana Series 7, Paper 3, Chapter 13.

United States Department of Labour/Women's Bureau. (2008). Quick stats on women workers, 2008. Retrieved August 25, 2009, from www.dol.gov/wb/stats/main.htm, last accessed on 21/03/2011.

Women workers in India in the 21st century—Unemployment and underemployment. (2004, February). Retrieved April 30, 2009, from www.cpinl.org.

Women's Economic Contribution through their Unpaid Work: The Case of India, ESA Fand Health Bridge.

www.cpiml.org/liberation/year_2004/febraury/WomenWorkers.htm, last accessed on 21/03/2011.

9

Gender Diversity in Indian Corporate Sector

Issues and Challenges

Anand Sharma

Faster inclusive and sustainable growth of any nation depends upon optimum utilisation of its physical and human resources. In this context woman is most significant human resource for inclusive and sustainable growth. UNDP estimates that women constitutes around half of global population, one-third of labour force, performs two-third of working hours but earns only 10 per cent of income and own only 1 per cent of wealth world over. These glaring facts indicate imperatives of women study in economic life of a nation. Although gender inequality exists in all walks of life but corporate sector suffers a lot. It is increasingly realised that promotion of gender equality is not only beneficial from society point of view but from business point of view as well because it leads to sustainable economic gains. Many studies and reports have revealed that huge gender gap exits in different forms and levels in corporate sector all over the world. Women faces different types of challenges such as recruitment bias, biased distribution of paid and unpaid work between male and female, sexual harassment, discouraging work environment, mid-career family and social guilt, low career progression at top level, etc. Some voluntary initiatives to bridge gender gap by leading companies inspires other to follow the suit to take benefits of gender equality still strong regulatory initiatives will push the cause. Recent changes in Company law 2013 stipulating minimum one women director will certainly improve women participation at top level leadership but still a lot is to be done.

Role of Women in Corporate Sector

Any society or country can not progress and flourish in sustainable way until and unless it recognises, motivates, trains and retains the best of its talent irrespective of its gender. Widespread gender gap in economic sphere of a nation or society is a huge loss to economic and social prosperity of a nation. Globally, it is realised that participation of women in corporate sector ensure sustainable development of organisation. In many countries, government legislations have also focused on minimum gender ratio in government as well as corporate sector. In order to promote gender equity women should be inducted at all levels in corporate sector i.e. junior, middle and top level positions.

Centre for responsible business, Barkley (2012) studied 1500 companies and found Companies with better gender diversity are more likely to achieve environmental, social and governance sustainability. It says these companies will ensure environment friendly practices, use of renewable energy, strong governance structure, more transparency, fair business practices, healthy product mix, congenial work environment, etc. Some Studies Women bring more aesthetic sense in the organisation. Women raise more questions than men thus they challenge the *status quo* and promote innovations in organisation.

CEO Kit (Chief Executive Women Australia) 2010 emphasize that Women influence or make 80 per cent of purchasing decisions. Thus if more women are inducted at different levels in consumer product organizations, it will certainly connect with the consumers in an effective way. Women may bring more aesthetic sense to product and its packaging. Women are more caring and responsible towards customers. Thus organizational climate and reputation will be positive if more women are inducted in corporate sector.

Various studies such as Ernst & Young (2011), McKensey (2007) revealed that companies with relatively balanced gender ratio especially at directors level performed better than industry average. Catalyst foundation (2007) found that on an average Fortune 500 companies with more women on their boards performed better than others. Companies with three or more women board directors, return on equity was 16.7 per cent compared to the average of 11.5 per cent; return on sales was 16.8 per cent, compared to the average of 11.5 per cent; and return on invested capital was 10.9 per cent compare to an average of 6.2 per cent by all companies. Indeed organizations like Credit Suisse, McKinsey and Walmart have shown that the presence of women at top levels of management and leadership has been correlated with better financial performance for the company. A Goldman Sachs report argues narrowing the gap between male and female employment rates would boost Australia's GDP by 11 per cent from current level. Gender equality ensures competitiveness depends upon whether and how its trains and utilises its women in corporate sector.

McKinsey and Company (2007) found that gender diversity in senior management correlates with "organizational excellence" as measured by a set of criteria including: leadership, direction, accountability, coordination and control, innovation, external orientation, capability, motivation, work environment and values. The study found that companies with more than three women in senior management functions score more for each organizational criterion of "excellence" than companies with no women at the top.

European Commission (2003) argues that benefits of balanced participation of women and men in business, particularly in management, ranges from improved staff recruitment and retention; improved creativity, innovation, and problem solving; to improved marketing strategies and outcomes. Many of these benefits are context specific and qualitative and therefore difficult to measure. Chartered Institute of Personnel and Development (CIPD) in the United Kingdom stress that gender equality enhances creativity and innovation, which are critical to competitive success. A 2005 survey showed that around 60 per cent of companies with diversity policies believed that innovation and creativity improved as a result. Recruiting women to key positions also allows companies to gain a competitive advantage through deeper cultural adaptation to the marketplace.

Status of Gender Gap in India

Although lots of rewards are attached to gender equality still huge gender gap exits worldwide. Gender Gap exits in different forms, magnitude and at different levels in corporate sector. It varies from one sector to another sector as well as one region to other region.

Various studies in India as well as in other countries show lot of variation in gender gap among different sectors of the economy and regions. Women are largely employed in education health and welfare sector whereas men are employed in manufacturing, mining and construction sector. Women tend to be concentrated more at lower or middle level. Women tend to leave career at middle of career due to mid-career guilt and family engagement thus could not reach to the top.

Economic Times quoted a recent report 'Women at Board 2013' that Women account for nearly 40 per cent of the total workforce of India Inc but presence of women is less than seven per cent in board of directors. It further says that three per cent of the boards have three female directors, while 44 per cent boards have only one woman director each.

Nigelwright Recruitment (2012) highlighted that top five companies of fortune global 500 (2011) had only 11 per cent women directors and top five companies of Deloitte 250 consumer product companies (2011) had only 13 per cent women directors in their board. It shows gender gap is more acute at top level. Even in developed country situation is not very good in terms of gender gap at top level positions. Although Harward Business School research says that now the situation is improving and there is a great deal of realisation among corporate sector that gender equality is key for sustainable growth.

ASI (Annual Survey of Industries, 2001 to 2010) reports that ratio of female participation in manufacturing sector was around merely 20 per cent for the decade 2001 to 2010. In manufacturing itself there is a huge variation in female participation for example Female participation in tobacco, wearing and leather apparels is around 58 to 32 per cent whereas it is as low as around 2 per cent in machinery manufacturing and metal industries. Within tobacco industry there is huge variation for example Bidi industry employs 68 per cent women whereas Cigarettes industry employs only 0.45 per cent women employees. State wise there is widespread gap in women participation in workforce. Kerala, Manipur, Karnataka, Tamil Nadu account for more participation of women as against very low participation in Punjab, Haryana, Rajasthan, UP and Bihar. It varies to the extent of 64 per cent in Kerala to merely 2.88 per cent in UP. These patterns are in tune with the level of women literacy, level of patriarchy and women health and empowerment etc.

Challenges to Women in Corporate Sector

According to ASI 2010 very huge wage differential exists in India at all India level wage differential ratio is 0.48, thus a female employee earns less than half of wages as compared to their male counterparts for similar kind of job. Ernst and Young Australia (2011) report on Women in leadership—Engaging Australian business revealed that despite Australian legislation mandated that women should receive "equal pay for work of equal value" in 1969, over 40 years later, the gap between men and women's pay is currently at 17 per cent. This is even more apparent at the executive level, with female CEOs earning two thirds the median wage of male CEOs and female chief financial officers and chief operating officers earn just half the median wage of their male counterparts. According to the National Centre of Social and Economic modelling, this wage gap deters women from joining the work force, to the detriment of $93 billion or 8.5 per cent of GDP each year.

Sexual harassment is a major problem for women participation in corporate work place. There is grim situation of sexual harassment at workplace in India. A 2010 Survey on workplace sexual harassment conducted by the Centre for Transforming India, a non-profit organisation, found that 88 per cent of women interviewed faced some form of harassment but many did not want to complain for fear of professional reprisals. Many others were not aware of what exactly constituted harassment. Some studies reveals in India, around every hour a woman is reported to be sexually harassed and every half an hour a woman is sexually molested. Magnitude of unreported cases is several times over the reported cases. To some extent it is realised that corporate sector is still not doing enough to make their work environment women friendly. Somehow long working hour, quick mobility, patriarchal mind set are deterrent for women in corporate sector.

Women network is essential which provides a platform to women to discuss, deliberate, cooperate, bargain and fight for their issues. Women cannot do socialising to please bosses after office hours thus they face lot of partiality and could not get the due recognition. Many times when women are straightforward they are transferred at odd places thus and harassed. Few networks like CII Indian women network are very essential platforms in this regard.

Women compromises from the beginning of the career by

accepting less rewarding jobs as their income is treated as supplementary in family income. They do not scuffle for more challenging jobs and satisfied with less earning jobs. At the same time they shoulder more responsibility than male in family thus at a point of time they cannot devote in their profession/work as much as men thus they are devoid of promotion opportunities. Lack of skill development and training opportunities is a major obstacle in women's career growth. At mid-career women develop mid-career family guilt thus they cannot focus on career. Due to family responsibility sometime women accept fewer wages for part time or less time consuming jobs which leads to low career progress resulting in low pension and less security for future.

The Way Forward: Towards Gender Balance in Corporate Sector

Women face bias from the beginning of career at recruitment stage. Studies reveal that men are more biased than women in a recruitment board. Thus, there should be women representation in any recruitment panel. In India although all recognised large scale companies announce that they are equal opportunity employers. Government ensures that in all appointment interviews at least one women representative is there in the interview board. Thus removing gender bias in recruitment is the first step in this direction.

24×7 mobile corporate cultures discourage women to participate in corporate workforce special at challenging positions. In order to take advantage of gender equality. Companies need to re-engineer the processes, actions and tasks in a flexible way so that women are encouraged to work. Performance appraisal system need to be revamped based on results not on presence in the organisations. Work from home and encouraging spouse employment is key to conducive work environment. Flexible and transparent organisations will encourage women in corporate.

In all societies whether advanced or developing, women have to shoulder more family responsibilities than men. Companies need to provide an encouraging environment to women so that women can perform at her best. Child/day care centres should be part of any companies holistic planning. Preferential allotment of seats in nearby schools and company's residence will definitely encourage women to give its fullest. Family leaves should be given to both parents equally so that male members can contribute in looking after the family responsibilities. In long run these practices will yield better financial results for the company.

In India there are sufficient legislative measures in place to promote gender equity and elimination gender bias in workplace but their effective implantation is still wanting. Thus appropriate measures should be taken to implement all these legislation in letter and spirit. Gender sensitivity training to male counterparts.

Conclusion

Indian patriarchal society discriminates against women from womb to tomb in all forms and levels. Some efforts and interventions have made some positive impact on society. Eminent educationists like Prof. Mool Chand Sharma advocates moral education at all levels for a gender sensitive egalitarian society. India stood at 101 rank out of 136 countries in Gender Gap index 2013 by world economic forum. The overall gender gap score is 0.655 (on a scale 0 = inequality, 1=equality) for our country. Over the period of time although, some gender gap has reduced but still need to go a long way. Further, sub-indices indicate that India has performed better in educational attainment and health and life expectancy whereas, performed worst in political empowerment. Now, it is increasingly realised that promotion of gender equality is not only a regulatory issue rather it has a business sense. Some of world's largest companies have promoted gender equality in very innovative way. ANZ Bank has taken some initiatives such as ANZ women Network, career mentoring coaching and development etc. IBM, KPMG and Walmart have taken encouraging steps to enhance the cause of Gender equality Indian corporates should take lessons from these company to enhance profitability. Gender diversity has a strong case for future business in India.

References

Chaudhari Biwas, Panigrahi A.K., (2013), "Gender bias in Indian Industry", *The Journal of Industrial Statistics*, 2(1), pp. 108-127.

Kellie, A McElhaney and Sanaz Mobasseri (2012), *Women Create a Sustainable Business*, Barkley: University of California, pp. 3-4.

Lisa Wrath (2009), *Gender Equality and Corporate Sector*, United Nations ECE.

Meredith Scott (2011), "*Women in Leadership: Engaging Australian Business*", Ernst and Young Australia.

Nigel Wright Recruitment (2012), "Women on Corporate Board: Lessons from the Consumer Sector", United Kingdom.

Paludi Michele (2011). *Sexual Harassment Policies and Practices in Gender and Higher Education* Eds. by Bank, J. Barbara, Greenwood Publishing House, Westport, C.T., pp. 376-379.

Sharma, Mool Chand and Sharma, A. (2003). *Discrimination Based upon Sex, Caste and Disability*, NCERT and NHRC, published by NCERT.

World Economic Forum (2013). "The Global Gender Gap Index Report 2013", Genewa: Switzerland, pp. 222-223.

PART V
Women's Health: Gateway to Empowerment

10
Women Empowerment, Maternal Health and Child Health Care

Renu

Introduction

Women play a very important role in every society and women empowerment is the key indicator of the development. Women do the world's two-third work but receives only a tenth of world's income. The Human Development Report (HDR) in the year 1995 focused upon gender disparity highlighting that women receive unequal treatment all over the world. In India women's participation is very low as compare to emerging economies such as China and South Africa. Female participation rate is only 29 per cent of women over the age of 15. Half the working population in India is employed by the agricultural sector only. In this chapter we will discuss the relationship between women empowerment, maternal health and child care.

Meaning of Women Empowerment

Women's Empowerment can be viewed as means of creating a social environment in which one can make decisions and make choices either individually or collectively for social transformation. It strengthens the innate ability by way of acquiring knowledge, power and experience (Hashemi Schuler and Riley, 1996).

Women's empowerment is very essential for the development of society. Empowerment means individuals acquiring the power to think and act freely, exercises choice and fulfil their potential as full and equal members of society. As per the United National Development Fund for Women (UNIFEM), the term women's empowerment means:

- Acquiring knowledge and understanding of gender relations and the ways in which these relations may be changed.
- Developing a sense of self-worth, a belief in one's ability to secure desired changes and the right to control one's life.
- Gaining the ability to generate choices exercise bargaining power.
- Developing the ability to organize and influence the direction of social change, to create a more just social and economic order, nationally and internationally.

The *Rig-Veda* and the *Upanishad* bear the testimony of esteemed exalted womanhood. At that time there was no gender division in hunting, warfare, defense and political activities. Further, family was the unit of political structure, where the women would also join politics to rule over the household, and warfare at times of crisis. The Aryans in the early Vedic period were essentially pre-occupied with military and semi-military operations and they were greatly dependent upon womenfolk (Mukharji Prabhati, 1978).

In the later Vedic period, there was a process of deterioration in the women status when agricultural civilization started and conditions of private property emerged. The existing political role of women was drastically reduced. In this period the role of women confined to the household only.

Polices for Women Empowerment

Son-preference, dowry murders, bride burning, spousal violence, orgy of rape and molestation, reification of woman as an object of sexual gratification and sex segregation indicate that Indian women, even in the first decade of the twenty-first century, still have a long way to go to attain gender justice. With reference to the foregoing, it is concluded that the plight of women in India is really not yet over. As India has woken up to the various categories of humiliation, atrocities, tortures and individual and mass assault to which women are subjected, many an Act/Rule/Plan/Programme has been ratified and implemented to engender the State of India. Consequently, various women empowerment specific policies and plans have been executed. Naturally therefore, the Eighth Five-Year Plan (1992-1997) marks a definite shift from 'development' to 'empowerment' of women. Special Marriage Act, 1954; Hindu Marriage Act, 1955; Hindu Succession Act, 1956; Hindu Minority and Guardianship Act, 1956; Hindu Adoption and Maintenance Act, 1956; Immortal Traffic Prevention Act, 1956; Dowry Prohibition Act, 1961 and 1984; Maternity Benefit Act, 1961; Medical Termination of Pregnancy Act, 1971; Child Marriage Restraint (Amendment) Act, 1978; Family Court Act, 1984; Indecent Representation of Women (Prohibition) Act, 1986; Commission of Sati (Prevention) Act, 1987; The National Plan of Action for Women, 1976; National Perspective Plan for Women, 1988; Shramashakti, 1988; National Commission for Women, 1990; Support to Training and Employment Programme for Women, 1987; Rashtriya Mahila Kosh; Mahila Samridhi Yojana; Indira Awaas Yojana; Jawahar Rozgar Yojana; Streeshakti Mission; DWCRA; TRYSEM; National Rural Health Mission; National Rural Employment Guarantee Scheme; The 73rd and 74th Constitutional Amendment Acts of 1993 and the support services launched and effectualized by the Government, of India bear ample testimony to desire and preparedness of the State of India to facilitate empowerment of women in India (Jugal Kishor Mishra, 2006).

Reasons for Empowerment of Women

Today we have noticed different Acts and Schemes of the Central Government as well as state government to empower the women of India. But in India women are discriminated and marginalized at every level of the society whether it is social participation, political participation, economic participation, access to education, and also reproductive healthcare. Women are found to be economically very poor all over the India. A few women are engaged in services and other activities. So, they need economic power to stand on their own legs on par with men. Other hand, it has been observed that women are found to be less literate than men. According to 2001 census, rate of literacy among men in India is found to be 76 per cent whereas it is only 54 per cent among women. Thus, increasing education among women is of very important in empowering them. It has also noticed that some of women are too weak to work.

They consume less food but work more. Therefore, from the health point of view, women folk who are to be weaker are to be made stronger. Another problem is that workplace harassment of women. There are so many cases of rape, kidnapping of girl, dowry harassment, and so on. For these reasons, they require empowerment of all kinds in order to protect themselves and to secure their purity and dignity (Dhruba Hazarika, 2011).

Data Source and Methodology

In the present study data has been taken from National Family Health Survey-3, District Family Health Survey-3 and the data on female literacy has been taken from article on Spatio-Temporal Pattern of Literacy in Haryana, written by Jitender Malik (2012).

Study Area

We have taken Haryana as our study area. We have taken 20 districts namely Panchkula, Ambala, Yamunanagar, Kurukshetra, Kaithal, Karnal, Panipat, Sonipat, Jind, Fatehabad, Sirsa, Hissar, Bhiwani, Rohtak, Jhajjar, Mahendergarh, Rewari, Gurgaon, Faridabad and Mewat. Though there are 21 districts in the State. Palwal district has added in 2008. NFHS data has collected for the year 2007-08. Therefore, Palwal district has not included in the study area.

Relationship between Women Empowerment and Maternal Health

There are many determinants of women empowerment but education plays crucial role in women empowerment. In the Indian history, gender discrimination with female child started with the womb and continues through her life till graveyard. Many times female child are aborted and they are not allowed to go to school. Women empowerment and maternal health care are closely related to each other. In India female literacy is much lower than the male literacy. According to 2011 census, female literacy was 66.77 per cent as compare to male literacy 85.38 per cent in Haryana state. Education plays a very important role in the development of the society especially for the women development. We have taken the data on female literacy and six variables on maternal health and find out the relationship of these variables with female literacy. Variables on maternal health care are following:

1. Any anti-natal check up,
2. Percentage of women who had institutional delivery,
3. Percentage of women who had safe delivery,
4. Percentage of women using any contraceptive method,

Table 10.1: Female Literacy Rate and Indicators of Maternal Health

District	*Female Literacy Rate*	*Any Anti-Natal Check-up*	*% of Women who had ID*	*% of Women who had safe delivery*	*% of Women using any Contra-ceptive Method*	*% of Women aware of ORS*	*% of Women Seen Vaccination card*
Panchkula	77.48	91.9	64.3	67.8	66.7	56.0	61.10
Ambala	76.64	84.3	55.4	62.9	65.4	50.8	61.10
Yamunanagar	71.99	90.8	52.3	58.4	63.8	42.5	55.80
Kurukshetra	69.18	92.0	64.2	67.8	65.6	43.2	54.80
Kaithal	60.69	95.1	48.0	57.4	67.0	52.8	54.90
Karnal	68.29	90.3	51.3	57.1	64.3	39.4	52.00
Panipat	68.23	87.2	39.0	48.4	59.1	37.8	22.70
Sonipat	70.88	95.5	53.7	61.0	60.8	44.0	45.70
Jind	61.58	93.2	42.1	48.3	66.2	40.5	37.40
Fatehabad	59.29	91.0	48.6	58.1	67.3	29.2	35.30
Sirsa	61.16	92.8	53.5	69.5	69.4	55.7	48.80
Hissar	62.31	92.9	48.6	54.5	67.6	38.7	47.50
Bhiwani	64.60	91.0	35.7	44.8	68.3	37.8	24.10
Rohtak	71.19	96.6	52.8	58.9	66.8	59.1	35.80
Jhajjar	70.96	92.1	48.0	57.9	61.5	42.7	43.10
Mahendergarh	67.25	95.2	56.8	65.1	71.3	42.3	42.20
Rewari	70.54	96.2	65.0	73.5	69.8	63.5	39.40
Gurgaon	77.64	94.1	52.3	56.8	65.0	61.1	37.90
Faridabad	75.17	81.5	39.1	42.7	54.4	33.5	36.50
Mewat	37.58	54.2	14.8	16.3	27.9	16.6	4.90

ID: Institutional Delivery; ORS: Oral Rehydration Salt

Number of Women (Unweighted cases)

Number of Children (Unweighted cases)

Meaning of Full Vaccination includes 1 BCG, 3 injections of DPT, 3 Doses of Polio and measles.

15-44 (Represents figure for currently married women aged 15-44 years.)

Among the six variables, all females are in the age group of 15-44 except female literacy rate and women having knowledge of ORS.

5. Percentage of women aware of ORS, and
6. Percentage of women who had seen vaccination card.

The Table 10.1 provides the data on the female literacy rate and on the indicators of maternal health care. From the above table we can easily see that in Gurgaon, Panchkula and Ambala the female literacy rate is high. We calculated the correlation between these results. Correlation value exists between –1 and +1. If it's close to –1 then there is a negative linear relationship between the two variables and its +1 then there is a positive linear relationship. In this chapter we separately calculated the correlation between female literacy rate and the indicators of maternal health care. We found a positive relationship between all the variables. Among the six variables, we found the highest correlation value (0.69) between female literacy rate and the women who had institutional delivery.

It is estimated that each year approximately one-third of a million women worldwide die due to pregnancy-related conditions. 99 per cent of these deaths occur in developing countries and approximately three-quarters of them are considered avoidable. The more socially and economically advantaged people are, the better their health. Years of formal education are a well-recognized indicator of social position and have been frequently used in international surveys to explore social inequalities. These studies show that people with progressively more advanced levels of education have better health and longer lives than those without. But it has been argued that women's education should not be treated merely as a proxy for the social determinants of health but as an important force in its own right. Women's educational levels (relative to those of men) have been found to be associated with maternal death. There is a positive relationship between levels of maternal education and health service use, even in adverse family or socio-economic situations. Furthermore, lack of education is highlighted as one of a number of stressors (along with limited money and decision-making power) affecting women during pregnancy and childbirth, creating vulnerability and increasing the likelihood of negative outcome. It is possible that much of the health disadvantage associated with low levels of maternal education can be addressed through universal access to quality health services; however, this hypothesis has not been tested empirically (Karlsen, 2011).

Awareness of ORS among women plays very important role in the prevention of diarrhea disease. In India every year 2.1 million

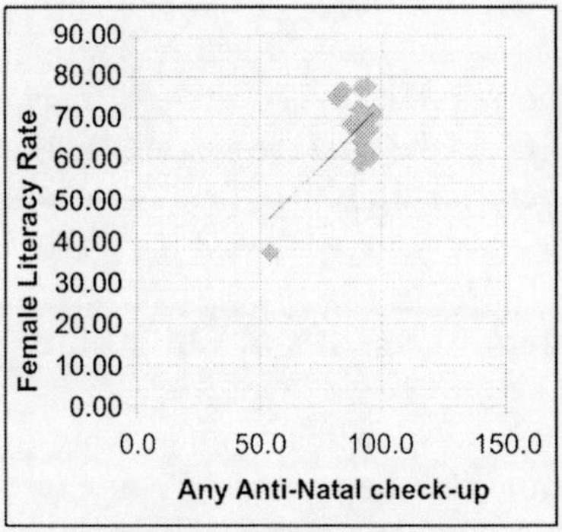

Fig. 10.1: Correlation: 0.62

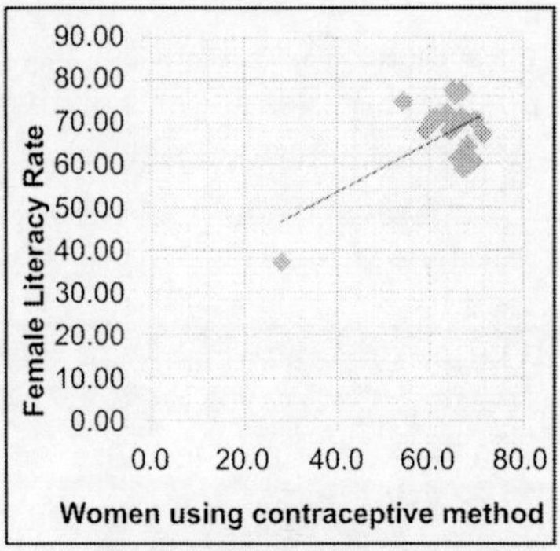

Fig. 10.2: Correlation: 0.59

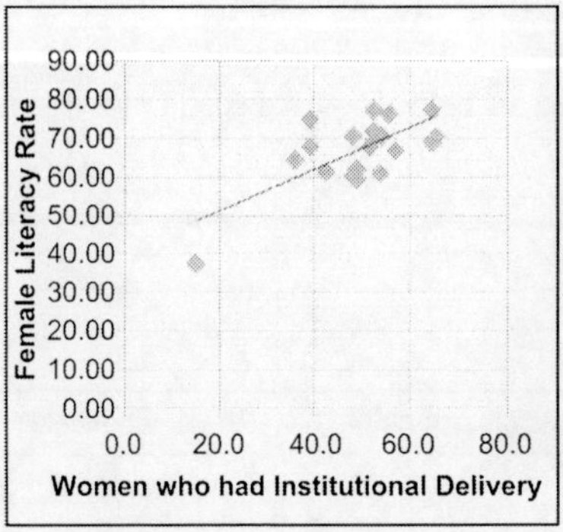

Fig. 10.3: Correlation: 0.69

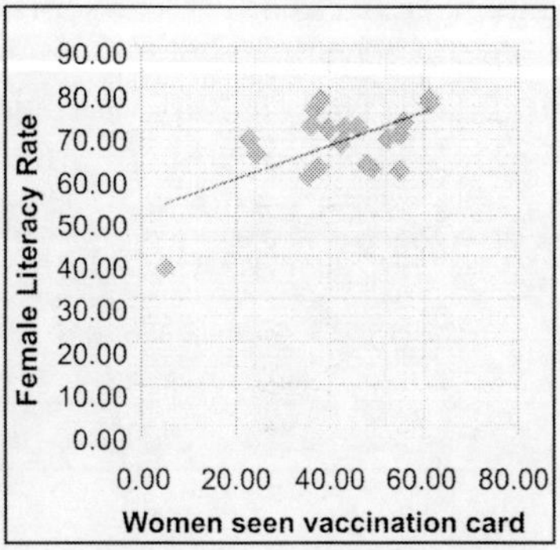

Fig. 10.4: Correlation: 0.60

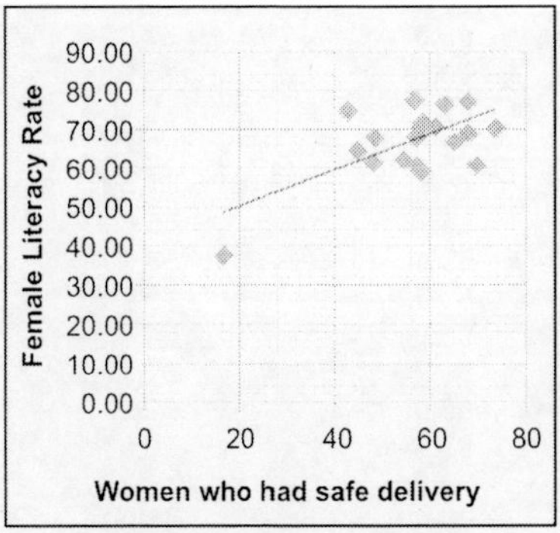

Fig. 10.5: Correlation: 0.64

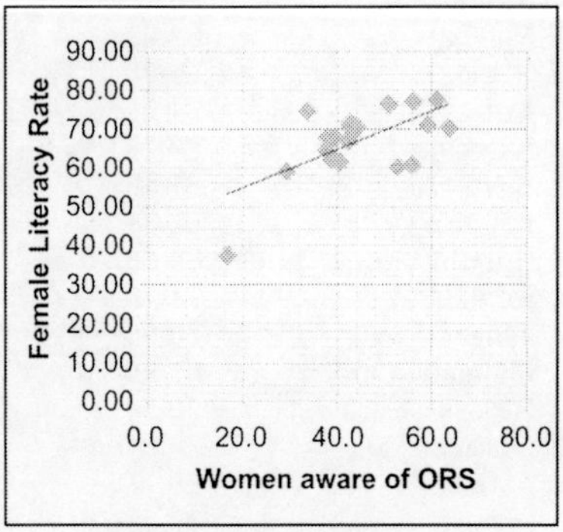

Fig. 10.6: Correlation: 0.63

children under the age of five dies because of this disease. Diarrhea thus accounts for about 23 per cent of under five deaths. Through our study we also found positive correlation (0.63) between female literacy rate and women aware of ORS. In the rural areas where market is not developed or the market is very far from the villages, general awareness of making ORS at home is very necessary.

Relationship between Women Empowerment and Child Care

There is series of literature on the fact that the women who are educated can taken care of their child in a better way. Women with more than a primary schooling had a smaller gender bias in sending children to school than women with less than primary schooling. But disparities in education between various social groups defined by region, area, caste, sex, class, disabilities etc. still exist. In the present study we have taken two variables on child care namely percentage of children who are fully vaccinated and children received colostrums within 24 hours after their birth.

Table 10.2: Female Literacy Rate and Indicators of Child Healthcare

District	*Female Literacy Rate*	*Children Received*	*Children received full*
	(%)	Colostrums (%)	Vaccination (%)
Panchkula	77.48	86.0	78.10
Ambala	76.64	91.5	79.10
Yamunagar	71.99	80.1	70.00
Kurukshetra	69.18	75.1	67.80
Kaithal	60.69	67.9	72.50
Karnal	68.29	86.6	75.20
Panipat	68.23	85.3	57.00
Sonipat	70.88	90.6	73.00
Jind	61.58	65.2	55.40
Fatehabad	59.29	68.9	62.80
Sirsa	61.16	71.6	61.30
Hissar	62.31	94.7	55.80
Bhiwani	64.60	63.4	58.40
Rohtak	71.19	86.8	75.70
Jhajjar	70.96	95.9	64.80
Mahendergarh	67.25	83.2	67.70
Rewari	70.54	85.0	67.30
Gurgaon	77.64	82.8	70.50
Faridabad	75.17	93.8	46.40
Mewat	37.58	73.2	11.00

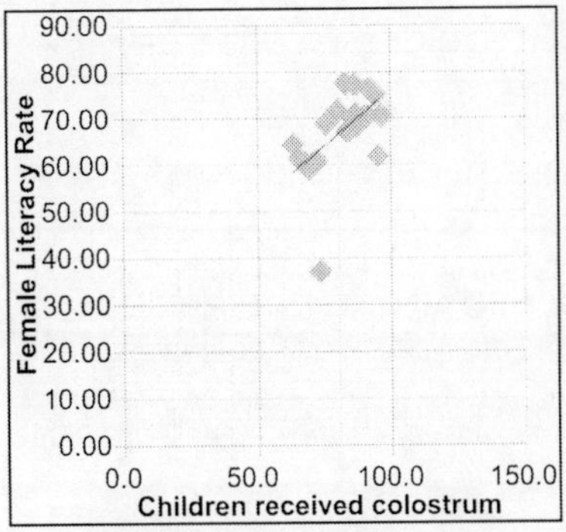

Fig. 10.7: Correlation: 0.53

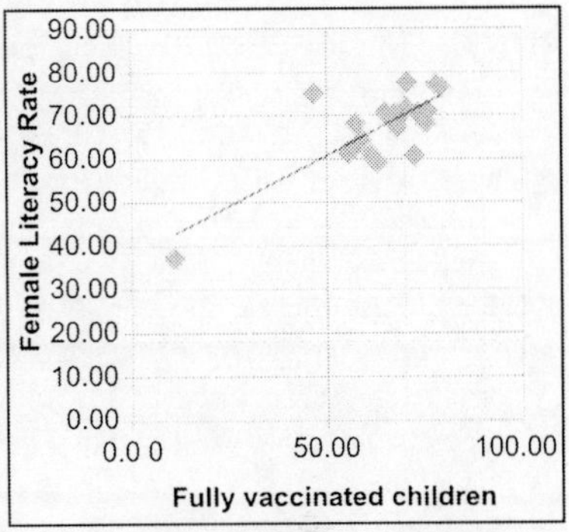

Fig. 10.8: Correlation: 0.77

Table 10.2 shows the female literacy rate and indicators of child healthcare. We have found the strong relationship between female literacy rate and the fully vaccinated children (0.77). It means that women who are educated can have easy access to primary health centres and vaccination card and able to prevent their children from dangerous diseases. However, we found the positive relationship between female literacy rate and the children received colostrums but the correlation value as such is not high as compare to other indicators.

Conclusion

Empowerment means an individual have the specific power to execute the decisions. In India, empowerment of women has a specific goal. To achieve this goal she has to come forward and fight to achieve her rights. Education of women is a powerful tool to bring positive change in the society. Therefore, in our country Government should emphasize on opening of more schools, colleges and university especially for women. Government should also pay attention to girl education and on reducing the gender discrimination.

References

Geetanjali, Kunuku (2011), *Women Empowerment: An Empirical Analysis*, published by Satish Upadhyay, Satyam Law International, New Delhi-110002.

Hazarika, Dhruba (2011), "Women Empowerment in India: A Brief Discussion", *International Journal of Educational Planning and Administration.* ISBN 2249-3093, Volume 1, No. 3, pp. 199-202.

Jitender, Malik (2012), "Spatio-Temporal Pattern of Literacy in Haryana", *International Journal of Reviews, Surveys and Research.* Vol. 1, Issue 1, September.

Karlsen, Say, Souza, Hogue, Calles, Giilezoglu and Raine (2011), *The relationship between maternal education and mortality among women giving birth in health care institutions: Analysis of the cross sectional WHO Global Survey on Maternal and Perinatal Health*, published by BMC Public Health.

Misra, Jugal Kishore (2006), "Empowerment of Women in India", *The Indian Journal of Political Science*, Vol. 67, No. 4, October-December, pp. 867-878.

Report: District Level Household and Facility Survey, Haryana (2010), International Institute for Population Sciences and Ministry of Health and Family Welfare.

11
Role of Healthcare Services in Women Empowerment

Chitra Choudhary

Introduction

Healthy man power is a basic pre-requisite for development of the nation. WHO states, "The enjoyment of the highest attainable standard of health is one of the fundamental rights of every human being without distinction of race, religion, political belief, economic and social condition". Health contributes to higher productivity and socio-economic development which in turn provides them with higher wages and better prospects of life. Thus social as well as economic development achieved by a nation is often determined on the basis of the level of health and the system of healthcare and health services prevalent in the society. Current health status of the women of India indicates that the growth pattern has so far not been inclusive as a large chunk of the population is out of the purview of the health system. Largest number of undernourished mothers and children live in India. Of the 1.3 billion people who live in absolute poverty around the globe, 70 per cent are women. For these women, poverty does not just mean scarcity and want. It means rights denied, opportunities curtailed and voices silenced. Significant progress has been made over the past few decades in providing healthcare to populations in developing countries but this progress has been uneven; women in particular, have not had an equal share. Women's inadequate access to healthcare is also reflected in mortality statistics. Women have continued to occupy a secondary and passive role in the patriarchal structure in Indian society.

Status of Women's Health in India

India with about 17.5 per cent of the world population accounts for about 25 per cent of the maternal deaths in the world. Every year about 1,25,000 Indian women die from pregnancy related causes many of which are preventable. Poor maternal health results in low birth weight and premature babies. Less than two-third of mothers received antenatal checkups, 58 per cent received iron and folic supplements (1998-99). More than a third of women in the country had a Body Mass Index (BMI) of less than 18.5. Anaemia is a major health problem. The prevalence of anaemia for ever married women has increased from 52 per cent in NFHS-II to 56 per cent in NFHS-III. Pregnant women are much more likely than non-pregnant women to be moderately to severely anaemic. Not only that the overall health status of women in India is quite unimpressive, there are vast disparities in the achievements across the states of the country. Despite an increase in institutional deliveries, 60 per cent of pregnant women still deliver their babies at home. The position of women is worse in "BIMARU" states. In India more than two-third of all maternal deaths occur in BIMARU states like Uttar Pradesh, Madhya Pradesh, Rajasthan, Orissa and Assam. There is an important link between women's status and population parameters such as fertility, Infant child mortality, life-expectancy, etc. High rates of fertility and Infant child mortality deplete women's health. National population policy 2000, specifically identified the low status of women in India as an important barrier to the achievement of population and maternal and child welfare goals (Ministry of Health and Family Welfare, 2000). Nearly 50 per cent women get married before they attain 18 years of age and 57.9 per cent pregnant women and 56.2 per cent married women suffer from anaemia. MMR is quite high at 301 maternal deaths per 100,000 live births in 2006. One-third of all malnourished children live in India and 46 per cent of children under-3 years are underweight. Thus the status of women health is largely reflected by the indicators like female mortality and morbidity, disease burden, reproductive health and encompassing reproductive behaviour, maternal mortality and morbidity, nutrition, poverty and violence against women and its consequences for the healthcare system of women. Indian women have high mortality rates during childhood, reproductive years and particularly in pregnancy (Kateja, 2008). According to the report, 5.2 million people in the (15-49) age-group in India are suffered by HIV/AIDS, and among the affected 38 per cent are women Severity of malnutrition problem presents a serious threat to health of girls and women. It is important therefore to understand how women are particularly impacted and their health outcomes. There is a critical need to look at women's health holistically.

Health Status of Women in Rajasthan

Rajasthan has made real progress over the past 60 years in achieving more equitable distribution between women and men of the benefits of development. Socio-economic indicators such as education, health and work participation or in more subtle process of power, decision-making and self-esteem the inferior position of women has been consistently documented. Status of women, as reflected by various socio-economic indicators, (mainly healthcare) is low in the state across all the districts. NFHS-III data indicate that majority of women have reproductive health and pregnancy related problems, but only 16.6 per cent of all mothers received antenatal care, 32 per cent of all deliveries took place in institutions and only 29 per cent received post natal care. Low coverage of safe deliveries and home deliveries assisted by doctor/nurse/ANM, is a cause of concern. The situation is more deplorable in rural areas with merely 5.8 per cent institutional deliveries (SRS, 2003). A holistic approach to women's health, which includes both nutrition and health services need to be adopted and special attention should be given to the needs of women and the girl at all stages of the life cycle.

Objectives of the Study

(1) To identify the factors determining the health status of women.
(2) To examine the extent of relationship between demand for health and socio-economic factors.
(3) The study attempts to unravel the mysteries behind poor health status of women in Rajasthan.
(4) To state the measures for women's health status.

Data Sources and Methodology

The chapter provides a snapshot of women's standing in 30 distícts of Rajasthan, using the secondary data as provided by the various years of Census of India 2011, Statistical Abstarct 2011 (Rajasthan) and Annual Health Report 2012-13. Principal component analysis is carried out over the period of 2011database. Various other indicators which significantly contribute to these three mortality indicators are used which are as follows—access to safe drinking water, toilet facility, electricity, roads, mothers who received three or more antenatal care and at least one tetanus toxiod injection, mothers who consumed IFA for 100 days or more, Institutional delivery and safe delivery, Family planning practices (any method per cent), female literacy, female work participation rate and female mean age at marriage.

The inter-district differences in Women's health status have been examined in terms of three mortality indicators. Infant Mortality rate (female)—It is the number of deaths of female children less than one year of age per 1000 live births.

(A) Under-5 Mortality Rate (female) (U5MR)–It is the probability per 1000, that a newborn baby will die before reaching age five, subject to current age-specific mortality rates.

(B) Maternal Mortality Ratio (MMR)–It refers to the death of a woman while pregnant or within 42 days of termination of pregnancy, irrespective of the duration and site of the pregnancy, from any cause related to or aggravated by the pregnancy or its management at per 1,00,000 live births.

Various indicators which significantly contribute to these three mortality indicators are used which are as follows—access to safe drinking water, toilet facility, electricity, roads, mothers who received three or more antenatal care and at least one tetanus toxiod injection, mothers who consumed IFA for 100 days or more, Institutional delivery and safe delivery, Family planning practices (any method %), female literacy, female work participation rate and female mean age at marriage. A strong association exists between level of women's education and use of reproductive-maternal health services (Kateja, 2008). Education improves women's status, increases age at marriage, reduces unwanted fertility, and improves utilization of health services.

Table 11.1: Mortality Indicators of Rajasthan's District (2011-12)

Districts	*IMR (f)*	*U-5MR (f)*	*MMR*
Ajmer	62	81	223
Alwar	55	81	152
Banswara	60	101	265
Baran	57	74	222
Barmer	75	90	222
Bharatpur	53	83	189
Bhilwara	62	81	223
Bikaner	53	79	191
Bundi	66	86	222
Chittaurgarh	63	73	265
Churu	51	66	191
Dausa	64	92	152
Dholpur	62	83	189
Dungarpur	65	85	265
Ganganagar	58	78	191
Hanumangarh	48	68	191
Jaipur	57	77	152
Jaisalmer	57	82	222
Jalore	78	98	222
Jhalawar	65	82	222
Jhunjhunu	53	73	152
Jodhpur	52	70	222
Karauli	74	90	189
Kota	37	50	222
Nagaur	60	80	223
Pali	56	72	222
Rajsamand	65	86	265
Sawaimadhopur	70	86	189
Sikar	58	84	152
Sirohi	68	91	222
Tonk	54	78	223
Udaipur	66	93	265

Source: Annual Health Survey (2011-12) and Statistical Abstract 2011.

Female schooling improves the chances that women will obtain employment, reduces their demand for children, and improves health-seeking behaviours. Similarly, where females are valued as productive workers, it may result in better treatment of female infants and children. Women's empowerment (reflected by all above mentioned three mortality indicators) depends on a host of socio-economic variables regarding sanitation, availability of medical care facility and so on. All the variables are inextricably interlinked.

Table 11.2: District-wise data (2010-11) with regard to socio-economic access to healthcare and other factors

I*	II*	III*	IV*	V*	VI*	VII*	VIII*	IX*
56.42	17.5	35.46	68.8	96.5	12.2	69.3	74.0	55.3
56.78	17.7	41.54	52.0	93.1	12.1	74.5	78.8	72.6
43.47	18.1	45.51	42.6	87.9	10.6	80.4	83.8	75.8
52.48	17.5	40.02	65.2	91.8	7.7	89.6	91.1	62.2
41.07	18.0	43.25	25.7	53.4	5.3	34.5	53.9	58.8
54.63	18.2	39.62	42.5	91.9	8.2	70.2	72.8	55.9
47.93	15.9	43.57	54.8	91.4	18.4	62.2	70.4	61.2
53.77	18.4	39.79	50.9	86.7	15.1	54.3	64.0	61.7
47.00	15.9	40.79	47.7	80.5	10.5	80.4	84.6	52.8
46.98	16.3	44.09	44.0	89.4	9.1	75.4	80.6	68.8
54.25	17.8	43.01	41.1	80.5	12.9	53.6	65.2	63.5
52.33	16.8	41.45	49.6	85.2	9.1	82.2	83.7	64.7
55.45	18.1	36.99	33.5	72.8	7.4	83.6	84.8	49.0
46.98	18.6	42.34	42.1	86.8	4.7	63.5	67.4	73.8
60.07	20.2	39.13	54.3	85.6	12.8	76.9	79.7	79.2
56.91	18.8	41.31	37.6	65.5	25.4	56.8	67.4	78.8
64.63	18.3	32.14	73.7	95.9	23.8	90.9	92.2	69.9
40.23	17.7	40.62	23.4	67.9	8.2	35.8	48.6	55.1
38.73	18.5	44.81	38.3	68.6	10.8	46.7	68.2	57.7
47.06	16.8	42.69	51.1	90.3	8.1	77.8	82.0	64.9
61.15	18.5	38.86	46.9	93.3	22.2	80.2	84.9	74.8
52.57	17.6	38.54	38.4	74.8	13.9	56.4	63.4	63.3
49.18	16.5	41.36	42.5	87.3	4.7	85.3	85.7	51.7
66.32	19.2	31.82	70.5	94.5	15.3	84.6	86.8	69.2
48.63	17.7	43.15	29.6	93.8	5.2	74.9	80.9	61.8
48.35	18.6	39.02	46.6	81.4	15.8	63.1	72.5	54.9
48.44	17.7	41.39	45.2	89.7	12.5	64.8	74.4	65.1
47.08	16.8	40.71	47.8	86.7	8.5	80.8	82.8	57.9
58.76	18.4	35.19	50.2	83.4	8.3	81.2	86.8	69.3
40.12	19.2	37.59	37.9	76.0	13.7	77.4	81.8	57.8
46.01	16.5	44.09	48.6	81.9	9.6	76.3	81.3	51.3
49.01	18.7	33.45	40.0	76.5	16.2	57.6	62.0	70.1

Note: I* female literacy, II* Mean age at marriage, III* Female work participation rate, IV* Mothers who received three or more Antenatal care (%), V* Mothers who received at least one tetanus toxiod injections, VI* Mothers who consumed IFA for 100 days or more (%), VII* Institutional Delivery (%), VIII* Safe Delivery (%), IX* Family Planning practices (any method %)

Source: I, II III from census of India 2011 and IV-VIII from Annual Health Survey 2011-12.

Findings

Though the data of MMR is available with regard to seven divisions of Rajasthan, so analysis and conclusions are made on that basis. Seven Divisions of Rajasthan are as follows:

- First division comprises of our districts named as Bikaner (Ganganagar, Hanumangarh, Bikaner, Churu).
- Second division comprises of five districts named as Jaipur (Jhunjhunu, Alwar, Dausa, Jaipur, Sikar).
- Third division comprises of four distiicts named as Bharatpur (Bharatpur, Dholpur, Karauli, Sawaimadhopur).
- Fourth division comprises of four districts named as Ajmer (Nagaur, Ajmer, Tonk, Bhilwara).
- Fifth division comprises of six districts named as Jodhpur (Jodhpur, Jaisalmer, Barmer, Jalore, Sirohi, Pali).
- Sixth division comprises of four districts named as Kota (Bundi, Kota, Baran, Jhalawar).
- Seventh division comprises of five districts named as Udaipur (Rajsamand, Udaipur, Dungarpur, Banswara, Chittaurgarh).

Descriptive statistics has been calculated and presented in the Table 11.3.

Table 11.3: Descriptive Statistics

	Mean	*Std. Deviation*	*Analysis N*
Imrf	60.1250	8.36564	32
U5MRF	81.0313	9.99834	32
Flit	51.0500	6.94682	32
Fmmarr	17.8281	1.00297	32
Electricity	64.95	15.273	32
SDW	67.05	14.642	32
TOILETFA	32.27	20.192	32
Road	43.24	14.795	32
ANC	46.35	11.704	32
Tetanus	83.78	10.073	32
ID	70.04	14.614	32
SD	76.14	10.629	32
FP	63.40	8.324	32
MMR	209.91	34.673	32
Fwpr	40.1284	3.57293	32
IFA	11.82	5.265	32

Principal Component analysis is a variable reduction technique which maximises the amount of variance accounted for in the observed variables by a smaller group of variables called components. KMO is an index for comparing the magnitude of the observed correlation coefficient to the magnitude of the partial correlation coefficients. Bartlett's test is used to test the hypothesis that the correlation matrix is an identity matrix which would indicate that your variables are uncorrelated. Communalities is the proportion of each variables variance that can be explained by the principal components. Both the undershowed tables reflect the appropriatness of all variables.

KMO and Bartlett's Test

Kaiser-Meyer-Olkin Measure of Sampling Adequacy.		.588
Bartlett's Test of Sphericity	Approx. Chi-Square	423.684
	Df	120
	Sig.	.000

Communalities

	Initial	Extraction
Imrf	1.000	.611
U5MRF	1.000	.727
Flit	1.000	.902
Fmmarr	1.000	.730
Electricity	1.000	.785
SDW	1.000	.798
TOILETFA	1.000	.851
Road	1.000	.724
ANC	1.000	.751
Tetanus	1.000	.816
ID	1.000	.866
SD	1.000	.825
FP	1.000	.836
MMR	1.000	.729
Fwpr	1.000	.539
IFA	1.000	.583

Extraction Method: Principal Component Analysis.

Table 11.3: Ranking of Districts on the basis of Principal Component Analysis

Districts	*Factor score*	*Rank*
Ajmer	0.78766	7
Alwar	0.85972	6
Banswara	0.52551	10
Baran	1.28395	2
Barmer	-2.62228	30
Bharatpur	0.26283	15
Bhilwara	0.52935	9
Bikaner	-0.85575	23
Bundi	0.46319	12
Chittaurgarh	0.78932	7
Churu	-0.88334	24
Dausa	0.91337	4
Dholpur	-0.23001	20
Dungarpur	0.02552	19
Ganganagar	0.02972	18
Hanumangarh	-1.44031	28
Jaipur	1.26039	3
Jaisalmer	-2.49147	29
Jalore	-1.382	27
Jhalawar	0.90221	5
Jhunjhunu	0.7321	8
Jodhpur	-0.93935	26
Karauli	0.46236	13
Kota	1.13935	1
Nagaur	0.17541	17
Pali	-0.32347	21
Rajsamand	0.48572	11
Sawaimadhopur	0.19542	16
Sikar	0.4612	14
Sirohi	-0.48218	22
Tonk	0.26208	14
Udaipur	-0.89625	25

Note: Self-Computed.

Conclusions

The chapter reveals that in which districts better healthcare and sanitation facilities are available, along with female literacy, female work participation rate and mean age at marriage, those districts fare well on all the above mentioned three mortality indicators. Within the Kota division, Kota ranked first, while Bundi, Baran and Jhalawar ranked as twelfth, second and fifth. In Jaipur division, Jaipur ranked as third, while Alwar, Dausa, Jhunjhunu and Sikar ranked at sixth, fourth, eighth and fourteen. Among the Bikaner division, Ganganagar

(18) fared well against Hanumangarh (28), Bikaner (23) and Churu (24). Within the Bharatpur division, Dholpur listed on tweenteh number while Sawaimadhopur, Bharatpur and Karauli have sixteen, fifteen and thirteen rank respectively. Out of Ajmer division, Ajmer (7) remained on top irrespective of Bhilwara (9), Nagaur (17) and Tonk (14). Within the Jodhpur division, all the disticts have lower ranking. Among the Udaipur division, Chittaurgarh (7) listed on top in comparison to Banswara (10), Rajsamand (11), Dungarpur (19) and Udaipur (25). The analyses found that there lies a great extent of disparity within all the divisions. Among all the divisions, Jaipur division fared well although differences are also there. Thus the study suggests that not only healthcare services but also other socio-economic variables have significant bearing on all the three mortality indicators reflceting women empowerment. It is impossible for her to provide high quality child care if she herself is poor and oppressed, illiterate and uninformed, anemic and unhealthy, has five or six other children, lives in a slum or shanty, has neither clean water nor safe sanitation. It is therefore proposes to adopt multisectoral approach, in order to empower women.

References

Annual Health Survey (2010-11): Rajasthan, Vital Statistics Division, Office of the Registrar General and Census Commissioner, New Delhi.

Census (2011): Census of India—Provisional Population Totals, Directorate of Census Operations, Jaipur, Rajasthan.

GOI: Report of the working group on empowerment of women for the 11th plan, Ministry of Women and Child Development, Government of India.

Kateja Alpana (2008): *Maternal Health in Rajasthan*, Royal Publication, Jodhpur.

Kateja Alpana and Ramakrishnan Sandhya K. (2008): *Infant Mortality in Rajasthan*, Royal Publication, Jodhpur.

Lakshmana, L.M. (2010): "Women's Health, Education and Empowerment: India's Status and Challenges", *International Journal of Development and Social Research*, Vol. No. I.

NFHS-II (1998-99): National Family and Health Survey, International Institute of Population Sciences (IIPS), Mumbai.

NFHS-III (2004-05): National Family and Health Survey, International Institute of Population Sciences (IIPS), Mumbai.

Statistical Abstract (2011): Directorate of Economics and Planning, Yojana Bhawan, Jaipur, Rajasthan.

Statistics of Women in India (2007): *Department of Women and Child Development,* Ministry of Human Resource Development.

12

Life Stress and Behavioural Dysfunction of Married Women

A Case Study of Working Women and Housewives in the National Capital Region (NCR)

Sunita Tanwar

Introduction

In the current situation women education and employment are much important for the development of the society, so their orientation is very important, which is a crucial challenge as there are many social and familial responsibilities for women. If family member's does'nt support, women employment becomes very difficult. A woman plays a very important role as a daughter, a wife, a mother, a sister etc., so these responsibilities are too expected to the women intensively in comparison to men. The present study is an attempt to understand the comparative life stress and behavioural dysfunction of married working women with a housewife in NCR.

Working women may be prone to depression because of the double burden of housework and a job outside the home. As they have to work in two environments, one is the office environment and the other is home environment. Both are vastly different from one another. Stress arising from marital relationships is manifested in chronic disorders such as depression, insomnia and hypertension. Since a relationship depends on the nature of the persons involved, it helps to seek the middle path when the inherent individual differences surface. It often helps to change one's attitude, go for counselling or talk openly with the spouse about problems facing in the relationship.

One of the most important relationships between a man and women is marriage. It involves emotional and legal commitment that is quite important in any adult life. There is no doubt that the choice of marital partner is one of the most important decisions one makes in his/her lifetime. People marry for many reasons, like; love, happiness, companionship, and the desire to have children, physical attraction, or desire to escape from an unhappy situation (Bernard, 1984). All the marriages are aimed at happiness in one or another way. Most couples marriage is filled up with expectations. Some of the expectations will be realistic while others unrealistic. This is due to the complex nature of marriage and the complex nature of individuals involved in the same. Marriages are the intermixing of two universes (Veenboven, 1983). If these two are not supporting to each other, misunderstanding will start and result into marital maladjustment.

Marital adjustment calls for maturity that accepts and understands growth and development in the spouse. If this growth is not experienced and realized fully, death in marital relationship is inevitable. A relationship between couples is not instantaneous rather a slow progress. "It is like the undetected cancer that kills silently and softly".

In the above situations women's life becomes very difficult, as she perceived herself in stress. It has been found in many studies, as the Hashmi, Khurshid and Hassan (2007) aimed at exploring the relationship between marital adjustment, stress and depression. Results indicated highly significant relationship between marital adjustment, depression and stress. The findings of the results also show that working married women have to face more problems in their married life as compared to non-working married women. The results further show that highly educated working and non-working married women can perform well in their married life and they are free from depression as compared to educated working and non-working married women.

Study on marriage and marital adjustment in USA presents social activities and recreation, training and disciplining of children, religion, in law relationship, financial matters, sexual relationship, communication, mutual trust and companionship as the areas of marital adjustment (Simth, 1961). In an another study on 581 couples and 25 per cent of them disclosed that at some time in the adjustment process, they discussed discovering and 18 per cent had seriously considered it (Leffcourt, 1976). There is a list of six areas of marital adjustment, which is defined by the psychologist, such as, religion, social life, mutual friends, in laws, money and gender (Lazarus and Delingis, 1983). Another psychologist defines ten areas of marital adjustment, i.e. values, couple growth, communication, conflict resolution, affection, roles, cooperation, gender, money and parenthood (Margolin, 1980).

There is evidence that the pressures of managing multiple roles in women are the greatest, and the psychological benefits of employment are the least, under conditions of heavy family responsibilities that is, when young children are at home (Blood, 1960). But beyond specific factors such as these, what is important to marital satisfaction over the course of marriage is the ability of partner to adjust to a variety of changes and to cope with a number of stresses. Marital role can be defined as set of attitudes and behaviours a spouse is expired to demonstrate in the content of the marriage relationship (Gore and Manigione, 1983). A marital role comprises of cultural expectations associated with the husband or with a wife. A husband is expected to act as head of family while wife is expected to make home and companion, or the wife may be expected to be the strong one, upon whom the husband can rely (Campbell, Converse & Rogers, 1976).

Perhaps half of the adults suffering from severe stress blame the deteriorating relationships on their spouse. Looking at the growing rate of divorces, court cases for alimony, physical abuses and single parents; it does seem as if handling a relationship can be a tricky and often taxing issue. The possible causes can be endless. More often than not, stress arising from marital relationships is manifested in chronic disorders such as depression, insomnia and hypertension. Since, a relationship depends on the nature of the persons involved, it helps to seek the middle path when the inherent individual differences surface. It often helps to change one's attitude, go for counseling or talk openly with the spouse about problems facing in the relationship (Weiten, 1986).

On the basis of above description in the present study main problems specified as life stress, marital adjustment and behavioural dysfunction of married working and non-working women's, because this issue is very critical to the development of women's well-being point of view. Although a lot number of studies had been conducted related to this issue, but for the complete and recent understanding of women problems more studies are needed with different variables.

Objectives of the Study

In the light of review literature and above descriptions following specific objectives were specified—

(i) To study life stress of married working women and housewives.
(ii) To measure the marital adjustment of working women and housewives.
(iii) To assess the behavioural dysfunctions of married working women and housewives.
(iv) To assess the correlations of the above variables with one another.

Hypotheses

(i) There exists a high level of life stress in married working women compared to the housewives.
(ii) There exists a significant difference in behavioural dysfunction between working women and housewives.
(iii) There exists a significantly low level of marital adjustment of working women in comparison to housewives.
(iv) Life stress would significantly correlate with behavioural dysfunction and marital adjustment.

Sample

The sample of this study is to be constituted 200 housewives (100) and working (100) women belonging to Delhi NCR. The respondents were selected from rural and urban settings of the age range of 30 to 45 year.

Behavioural Measures

Life Stress Scale

Life stress scale was developed by Ravikant and Sanjeev Kumar

Gupta, (2009). This scale measures the six dimensions of life stress namely Sociability, Apathy, Health, Economical Status, Educational Status and Family Situations. Each dimension comprises of 8 items, dictonomous scale having two alternatives 'Yes' or 'No' indicating the overall life stress. Reliability of the scale was found as.67 on the basis of test-retest method. Face validity was established as 60 per cent based on perceptions of different experts of the field related to life stress.

Marital Adjustment Questionnaire

It was developed by the Pramod Kumar and Kanchana Rohatgi (1999) consisting of 25 highly discriminating 'Yes-No' type items. The scale measure three types of marital adjustment based on the Sexual Statement (4 items), Social Statement (9 items), and Emotional Statement (12 items) of the both husband and wife. The split-half reliability test was conducted, correlating odd-even items, applying the Spearman-Brown formula for doubling the test length, and was found to be .49 (N = 60) with an index of reliability of .70. The test-retest reliability was also studied. It was found to be .71 (N = 60) with an index of reliability of .84. The content validity was adequately assured as only those items were selected for the initial questionnaire for which there was 100 per cent agreement among the experts.

Dysfunction Analysis Questionnaire

This scale was developed by D. Prasad, S.K. Verma, A. Malhotra, and S. Malhotra, (1985). It measures five areas of dysfunction, such as social, vocational, personal, family and cognitive. 10 items included in each area, therefore, total 50 items are included in this scale. The correlations scores obtained between the two test sessions were highly significant for each dimension. Such as r = .70** (social), .87** (vocational), .84** (personal), .74** (family), and .86** (cognitive) were found. Split half reliability was also found very highly significant with r = ranged from .88 to .97.

Results

The result is obtained after data collection, data was scored and put to statistical analysis in order to test the formulated hypothesis of the study. In this way life stress of working women and housewives was assessed in relation to selected variables such as marital adjustment and behavioural dysfunction, and results have been described below.

Comparison of Working Women and Housewives on Different Variables

The comparison of scores of working and non-working married women on life stress, marital adjustment and behavioural dysfunction is performed through following Table 12.1.

Table 12.1 shows the comparison of working and non-working married women on life stress, which reveals that there is significant difference between working and non-working married women

Table 12.1: Means, Standard deviations and *t*-value of scores of working and non-working married women on different variables (N = 200)

Variables		*Subject*	*N*	*Mean*	*S. D*	*t - values*
Life Stress		Working Women	100	17.46	5.72	11.71**
		Housewives	100	11.62	5.44	
Marital Adjustment		Working Women	100	18.42	3.84	3.14**
		Housewives	100	19.44	3.41	
Behavioural Dysfunction	Social	Working Women	100	28.78	8.38	3.89**
		Housewives	100	25.94	7.96	
	Vocational	Working Women	100	29.18	8.22	4.75**
		Housewives	100	25.80	7.67	
	Personal	Working Women	100	26.64	8.21	3.33**
		Housewives	100	24.22	8.02	
	Family	Working Women	100	27.52	8.31	4.51**
		Housewives	100	24.34	7.43	
	Cognitive	Working Women	100	28.18	8.17	2.48*
		Housewives	100	26.40	7.86	
	Total	Working Women	100	140.30	31.11	5.21**
		Housewives	100	126.70	27.19	

*Significant at the 0.05 level.
**Significant at the 0.01 level.

Table 12.2: Correlations among life stress, behavioural dysfunction and marital adjustment

	Life Stress	*Marital Adjustment*	*DAQ s*	*DAQ v*	*DAQ p*	*DAQ f*	*DAQ c*	*DAQ total*
Life Stress	1							
Marital Adjustment	-.279*	1						
DAQ s	.279*	-.190	1					
DAQ v	.257*	-.132	.737**	1				
DAQ p	.282*	-.197	.659**	.763**	1			
DAQ f	.285*	-.183	.648**	.794**	.811**	1		
DAQ c	.298*	-.174	.687**	.729**	.805**	.813**	1	
DAQ total	.231*	-.158	.648**	.823**	.730**	.765**	.687**	1

* Correlation is significant at the 0.05 level.

** Correlation is significant at the 0.01 level.

(t = 11.71, $d.f$=198). The results support to hypothesis: (i) that working married women are under higher stress.

Comparison between working women and housewives on the all five separate dimension and total behavioural dysfunction shows the significant difference that means hypothesis: (ii) is proved, in which all the difference are significant at the .01 level of confidence (Social, t = 3.89**; Vocational, t = 4.75**; Personal, t = –3.33**; Family, t = 4.51** and Total, t = 5.21**) except the Cognitive dimension (t = 2.48*) which is significant at .05 level of confidence. Mean values shows that working women have more behavioural dysfunctions in comparison to housewives.

Table 12.2 also shows the significant difference between working women and housewives on marital adjustment (t = 3.14, $d.f$ = 198). The results further indicates that the mean value of non-working married women (M = 19.44) is significantly higher than the mean value of working married women (M = 18.42). This finding support the hypothesis that non-working married women are better adjusted than working married women.

Above results have clearly described the difference between working women and housewives on selected variables, but not reflect the relationship among these variables. So for knowing the relationship among different variables, correlation was conducted as shown in the Table 12.2.

Table 12.2 indicates that there is significant correlation between the different measures. Which shows that the Life Stress is significantly and positively correlated with different dimensions of Behavioural Dysfunction (Social = .279*, Vocational = .237*, Personal = .262*, Family = .265*, Cognitive = .298* and Total = .231*), but it is negatively correlated with the Marital Adjustment (–.279*). All the correlation values indicate that the significance of relationship is lower (at the .05 level of confidence). Results indicate that life stress of married working women may increase the behavioural dysfunction in different situations. On the other hand marital adjustment negatively affects the life stress, it means in the condition of increasing marital adjustment, life stress of working women will decreased, or in other words low level of life stress can enhance high level of marital adjustment. Different dimensions of Behavioural Dysfunction (Social = –.190, Vocational = –.132, Personal = –.197, Family = –.183, Cognitive = –.174 and Total = –.158) are also negatively correlated with marital adjustment. It shows that marital adjustment and behavioural dysfunctions are affected by each other, although its not proved statistically significant. The different dimensions and total behavioural dysfunctions are highly positively correlated to each other, which indicate to high reliability of scores on Dysfunction Analysis Questionnaire.

All the above descriptions support to the hypothesis-4 that Life stress would significantly correlate with behavioural dysfunction and marital adjustment, which is same for the working women and housewives. Although these variables are find significantly correlated to each other in some extant, but here it is not clear that who is the predictor/criterion variable, so it is the limitation of this study so other elaborative studies with regression analysis can be further conducted.

Discussion

Obtained results supports to the hypotheses, fully or partially in this study. The research was undertaken to investigate the life stress, marital adjustment and behavioural dysfunction among married working women and housewifes. The result indicates that housewives are better adjusted in their married life than working married women. Along with this they also do not feel life stress in their married life as compared to working married women (Hashmi, Khurshid and Hassan, 2007). Work-Family Conflict has been commonly defined as a "form of inter-role conflict in which the role pressures from work and family are mutually incompatible in some respect (Greenhaus, Beutell, 1985;

and Frone, 2003). Whereas, findings suggest that housewives do not face difficulties in their married life whereas married working woman have to face many marital adjustment problems in her married life (Nübling, Stobel, Hasselhorn, Michaelis, and Hofmann, 2006). She also cannot perform better her married life responsibilities because she is under stress and if a married woman feels stress in her life, it affects her household work, her relationship with spouse and other members of her family and their daily behaviour. Researchers studied that women feel more life stress and behavioural dysfunctions after marriage and these two factors affect their married life. Because of depression and stress they cannot tolerate their spouses' behaviour and immediately get irritated. This makes their life miserable and leads towards breakup (Bradbury and Fincham, 1990).

According to the researches working married women cannot properly adjust with their married life because they have many tasks to perform at a time (Hops and Patterson, 1972). Working married women found themselves moving from one job to another job under a frequently changing cast of bosses. Reduced autonomy and an ever-increasing workload, combined with the added burden of having a small child at home, made their job's huge claim on time and emotional energy intolerable. That's why they cannot perform well at home (Hicks and Platt, 1969; Hofferth, 1979). Working married women would report more stress and less satisfaction than house wives (Burke and Weir, 1987), because work sometimes serves as to put a woman into an unhappy situation, sometimes getting stuck in a situation that increases stress, and heavy work puts a bad effect on their lives and it creates stress in their personalities (Cooper, 1981).

The findings of this study indicate that working women have to face more life stress than those women who are housewives (Sarwar, 1994). It may be possible due to many reasons. First of all, working women can get more jobs related problems with household responsibilities (Yildirim, and Aycan, 2008; Pal, and Saksvik, 2008), and second, different behavioural dysfunctions, which may be produced by different and contradictory responsibilities of office and family or due to work-family conflict (Hill, 2005). But results further indicate that both working women and housewives have marital adjustment problems in their married life, although it is significantly higher in case of working women (Isabelle, Matthias, Hans-Martin, Schwappach, and Rieger, 2008). Due to multiple job responsibilities they cannot give proper attention to their home and their married life, resulting into marital maladjustment in comparison to housewives.

Thus, present study suggests that women have many responsibilities in family and if not supported by family they suffer from many life stresses, marital life problems and behavioural dysfunction especially in case of working women. If we the support to women then they contribute in the development of family, society and finally country with their complete efficiency.

References

Bernard, J. (1984). *Work and Family: Changing Roles of Men and Women.* Palo Alto, CA: Mayfield.

Blood, R.O. (1960). *Husbands and Wives.* Wolfe DM, New York.

Bradbury, T.N., and Fincham, F.D. (1990). Attributions in Marriage: Review and Critique. *Psychological Bulletin*, 107, 3-33.

Burke, R.J., and Weir, T. (1987). Relationship of Wives Employment Status to Husband, Wife and Pair Satisfaction and Performance. *Journal of Marriage and Family*; 38 (5), 278-287.

Campbell, A., Converse, P.E., and Rogers, W.L. (1976). *The Quality of American Life*. New York: Russel Sage Foundation.

Cooper, C.L. (1981). *The Stress Check.* Englewood Cliffs: Prentice-Hall.

Frone, M. (2003). Work-family balance. In J. Quick, and L.E. Tetrick (Eds.) *Handbook of Occupational Health Psychology*, Washington, D.C.: American Psychological Association.

Gore, S., and Manigione, T.W. (1983). Social roles, sex roles, and psychological distress: Additive and interactive models of sex differences. *Journal of Health and Social Behaviour*, 24, 300-312.

Greenhaus, J., and Beutell, N. (1985). Sources of conflict between work and family roles. *The Academy of Management Review*, 10, 76-88.

Hashmi, H.A., Khurshid, M., and Hassan, I. (2007). Marital adjustment, stress and depression among working and non-working married women. *Internet Journal of Medical Update*, 2(1), 19-26.

Hicks, M., and Platt, M. (1969). *Marital Happiness and Stability: A Review of Research in the 60's*. New York: Wiley.

Hill, E. (2005). Work-family facilitation and conflict, working fathers and mothers, work-family stressors and support. *Journal of Family Issues,* 26 (6), 793-819.

Hofferth, S.L. (1979). Effects of women's employment on marriage: Formation, stability and roles. *Marriage and Family Review*, 2, 27-36.

Hops, H., and Patterson, G.R. (1972). *Marital Interaction Coping System*. Weiss R.L., London: Greenwood Press.

Isabelle, F., Matthias, N., Hans-Martin, H., Schwappach, D., and Rieger, M.A. (2008). Working conditions and work-family conflict in German hospital physicians: Psychosocial and organizational predictors and consequences. *BMC Public Health,* 8, 353, doi:10.1186/1471-2458-8-353.

Lazarus, R.S., and Delingis, A. (1983). Psychological stress and coping in aging. *American Psychologist,* 38, 245-254.

Leffcourt, H.M. (1976). *Locus of Control: Current Trends in Theory and Research.* New York: Willey.

Margolin, G. (1980). Behaviour exchange in happy and unhappy marriages. A family life cycle perspective. *Behaviour Therapy,* 12, 329-343.

Nübling, M., Stobel, U., Hasselhorn. H., Michaelis, M., and Hofmann, F. (2006). Measuring psychological stress and strain at work: Evaluation of the COPSOQ Questionnaire in Germany. *GMS Psychosocial Medicine*, 3, 1-18.

Pal, S., and Saksvik, P. (2008). Work-family conflict and psychosocial work environment stressors as predictors of job stress in a cross-cultural study. *International Journal of Stress Management*, 15, 22-42.

Sarwar, A. (1994). *Marital Adjustment and Depression Among Working and Non-Working Women.* Unpublished M.Phil. thesis. National Institute of Psychology, Quaid-i-Azam University, Islamabad.

Simth, H.C. (1961). *Personality Adjustment.* New York: McGraw-Hill.

Veenboven, R. (1983). The growing impact of marriage. *Social Indicators Research,* 12, 49-63.

Weiten, W. (1986). Psychology applied to modern life. *Adjustment in the 80's* (2nd edition). California: Words Worth.

Yildirim, D. and Aycan, Z. (2008). Nurses' work demands and work-family conflict: A questionnaire survey. *International Journal of Nursing Studies,* 45(9), 1366-78.

PART VI
Women Empowerment: Through the Lens of Literature

13

Empowering Women

The Role of Literature, Language, Law and Culture

Bir Singh Yadav

Since age long woman has been the victim of oppression, suppression and expression in the patriarchal social set up wherein the prevailing gender rules are recognized as preordained, consequently the stereotypical representation depicts her as weak, meek, docile, innocent, seductive, irrational as well as sentimental that imprisons her in inferior and subordinate frames. Her image is the outcome of a specific cultural construct in male-dominated society that treats her as sex object and child-bearing and rearing machine. This ideological construct has become instrumental for her exploitation as all the social inequalities between man and woman is not natural or predestined but created by man in order to retain power in varied forms in the society. The institutions of religion, family, education, arts and knowledge system in the form of social and cultural structures re-enforce this inequality in such an effective way that without seeming oppressive they convince woman and seek her consent for her being in the subordinate role by naturalizing this unequal power relation-ideology in the society. Hence, at the very outset when we think of empowering woman, it is essential to unpack these ideologies of domination with critical tools in order to release her from the age-old iron-cage of bondages to which she has become habituated and accepted it as her fate.

Undoubtedly literature, language, law, religion and culture with male politics and ideology have been the major contributory factors for the deteriorated condition of women in the society, but with their holistic approach they may also be the effective means in the move of empowering women. To redeem woman from her image of 'femininity' Feminism with its multi-layered semantic configuration in literature taking the Black critics, Marxist feminists and deconstructionists in its fold has played a crucial role. The Black critics express their serious concern over the silence of feminist critics about the black and the third world woman. Marxists take oppression; French feminist critics stress on psychological repression and American feminist criticism takes expression as the root cause of woman's inferiority in the society. Taking it a special kind of political discourse, Toril Moi, in critical and theoretical practice, is committed to the struggle against patriarchy and sexism.

Though women empowerment move took its formal launch from the USA in the late 1960s with the establishment of 'Women Study' as a discipline, consequently it showed its influence in the other first world nations in 1970s; yet besides some scattered and unacknowledged efforts, feminism got its inception with Mary Wollstonecraft's *A Vindication of the Rights of Woman* (1792) in which she rejected the socially accepted view that "women are naturally inferior or weaker to man". She suggested that women should get the status of 'companion' rather than being mere wives to their husbands. She found lack of education and sentimentalism responsible for keeping women subordinated; hence she emphasized the importance of rationality and reason over sensibility and feeling. Margaret Fuller, a radical thinker, editor and journalist in her book *Women in the Nineteenth Century* (1845) rejecting the feminine roles stated that 'there can not be a completely 'masculine' male just as there is no truly 'feminine' female'. Exploring gender relations, Virginia Woolf in her works *Room of One's Own* (1929) and *Three Guineas* (1938) attacked the patriarchal education system and reading practices which prevented women readers from reading as women; hence, she was the first woman to propound a woman centric notion of reading and education. Simone De Beauvoir in her seminal work *The Second Sex* (1949) pointed out the mystification and stereotyping of women as "instrumental by man in establishing patriarchy"; hence it was her in-depth insight that revealed that woman was constructed as such by man and society. Moreover, her most emphatic encapsulated sentence that has become a dictum that "one is not born, but rather becomes, a woman" (Beauvoir, 1973:31) gave a new impetus to the feminist thinking. Peeping into the exploitative philosophy she finds the marriage as an oppressive and exploitative economic arrangement through which women allow men to subordinate them which also re-enforces sexual inequalities and binds women to domesticity. She also argues that "This humanity is male and man defines women not in herself but as relative to him; she is not regarded as autonomous being" (Beauvoir, 1997:16). Thus in biological, psychological, historical and social context she traces the marginalized position of woman and as she rejects this 'otherness' she takes the subject position in the society. She also stresses the point that there is no such thing as 'feminine nature' and in the light of 'mind over matter' philosophy she suggests that the only way to female's emancipation lies in woman's release from her bodily identifications. She is hopeful that with the advancement of science and technology woman would be freed from being a domestic and reproductive chattel and she would be equal to man in thinking, working and acting. Kate Millet's *Sexual Politics* (1969) presenting women's treatment in art and literature makes clear that sex is natural and gender is social construction.

Phallocentric literary criticism paved way to a new and revolutionary field of criticism known as 'gynocriticism' – an alternative concept to female centered criticism propounded by Elaine Showalter, an American feminist thinker and author of *A Literature of Their Own* (1977). In her essay "Towards A Feminist Poetics", Showalter divides feminist criticism into two distinct varieties: woman as reader—"consumer of male produced literature" and "woman as writer-producer of textual meaning" (Seturaman, 403). Further tracing the history of women's literature, she shows three stages termed as:

> *Feminine, Feminist and Female stages*—During the Feminine phases, dating from about 1840 to 1880: women wrote in an effort to equal the intellectual achievements of the male culture; and internalized its assumptions about female nature... In the Feminist phase, from about 1880 to 1920 or the winning of the vote: women are historically enabled to reject the accommodating posture of femininity and to use literature to dramatize the ordeals of wronged womanhood. In the Female phase on going since 1920, women reject both imitation and protest—two form of dependency—and turn instead to female experience as the source of an autonomous art. (Seturaman, 405)

In this way if we are confined only to the stereotyping of women and their limited roles they play in literary history, we do not know what women have felt and experienced but we know only 'what men have thought women should be'. This critique also has a tendency to naturalize woman's victimization; therefore, feminist debates posit the omnipresence of systematic or institutionalized nature of women's oppressions. They try to know how oppressions had become institutionalized, how it functioned and how it could be changed. Showalter calls this analysis the feminist critique which is historically grounded inquiry probing into the ideological assumption of literary phenomena. It presents the images and stereotypes of women in literature, the omissions and misconceptions about women in criticism and the fissures in male constructed literary history. It also includes the exploitation and manipulation of female audience especially in popular culture and films; and with this analysis of woman as sign in semiotic system, the feminist critique focuses on woman as a reader of male produced and male oriented text. The subject under consideration is not a woman's experience but 'what men have thought woman should be'.

The second type of feminist criticism depicts woman as writer—woman as the producer of meaning in the light of history, themes, genres and structures of literature by women. Its focus is on the psychodynamics of female creativity; linguistics and problem of a female language and literary history and Showalter used the term gynocritics for this specialized discourse. The feminist critique is male-oriented representing the stereotyping of women without revealing what women have felt and experienced in their real life.

Gynocriticism starts from this point to construct a female framework for analysis of women's literature, to develop new models based on the study of female experience rather than to adopt male models and theories. Gynocriticism has its beginning at the point when we free ourselves from linear absolutes of male literary history, stop trying to fit women between the lines of the male tradition and concentrate on the nearly visible world of female culture. In the second stage Showalter sees a tendency in women's writing to lash out against the traditional standards and values. The woman writer of this phase expanded their sphere of influence by making inroads into social work. They expressed genuinely radical female protest against marriage and women's economic oppression. Through, the rejection of male-imposed definition and self-imposed oppression they opened the doors for the exploration of female identity, feminist theory and the female aesthetics. The third phase on going since 1920s is characterized by a self-discovering and some freedom from some of the dependency of 'opposition' as a means for self-definition.

The main thrust of the essentialism sprouts from the core query—"Is a woman a woman because she is biologically female or because she behaves like a woman?" (Waugh, 322). The argument put up by the essentialists is that woman being biologically different from man, is also psychologically and emotionally different and this difference can not be overcome. Simultaneously, they argue that women, not being man, should not take it in a shameful or derogatory sense and feminists should work to liberate women from a system of male-centered values and beliefs. On the other hand anti-essentialists think that the biological difference perpetuates a misogynistic belief system that has been working in a traditional way in excluding women from the male sphere. Shulamith Firestone, an American radical feminist in her text *The Dialectic of Sex* (1970) argues that technology could be used to free woman from her biological system and with the end of biological difference, the cultural differences would also be abolished and woman would get equal status to men. Firestone thinks that woman owing to her reproductive system always feels inferior to man.

Like Simone De Beauvoir Mary Daly, the American feminist theologian and a feminist critic of Christianity in her book *Gyn/Ecology* (1978) strongly advocates that "religion, law and science were all methods of patriarchal control working to define and limit women." She further argues that "the image of 'God the father' was constructed to validate the rule of the father in patriarchy" (Waugh, 324). She also challenges language being used as a tool of patriarchy as she finds women silent in patriarchal language. She points out that both religion and language have developed without a concept of female subject. She recommends the flow of patriarchal discourse and she has also written a feminist dictionary to support her project. She also explained that "women had a natural tendency towards pacifism and nurture that enabled them to live in harmony with the environment, unlike men, who compete with nature struggling to dominate the environment as they dominate women" (Waugh, 325). Highlighting women's involvement in anti-war and anti-nuclear protests in the essay "Feminisms" Fiona Tolan argumentatively stresses that "all kinds of violence—from rape to war to deforestation—were connected expression of male colonial aggression" (Waugh, 325). In this way, women, nature and the third world are all victims at the hands of an exploitative male capitalistic technology. Keeping in view the radical Lesbian Theory Daly has also argued that by refusing heterosexuality, woman could fatally undermine patriarchy.

Kate Millet in her text *Sexual Politics* (1969) suggests that patriarchal society works to inculcate male supremacy through a variety of covert means. She highlights how the entire social and cultural system in patriarchy functions in a well designed way according to sexual politics as it goes on encouraging women to internalize their own inferiority until it becomes psychologically rooted. Psychoanalysts Jullia Kristeva, Lucy Irigaray and Helen Cixous representative of French feminism in Britain and North America, like Beauvoir, also traced a progression of male supremacy as it has become so ingrained in western ideology as now seems natural and unquestionable. She found the apparently gender-neutral system of law, science and religion actually expressing male-thought, representing a masculine world-view.

Feminists think that Freudian theory has also contributed to perpetuate the belief that inferiority is an inherent quality of the female as Freud asserts that "anatomy is destiny" but his radical theory that patriarchal law is instilled into the child during a period of socialization provides a fresh energy to feminism. Highlighting the sprouting sense of male superiority Freud thinks that the crises in a male child's life begins when he learns that he must reject his mother and accept the authority of his father because father stands for social law and order, the acceptance of it reduces the mother (woman) to margin. In this way Oedipal Complex also contributes to gender identification.

Many Freudian Feminists feel that the patriarchal character of language also contributes to gender discrimination. Language is governed by men and it does not give 'a subject space' to women, hence leaves women speechless. Fiona Tolan asserts that:

> Using language, the child begins to construct and maintain a stable self identity in which self and other are distinct, where previously the child and the mother had been indistinguishable. It is through language that the authority of the father is maintained and the connection with the female (which threatens the autonomy and self identity of the child) is

> severed. The emphasis on language reinforced the message that sexuality was socially constructed; like Freud, Lacan identified a period before gender difference." (Waugh, 334-35)

Showalter, perceiving a parallel difference between the feminist problem of women's language and the language issue of a decolonized state, thinks that the entire issue of women's language and its advocacy is political as it has taken the shape of power struggle. As long as women remain silent, they will be kept outside the historical process. Therefore, what they need is genderlect spoken by women in the society. In the absence of which she feels that "women's literature is haunted by the ghosts of repressed language". Crossing the boundaries of Freudian theory, Showalter also takes into consideration the theories of other eminent psychologists and explores the positive aspects of feminist psychoanalysis in the form of the increased interest in the study of mother-daughter relationship that is a helping hand to women empowerment.

In order to explore the full meaning of the text gynocentric reader goes beyond the surface of the text as the intensive reading of *The Mad Woman in the Attic* reveals the rage of the repressed sexuality and the frustrated voice hidden behind—'the Angel in the House' that every woman is supposed to be. They recognized this social repression coming entirely through unconscious expression from the house of women.

Freudian concept also illustrates women's relationship to language, fantasy and culture through penis envy, castration complex and oedipal phase. Lacan also thinks that the girl child acquires language at the same time at which she recognizes the male as superior sex, hence to a woman the reminder of her own gender becomes a painful and weakening experience as it starts conditioning at an early age to fear patriarchal authority that leads to a process which Gilbert and Gubar call the phenomena of "inferiorization". Julia Kristeva also explains it through the "semiotic" and 'symbolic'—the two opposite states in which the symbolic always tries to repress the semiotic. It assumes the form of conflict between the conscious and the unconscious as Fiona Tolan remarks that

> "The idea of irrepressible unconscious was significant for feminism: it demonstrated that conscious/symbolic state (patriarchal order and control) was neither as natural nor as

> stable as would be believed, and consequently, that it could be overthrown". (Waugh, 335)

Making an entry in the social realm Kristeva concludes that symbolic is the social state in which bodily desires are controlled and repressed and the authority of the father is recognized. She thinks that the semiotic may be repressed but can not be eliminated and as it surfaces it disrupts the symbolic order—the entire patriarchal system. The process of repressing the semiotic by the symbolic always remains continue but the semiotic (unconscious) always goes on reflecting the reality, therefore, semiotic form of impressible unconscious is crucial for feminists generating social reality.

Translation theory through decoding and recoding to the 'base', as Nida and Chomsky think, also strikes the core of the issue. In a deconstructive move retrogressively we move to a stage where gender loses its meaning and all texts (male/female) become sexless and equal rejecting altogether the difference between masculine and feminine.

Taking culture as a binding force, Showalter in her essay "A Theory of Culture" presents a reflection of women's body, language and psyche in relation to the social context in which they occur. She thinks that all language is the language of the dominant group and power is fused with the language. She makes it clear that women's beliefs find expression through rituals and arts. In reality women's writing is a double voiced discourse containing a dominant and a mute story simultaneously. Men's writing, as she thinks, carry no meaning for women as she asserts, "Renaissance was not Renaissance for women, nor were Romanticism and Modernism". Ardner's model also shows that much of muted circle 'y' falls within the boundaries of the dominant circle 'x', hence all the male consciousness is within the circle of dominant structure and is structured by language. Hole and Bulge's culture model also shows that female tradition in society is positive source of strength as well as a negative source of powerlessness. She also challenges the psychological theories of Freud, Lacan and Bloom by positing theories of new 'white fathers' like Ardner and Gruz. Referring to Theodor Reik Freudian concept of writing with urination Showalter concludes that women can write more easily because they have bigger bladders.

According to Gilbert and Gubar, in patriarchal western culture the author is compared to a father, being creator he is supposed to represent the authority to set aesthetic standards whereas on the other side women lack the authority symbolized by the phallus, the organ of procreation, therefore, they are not in a position to create text. But Showalter contradicts it by thinking that text is created in brain, moreover, literary creation can be likened to gestation labour and delivery which are related to women. It hardly bears any resemblance with insemination, a male activity. She does admit that the main difference between men and women lies in body on the basis of which man exercises his power over women; consequently woman is marginalized and treated as 'other' but she stresses that this difference must be in the body of her writing and not the writing of her body.

Taking language issue we also agree with Lacan's proposition that the symbolic (social order) is conceived through language and language is masculine reflecting a male ideology and the male view of the world. Kristeva also points out the patriarchal foundation of western philosophy as it is founded on the repression of difference, any thing (feeling, thought or action) that deviates from the prescribed or established norms (may be right or wrong) is labeled as criminality, perversion or abnormality/madness and thereby is prohibited on this logistics. Therefore, as long as the male norm in the language remained forceful as the main/sole voice, female difference was suppressed. Consequently, we see that woman as subject (subjective woman) has no place in the male view but rather she is trained as 'other' as French feminists say that woman is mute in language because she does not exist as speaking 'I' in language. In this way Ecriture feminism becomes political and taking a deconstructive turn by disrupting the order and law of language, the writer also disrupts the social structures, hence the deconstruction of masculine language leads to the disruption of patriarchy which resultantly provides rightful position to women. Similarly, the image of God/father/ author in language represents masculine domination which needs to be subverted into anti phallic language.

Feminism has its beginning with liberation demanding equality for women at the first stage, at the second stage they reject the difference between masculine and feminine or some radical feminists reject patriarchy in favour of matriarchy. But anyhow the first two stages respond equality and the third phase known as 'post-modernism' in deconstructionist view based upon the concept about the 'fluidity of gender' as Judith Butler in her book *Gender Troubles* (1990) argues that masculine and feminine are artificially constructed binary gender categories based on imposed heterosexuality which could be deconstructed into multifarious possible gender positions. What direction this shift in the post-feminist move will take is uncertain to predict. If the category of women gets extinction in the 'post-feminist' era the feminist move will automatically become insignificant or it may lead to generate some powerful structure-nothing can be said.

Several kinds of issues from the field of literature, religion, scriptures and law are cropping up in this era of postmodern feminism. In *Paradise Lost* placing Eve in the context of postmodern woman Richard A. Poser commenting on the test of Eve's character in "Penal Theory in *Paradise Lost*" states that "Milton's Eve is intelligent" because "she has an enquiring mind" (Posner 260) but she is "left in the dark double" (Posner, 261) as she has to obey the duty of Adam without knowing the reason. He further states that rejecting the perfect obedience to male authority "she wanders off against Adam's wishes and is promptly 'seduced'. Even worse from the standpoint of maintaining male authority, she eats the forbidden fruit in the belief that acquiring knowledge will put her on a more equal footing with Adam" (Posner, 261) as Milton writes in *Paradise Lost*

> .....so to add what wants
> In Female Sex, the more to draw his Love,
> And render me more equal, and perhaps,
> A thing not undesirable, sometime
> Superior: for inferior who is free. (IX.817-825)

On the other hand, C.S. Lewis in *A Preface to Paradise Lost* showing man's uxorial nature comments that "Adam eats the fruit because he can not bear to live without Eve. Uxoriousness leads him into sin" (Lewis, 126) and Posner also seems to conclude that "independent minded woman and uxorious man are ultimate source of human misery". (Posner, 261) But we also have Shakespeare who in *The Tempest* in case of Prospero shows that fall is fortunate if it is for the sake of knowledge, then why not so in case of Eve? And if it is so then it leads to the conviction that every fall hath a rise and every rise hath a fall. Then the query crops up whether the modern Eve aspiring full freedom is rising to fall and modern Adam's uxorial nature will be the contributory factor to it. But Milton also gives clue to patriarchal system as he asserts in *Paradise Lost* addressing Eve that she is to be made subject "to thy Husband's will/Thine shall submit, he over thee shall rule" (X.195-196) and giving inkling to essentialism it is also made clear that Adam and Eve were unequal before the fall. Adam's physical appearance "declared absolute rule" while Eve's appearance "implied subjection", Adam had been created "for God only, she (Eve) for God in him [Adam]". (IV.295, 296, 299-301, 307-308, 330) Adam, being the son of God, is only for God or the sole proprietor of spiritualism and Eve, being the daughter of man, should see God in him (Adam), hence she is subjugated as a sex object which leads to a mind-matter relationship. In epics, scriptures as well as in religions on account of woman's deprivation from God and spiritualism, she is depicted as something –'other' in darkness that needs protection from temptation as in the conversation that takes place between them after fall, Adam reminds her that "had she not insisted on going off to garden by herself, he would have protected her from temptation" (Posner, 264). Eve (modern woman avant la lettre) replies: "was I to have never parted from thy side? / As good have grown there still a lifeless Rib". (IX.1153-1154) It shows procreative as well as divine motherly image of female sex with which God has created her. God may not be physically everywhere but through mother He is everywhere. But what wrong has taken place in the mind of the postmodern woman is that she wants to detach herself from the divinely mother role with the help of modern science and technology and slyly attempts to attract and ensnare man by her physical nudity projecting herself completely in the role of self-styled *apsra* which gives her an image of the beautiful blonde of the earth—the matter. Consequently, the relationship between man and woman seems mind–body relationship as Eve asks Adam "Why didst not thou the Head/Command me absolutely not to go?" (IX. 1155-1156). But Milton stressing the freedom and equal status of the female advocates through Adam "Force upon free Will hath here no place" (IX.1174) Milton highlighting the ideal state in Eden before the fall tells that man can not force a woman to do anything against her will. But as they expelled from Eden, woman's additional punishment is subjection to man's physical force as Posner remarks:

> The subjection of woman to man's force and man to another man's force are consequences of the fall's having deprived humankind of the ability to conform to the natural law. A

> government of men must take the place of a government of (natural) laws. (Posner, 264)

Eve also explains it to Şatan, the prohibition against eating the fruit of the Tree of the Knowledge of Good and Evil was "Sole Daughter of [God's] voice; the rest we live/Law to ourselves, our Reason is our Law" (IX.650-654) Milton in *The Christian Doctrine* makes it clear by stating that in Eden "it was the disposition of man to do what was right, as a being naturally good and holy." Made in the image of God, man had "implanted and innate in him… the law of nature, which is sufficient of itself to teach whatever is agreeable to right reason, that is to say; whatever is intrinsically good." (Milton, 1985, 993) But that was lost in the fall as a result of which human coercion usually in tyrannical form through the command of men and women "do what was right" started as Milton asserts:

> Since thy lapse, true Liberty
> Is Lost, which always with right reason dwells
> Twinn'd, and from her hath no dividual being:
> Reason in man obscure'd or not obey'd,
> Immediately inordinate desires
> And upstart Passions catch the Government
> From Reason, and to servitude reduce
> Man till then free. Therefore, since he permits
> Within himself unworthy Powers to resign
> Over free Reason. God in Judgment just
> Subjects him from without to violent Lords;
> Who oft as undeservedly enthrall
> His outward freedom. (XII. 83-95)

Women are still the object of male violence and when they respond to male violence with violence, they have to justify themselves to a world that continues to see women as responsible for relationship and obliged to conform to 'ladylike' stereotypes. In the field of law and literature the feminists intend to examine how both the disciplines continue to assure either that women are irrelevant or that their role is to be the object of male desire. The realities lie in the actual experience of women. A fair analysis of the structures of families,, religions, governments and political writings from Plato and Aristotle through Rousseau and beyond, shows how in a male centered culture a woman has to feel simultaneously loyalty to that culture and also anger at it for demeaning her as a woman. It is also difficult for women to define their feelings in the language which is chiefly made by men to express theirs. In *Jude the Obscure* Sue doesn't like marriage because marriage licenses the husband to have sex whenever he wishes even against his wife's desire. Consequently, marriage in most cases assumes the form of sex for money and protection. In male centered world women don't feel but they are taught to feel in a particular way; and even they are raped in marriage bed; resultantly woman becomes a provider and not a partner in the enjoyment. Literary scenes direct law, therefore, to empower woman it has provided a legal shape to it in the form of domestic violence against women. Thus most of the women lose their personhood upon marriage as her person being united with her husband's becomes one person that is not hers but it is him. The oppression of women by means of their reproductive capacities also remain intact. Those women who express their sexuality also remain at risk in male centered society, for men will continue to punish them for it.

In the male dominated society, parenting of the children in a particular way also results in great anger towards the mother figure especially in case of a girl child who recognizes that the mother has failed to empower her as the mother has the boy (son) to favour. This double parenting that creates gender imbalance and ill feeling results exclusively from female parenting. It is suffice to say that a brief encapsulated history of the feminist criticism that has its beginning with a study of images of women in literature, shows the ways in which women were represented, disempowered, forced into stereotypical molds. Values of social order are expressed in the ways of daily life and through the process of naturalization and internalization they are reduced to subordinate role which needs disruption for their empowerment.

In male centered social set up, a woman is judged by masculine law as if she were not a woman but a man. Ibsen in *A Doll House* and particularly in 'notes for a modern tragedy' had jotted down before beginning to write that play:

There are two kinds of moral laws, two kinds of conscience, one for men and one quite different for women. They don't understand each other, but in practical life, woman is judged by masculine law as though she weren't a woman but a man…The wife in the play ends by having no idea what is right and what is wrong; natural feelings, on the one hand, and belief in authority on the other lead her to utter distraction.... A woman can not be herself in modern society. It is an exclusively male society; with laws made by men and with prosecutors and judges who assess feminine conduct from a masculine standpoint.(466)

In order to empower woman virtually in this male dominated world literature, language, law and culture will have to play a significant role in her representation so that she can gain her rightful place in the society. The male will have to change his attitude and outlook towards the female not taking her as a 'thing' or 'the other' but she should be assigned her grace and dignity accepting her equally important human being as life partner without whom male is incomplete. Women will also have to make men understand her in right perspective not as a competitor in the game but as a companion in the divinely designed life scheme. With such a sense of understanding and sacrifice not with lust but with love, not with a feeling of domination and subjugation, but with mutual respect endowed with a sense of equality, both can be equally potent and powerful like two stars attracting each other without colliding may maintain the decorum of the sublime and civilized society reflecting the image of paradise on the earth.

References

Beauvoir, Simone De. (1977), *The Second Sex.* London: Vintage. Print.

Ibsen, Michael Meyer. (1971), *A Biography.* London: O.U.P. Print.

Ibsen, Henrik. (1965), *A Doll's House.* Trans. Peter Watts. London: O.U.P. Print.

Lewis, C.S. (1987), *A Preface to Paradise Lost.* O.U.P. Print.

Milton, John. (2000), *Paradise Lost.* New Delhi: UBS Publishers. Print.

——. (1985), *The Christian Doctrine.* London: O.U.P. Print.

Nayar, Pramod K. (2010), *Contemporary Literary and Cultural Theory.* New Delhi: Longman, Pearson. Print.

Posner, A. Richard. (1996), "A Penal Theory in Paradise Lost'. *Law and Literature: Text and Theory.* London: Garland Publishing Inc. Print.

Seturaman, V.S. ed. (2008), *Contemporary Criticism; An Anthology.* New Delhi: MacMillan. Print.

Showalter, Elaine. "Feminist Criticism in the Wilderness". *Modern Criticism and Theory.* Ed. David Lodge and Nigel Wood. (2010), New Delhi: Dorling Kindersley, 326-348. Print.

Tolan, Fiona. "Feminisms". (2009), *Literary Theory and Criticism.* ed. Patricia Waugh. New Delhi: O.U.P., 319-338. Print.

Waugh, Patricia. (2009), ed. *Literary Theory and Criticism.* New Delhi: O.U.P. Print.

14

Depiction of Indian Women's Anguish through Kamala Das's Works

Anil Kumar

The concept of society was developed by human beings in the due course of time. Society is an amalgamation of rituals, traditions, norms, and beliefs. All the members of society are expected to follow this unwritten rubric. The ultimate aim of all this devised system was the betterment of mankind in all its forms. It was for the upliftment of life that the phenomenon of society took place. All women and men were in the centre of this development. Society was for human beings not *vice-versa*. Later on, this same society imposed various sanctions on its members. People were reduced to a mechanical routine and limited sphere of thought. In this process of degradation, female members of society became more vulnerable. Society became a repository of discriminatory practices, hollow traditions, and worn-out ideas. Male members of society captured the driver's seat. Women were relegated to mere objects. Several duties and moral obligations were enjoined on them. They were not free to live their lives in their own ways.

Though in the Vedic period, women had more rights. They were free to choose their life partners, participated in religious rites, and received education. But, in later periods, especially after the invasion of Muslims, many restrictions like *parda partha* were imposed upon women. With the passage of time, these restrictions became traditions. In the nineteenth century, some reformers like Raja Ram Mohan Roy and others tried to improve the life and status of women. In the coming years, women participated in the freedom struggle and also voiced their problems, though it was unfortunate for them that their exclusive movement for rights subsumed in the movement for independence. At the time of independence, women were empowered with many rights in the Constitution of free India. Women and men were made equal in the eyes of law. Women started to fly high, carving out their place. Numerous government schemes for the welfare of women were started. Numerical data improved with the spread of education. There are women who are on the highest positions of this country. But most of Indian women's condition is not much improved even after sixty-six years of independence. They are subjected to rapes, acid attacks, domestic violence, dowry deaths, and child marriages, etc. Women are not allowed to go alone anywhere. Young girls are directed about dress codes, behaviour codes, and life styles. In our so called modern India, there are *Khap Panchayats* which *diktat* women about moral responsibility towards society. Girls are killed even before their births. Even the custodians of justice enjoy the flesh dance by women in the Patiala House Court Premises in New Delhi. All our cultural practices are replete with the discrimination against women. In a real sense, women are fighting to gain their lost ground in this man-dominated society.

This gloomy and unequal picture of society has been represented by many writers in various ways. Whether it is Prem Chand, Mahashweta Devi, Jayant Mahapatra, Mahesh Dattani, and Shashi Deshpande; all have depicted the imbalances of our society. Casteism, economic imbalance, maltreatment of LGBT community, women's subjugation, etc. are the issues from which society is suffering. But the most critical problem is the inhumane treatment and loss of identity which half of our population i.e. women is facing. Shashi Deshpande has aptly demonstrated this dilemma through her own condition:

> Yes, I did and I do write about women. Most of my writing comes out of my own intense and long suppressed feelings about what it is to be a woman in our society, it comes out of the experience of the difficulty of playing the different roles enjoined on me by society, it comes out of the knowledge that I am something more and something different from the sum total of these roles. My writing comes out of my consciousness of the conflict between my idea of myself as

> a human being and the idea that society has of me as a woman. All this makes my writing very clearly women's writing. (107)

Among the women poets, Kamala Das, now Kamala Suraiya (as she has changed her religion) is, perhaps, the first woman who freely talks about the bruises she received on her psyche in this male-dominated society. Born in a society where women are treated as mere commodities; where they are not allowed to sit in the presence of male-members of their family; where they are not allowed to mention sex, even among themselves, here is Kamala Das, giving uninhibited expression to the full range of female experiences and talking in a confessional voice of love, lust, sex, extra-marital relationships, illness, death, and decay.

Kamala Das herself is the means and inspiration for her poetry. In *My Story*, she writes that "a poet's raw material is not stone or clay; it is her personality. I could not escape from my predicament even for a moment" (157). And it is, therefore, that she unburdens her tormented soul through writing. In "Composition", she craves:

> I must let my mind striptease
> I must extrude
> autobiography. (*The Old Playhouse and Other Poems* 5)

Kamala Das is bold enough to the definitions given to women by men and rushes "into an area of confession where angels might well fear to tread" (Kaur, Preface viii). She seems to surpass even herself, carrying her frankness to almost frightening limits as in "*The Looking Glass*":

> Gift him all,
> Gift him what makes you woman, the scent of
> Long hair, the musk of sweat between the breasts,
> The warm shock of menstrual blood, and all your
> Endless female hungers. (*The Descendants* 25)

Therefore, unlike the conventional Indian woman, she comes in the line of Mamata Kalia and Gauri Deshpande to express herself freely. She has to face the anger of the society and her parents when she serialized her autobiography. She admits it in the Preface of *My Story*:

> My relatives were embarrassed. I had disgraced my well-known family by telling my readers that I had fallen in love with a man other than my lawfully husband. Why, I had even confessed that I was chronically falling in love with persons of flamboyant nature. (i)

Like Sylvia Plath, Judith Wright, and Anne Sexton, Kamala Das too, scrubs out her tormented soul by revealing her innermost experiences of life. She writes in the Preface:

> ... I wrote continually, not merely to honour my commitment but because I wanted to empty myself of all the secrets so that I could depart when the time came, with a scrubbed-out conscience. (*My Story* i)

Kamala Das is the representative of all women. There is a rare occasion when woman feels happy. She is everywhere in chains and is making efforts to free herself from the clutches of this male-dominated society. Her poetry depicts the predicament of an ordinary Indian woman who is always subjugated by male—first as a father, then as a husband, and finally as a son.

Like other average Indian women, Kamala Das has been a dissatisfied woman throughout her life, and this dissatisfaction comes forth in a mode of confession through her literary works, as she writes in *My Story*, "I myself had no control over my writing which emerged like a rash of prickly heat in certain season" (178). This confession is a kind of getting 'self-knowledge' as she says in "Composition":

> I also know that by confessing
> by peeling off my layers
> I reach closer to the soul
> and
> to the bone's
> supreme indifference. (*Old Playhouse* 7)

Like all other girls, Kamala Das had also expected from her husband a caring and loving nature as she confesses in *My Story*:

> I had expected him to take me in his arms and stroke my face, my hair, my hands and whisper loving words. I had

> expected him to be all that I wanted my father to be, and my mother. I wanted conversation, companionship and warmth. Sex was far from my thoughts. I had hoped that he would remove with one sweep of his benign arms, the loneliness of my life.... (84)

But the only lesson that she receives from her husband is about sex and lust. This goes a long way in turning her vision tragic and her verse melancholy. Her literary output dramatizes an 'aching disappointment' which is the result of her realization of the futility of her idealized notions about love and sex. It is through her poetry that she celebrates the most secret emotions of her life. In "*Loud Posters*" she asserts:

> I have stretched my two dimensional
> Nudity on sheets of weeklies, monthlies.
> Quarterlies, a sad sacrifice. I've put
> My private voice away, adopted the
> Typewriter's click as my only speech; I
> Click-click, click-click tiresomely into your
> Ears, stranger, though you may have no need of
> Me, I go on and on, not knowing why.... (*Old Playhouse* 47)

It was customary for a Nair girl to marry when she was hardly out of her childhood, and it was also customary for the much older husband to give her a rude shock by his sexual haste on the wedding-night. The same happens with Kamala Das as she is married at the fragile age of fifteen to an elderly man. She labels her first sexual experience with her husband on her wedding night as an "unsuccessful rape" (*My Story* 89). Talking about her husband's sexual brutality, she writes in *My Story*:

> Whenever he found me alone in a room, he began to plead with me to bare my breasts and if I did not, he turned brutal and crude. His hands bruised my body and left blue and red marks on the skin. (84)

A similar crude and hasty approach of the male to the female body is described in "My November":

> Like a sickle embedded
> In flesh or a crescent of the moon
> Is this pain beneath my left breast
> Which ruthless lover clasps its opulence
> In this brutal, so brutal way? (qtd. in Pandeya 68)

"This kind of situation", in P.K. Pandeya's words, "would later become tasteless marital sex leading to disillusionment and constant search for a fulfilling love experience" (68).

Throughout her poetic volumes, Kamala Das has contrasted two aspects of love—the real fulfilling love and the pure carnal or commercial love. Kamala Das advocates the first kind of love that means companionship and emotional attachment and that is free from 'mere' sexual gratification; while her male partner wants 'just' sex. This type of love she receives from her grandmother only, who becomes an archetypal ideal for unselfish and unconditional love for Das. Kamala Das's definition of love is very supreme as she defines in her essay *Obscenity and Literature* (1972):

> Love is beautiful whatever four lettered name the puritans call it by. It is the foretaste of paradise. It is the only pastime that involves the soul. (qtd. in S. Kohli 37)

It is a "beautiful anguish and Tapasya" (*My Story* 14). In her interview to Iqbal Kaur, she says:

> Love means caring for another, having plenty of time for another. I want a kind of love that is pervasive—all pervasive like ether—love which creates its own climate, a balming climate. (Das, "I Needed...." 163)

It is a kind of love that involves both body and soul. It is a kind of union between man and woman, where both mingle into each other, rising above their ego. But, in her conjugal life, Das never gets such type of fulfilling love. The man's love is full of dirt and filth, and is not pure and emotional. Therefore, the woman persona cries out in total disillusionment in "The Freaks":

> Can't this man with
> Nimble finger-tips unleash

Nothing more alive than the
Skin's lazy hungers? (*Old Playhouse* 1)

Her heart, that has dreamt of 'fulfilling-love', turns into "an empty cistern":

The heart
An empty cistern, waiting
Through long hours, fills itself
With coiling snakes of silence.... (11)

And it is only to save herself that she behaves like a freak:

I am a freak. It's only
To save my face, I flaunt, at
Times, a grand, flamboyant lust. (*Old Playhouse* 11)

The same thing is confessed in *My Story* when she writes, "I accepted with gratitude his tenderness, which was but lust, loud and savage, for it seemed like a good substitute for love" (112).

One seeks in love the completion of one's own personality but here, the fever of domesticity, routine of lust, artificial comfort, and male domination, completely dwarf Kamala Das's feminine-self. In "The Old Playhouse", where "the central burdern of the poem is the total loss of identity and freedom" (Kumar, 1960), Das voices her anguish and protests against her husband who has turned her into a 'caged-bird':

You planned to tame a swallow, to hold her
In the long summer of your love so that she would forget
Not the raw reasons alone, and the homes left behind, but
Also her nature, the urge to fly, and the endless
Pathways of the sky. (*Old Playhouse* 1)

She laments over the erosion of her personality which is the result of both the domestic-slavery and man's "monstrous ego":

You called me wife,
I was taught to break saccharine into your tea and
To offer at the right moment the vitamins. Cowering

Beneath your monstrous ego I ate the magic loaf and
Became a dwarf. I lost my will and reason.... (1)

In *My Story*, she writes in the same tone: "I kept myself busy with dreary house-work while my spirit protested and cried, get out of this trap, escape..." (98). Therefore, marriage comes to Das just as an 'intrusion' in her creative personality that has turned her into a 'trained circus dog'. With her characteristic ironic mockery, and deliberate self-conscious cynicism, she advises in "Composition":

Husbands and wives
here is my advice to you.
Obey each other's crazy commands,
ignore the sane.
Turn your home into a merry
dog-house,
marriage is meant to be all this. (*Old Playhouse* 8)

A muted sense of rebellion against imposed forbearance is equally evident in "The Stone Age", a poem that is all about "colonization of woman's mind (and body) by patriarchy" (Ahmed, 1959). This colonization of female body and mind is far more damaging and unjust than political imperialism from where there is always a scope for liberation. This is not the "stone age" of the noble savages, but of the deceiving male, always weaving "a web of bewilderment", and waiting with a trap to catch the gentle, dove-like woman, and like a python to strangulate her gradually reducing her to a soulless shape, a mere plaything with no emotion of her own: "You turn me into a bird of stone, a granite/Dove..." (*Old Playhouse* 51). "You stick a finger into my dreaming eye" signifies the harsh denial of individual freedom which accentuates the need for "a room for one's own" as advocated by Virginia Woolf in her article of the same title.

Kamala Das represents the plight of all women, particularly Indian women whose fates are none the less same as that of herself. Hence, she writes in "Someone Else's Song": "I am a million, million people/ Talking all at once, with voices raised in Clamour" (qtd. in Ahmed, 1963). Therefore, the struggle of her "self" ultimately becomes the struggle of the whole humanity, specifically of all women. In an interview given to British Council, Sylvia Plath has also stressed upon the universality of "personal experiences", as she says:

> ... I think that personal experience shouldn't be a kind of shut box and a mirror looking narcissistic experience. I believe it should be generally relevant, to such things as Hiroshima and Dachau, and so on. (qtd. in Martin, 1960)

Similarly, Kamala Das is speaking not only on her own behalf but also on the behalf of millions of Indian women who are too timid to speak out against their exploitation. Therefore, "who so touches her poem, touches a woman" (Raizada 118). Devinder Kohli is right when he writes in *Kamala Das*:

> Kamala Das is essentially a poet of the modern Indian woman's ambivalence, giving expression to it more nakedly than any other Indian woman poet with the possible exception of Amrita Pritam in Punjabi. (191)

In this way, Kamala Das comes forth as an ardent spokesperson for women's Liberation Movement in India. It becomes difficult for Kamala Das to accept man as 'Subject', the 'Absolute' and woman as the 'Object', the 'Other'. She laments over women's fate of remaining just a 'toy' to play in the hands of men. She expresses, in the poem "Toys", the idea that women's bodies are playthings and wombs are weeping blood. She cries out that a woman is always seen through man's eyes and is just a womb, an ovary, a female. She revolts against the definition of woman as a sexual being, a "second sex" that exists for fulfilling man's sexual desires. Commenting upon a woman's situation, Gloria Steinem writes:

> Women of every race are the only discriminated group with no territory, no country of their own, not even a neighbourhood. In a patriarchy a poor man's house may be his castle but even a rich woman's body is not her own. (qtd. in Mohanty 45)

And in Indian society, the situation is more painful, because here woman has to live merely as a subordinate to man, as D'Souza writes:

> In fact, according to the traditional Hindu code, woman is always deemed to be subordinate to man, first to her father,

> then to her husband, and finally to her son. (qtd. in Mohanty 48)

They are merely 'muted whispers' who all bear the same plight of being subjugated. Das writes in "Composition":

> We are all alike,
> we women,
> in our wrapping of hairless skin.
> All skeletons are alike. (*Old Playhouse* 6)

A woman has to pretend to be something else that she is not in real. In "*The Suicide*", Das uses both sarcasm and irony while expressing her restlessness with the shackles of feminity:

> But,
> I must pose,
> I must pretend,
> I must act the role
> Of happy woman,
> Happy wife. (*Descendants* 2)

In her thought provoking book, *The Second Sex* (1949), the great French feminist Simone de Beauvoir says, " Women are not born; they are made" (278). Similarly, Kamala Das opines that it is the society that requires a woman to find her total fulfilment in 'submissive domesticity'. She rejects gender-difference and instead of stooping to conquer, she is out to demolish the concept of male dominance and his egoistic superiority in her poetry:

> When a man is dead, or a woman,
> We call the corpse not he
> Or she but it. (*Descendants* 16)

One thing noteworthy in Das's poetry is that – though there is much lamenting and much weeping on the lost feminine-identity, there is an equal eagerness shown to regain this lost identity. The central crux of Das's poetry is to come out of this 'imposed subjugation' by man. In her interview to Iqbal Kaur, Das reveals the 'startling' purpose of her poetry:

> I needed to disturb society out of its complacence. I found the complacence a very ugly state. I wanted to make women of my generation feel that if men could do something wrong, they could do it themselves too. I wanted them to realize that they are equal. I wanted to remove the gender-difference.... (Das, "I Needed.... 167)

The same tone of rebellion against male-domination and his ego is evident in "The Conflagration", where she initiates woman to awake, arise and realize her 'self':

> Woman, is this happiness, this lying buried
> Beneath a man? It's time again to come alive,
> The world extends a lot beyond his six-foot frame.
> (*Descendants* 20)

This same desire to extricate herself from this 'soul killing' subjugation is evident in "The Prisoner". Here, the male's body is a prison to enslave the female from where she wants to free herself:

> As the convict studies
> His prison's geography
> I study the trappings
> Of your body, dear love,
> For I must some day find
> An escape from its snare. (*Old Playhouse* 29)

"An Introduction" is another poem that is "concerned with the question of human identity" and arises "pertinent questions relating to a woman's... identity..." (Kohli, "Kamala Das" [1980] 188). It is a struggle to come out of the identity crisis, aggravated by the attitude of the world of categorizers. The traditional society tries to clip off woman's wings of freedom:

> Dress in sarees, be girl
> Be wife, they said. Be embroiderer, be cook,
> Be a quarreller with servants. Fit in, Oh,
> Belong, cried the categorizers. Don't sit
> On walls or peep in through our lace-draped windows.
> Be Amy, or be Kamala. Or, better

Still, be Madhavikutty. It is time to
Choose a name, a role. (*Old Playhouse* 27)

But she asserts her identify by ignoring the categorizers' advice and requests them to leave her alone: "Why not leave/ Me alone, critics, friends, visiting cousins./ Everyone of you?" (27). She asserts herself by rejecting the traditional norms decided for woman.

Then...... I wore a shirt and my
Brother's trousers, cut my hair short and ignored
My womanliness. (27)

Though there is much aggression in Kamala Das against male-domination, yet she is against the binary male-female opposition posited by the Western Radical Feminists. Her overall stance is in no way anti-male as we find in Sylvia Plath's "Lady Lazarus":

Out of the ash
I rise with red hair
And I eat men like air. (*Collected Poems* 247)

On the contrary, Kamala Das is a feminist of her own kind who can never hate the male because she has loved them as her husband and her sons. Therefore, she is not propagating freedom in love when she writes in "I shall Some Day":

I shall someday leave, leave the cocoon
You built around me with morning tea,
Love-words flung from doorways and of course,
Your tired lust. I shall some day take
Wings, fly around, as often petals
Do when free in air.... (*Old Playhouse* 48)

Such type of freedom becomes her "dancing shoe" (*Old Playhouse* 4). On the contrary, she wants to be clutched in love as cancer clutches human body. Her freedom concept becomes more complex when in 1999, she changes her religion. She has accepted Muslim religion, a religion that is more rigid and orthodox on the part of woman. While a Hindu woman has choices in love even after her marriage, a Muslim woman can't even think about any other man than her husband. Therefore, Kamala Das wants freedom, not in love, but from domestic imprisonment and male domination, and wants to flourish in her full growth.

In this way, it is clear that Kamala Das indulges in self-awareness, self-exposure and self-introduction in order to redefine her 'self' poetically. Hers is a voice, not for her own self but for all women who have lost their self-identity somewhere in the domestic-slavery that is imposed by this male-dominated society. Sarojini Naidu was right when she suggested:

> I charge you restore to your women their ancient rights, for, as I have said, it is we, and not you, who are the real nation-builders. Educate your women and the nation will take care of itself, for it is as true today as it was yesterday and will be to the end of human life that the hand that rocks the cradle rules the world. (qtd. in Bhalla 12)

References

Ahmed, Irshad Gulam. (2005), *Kamala Das: The Poetic Pilgrimage*. New Delhi: Creative Books.

Beauvior, Simone De. (1989), *The Second Sex*. Trans. and ed. H.M. Parshley. New York: Vintage Books.

Bhalla, Amrita. (2010), *Shashi Deshpande*. New Delhi: Altlantic Publishers.

Deshpande, Shashi. (1996), "Of Concerns, Of Anxieties." *Indian Literature: Women's Writing in English, New Voices* 39.5: 104-108.

Das, Kamala. (1988), *My Story*. New Delhi: Sterling Publishers.

—. (1973), *The Old Playhouse and Other Poems*. Madras: Longman.

—. (1967), *The Descendants*. Calcutta: Writers Workshop.

Iyengar, K.R. Srinivasa. (2007), *Indian Writing in English*. Rev. ed. New Delhi: Sterling Publishers.

Kaur, Iqbal. Preface. Kaur i-xi.

—. (1995), ed. *Perspectives on Kamala Das's Poetry*. New Delhi: Intellectual Publishing House.

Kohli, Devinder (1975). *Kamala Das*. New Delhi: Arnold & Heinemann.

Kohli, Suresh. ed. (1973), *Sex and Violence in Indian Literature and Arts*. New Delhi: Sterling Publishers.

Kumar, Sunil. (1992), "The Poetry of Kamala Das: A Woman's Quest for Identity." *Quest for Identity in Indian English Writing: Part II Poetry*. Ed. R.S. Pathak. New Delhi: Bahri Publications.

Martin, Linda Wagner. (1999), *Sylia Plath: A Literary Life*. London: MacMillan.

Mohanty, Niranjan. "A Feminist Perspective on Kamala Das's Poetry." Kaur 45-49.

Pandeya, P.K. (1998), "The Woman's Voice in Kamala Das's Poetry." *Indian Literature Today*. Vol. II, Ed. R.K. Dhawan. New Delhi: Prestige.

Plath, Sylvia, (1980). *Collected Poems*. Ed. Ted Hughes. London: Faber & Faber.

Raizada, Harish. (1992), "The Confessional Note in the Poetry of Kamala Das." *Indian Poetry in English*, Ed. H.M. Prasad. Aurangabad: Primal Prakashan.

15

From Suppression to Assertion

A Study of Arundhati Roy's *The God of Small Things*

Rekha Kumari and Madhukar Sharma

Women are integral part of human civilization. No society or country can ever progress without an active participation of woman in its overall development, although the place and the role of woman in society have differed from culture to culture and from age to age. It is from equal status with men in ancient times through the low points of the medieval period to the promotion of equal rights by many reformers. Male chauvinism exists in our society since time immemorial. Women no doubt have acquired constitutional rights of equality with men but the change in social attitudes towards women is yet to be achieved. A woman is in actuality always cocooned and cornered in society and the first Indian law giver, Manu presented her subordinate lot as: "In childhood a female must be subjected to her father, in youth to her husband, when her lord is dead to her sons; a woman must never be independent" (Muller, 57). Gender discrimination is the least of worries for women in India, known otherwise as the fourth most dangerous country in the world for women. Other instances of violence against women has an astonishing and grim variety to it—with the frequent occurrence of glaring and brutal gang rapes, acid throwing, domestic violence stemming out of dowry, rape, harassment etc.

In spite of the significant change in women's position in society in the post-Independence era, she is still not totally emancipated. Women empowerment is the process by which women negotiate a more equitable distribution of power, a greater space in the critical decision-making processes in the home, in the community and in the economic and political life. It is against patriarchy. Changes in law pertaining to marriage, property, sexual harassment, dowry, rape and other forms of violence, so as to bring in laws favouring or supporting women's empowerment are necessary but not enough. Enabling women to actually access to the benefits of appropriate laws is the key task of the empowerment process. These contradictions can best be understood by examining the Indian social structure which comprises institutions like caste, joint family and religious values and practices consolidating women's subordinate position.

Literature being reaction is not immune from the contemporary social-cultural political scenario and in fact reverberate it. Writings of minorities and other marginal voices have found a perfect platform at literary scenario—be it feminist writings, queer theories, Dalit writings, tribal writings, prisoner writings and other fourth world literature writings. The development on all the fronts social, economical, political, technical and other developmental endeavors has brought significant changes in the status and role of women. One can see women holding responsible positions in public and private offices. The later part of last century has seen a remarkable shift in attitudes towards women. World over, literature has recorded transition in woman's stature. Now woman is not depicted as sacrificing herself at the altar of patriarchy. One such portrayal is ostensible in the oeuvre of Arundhati Roy, a political activist cum-world renowned post colonial contemporary writer who got Booker Award for her debut novel *The God of Small Things* (1997). The novel is set in Ayemenem, a southern State of Kerala and deals with the themes like global capitalism, neo-imperialism, eco-criticism, issue of untouchability and racial subalternity. It depicts the traumatic experiences of an anglophile family through the eyes of one of the fraternal twins Rahel, the daughter of Ammu. The plot of the novel orbits two events: unfortunate and untimely death of Sophie Mol and a forbidden relationship between an untouchable Velutha and a Syrian Christian divorcee woman Ammu. Through this novel, Roy depicts the woman interrogating and transgressing the hegemonic love laws. She deals with the three generations of women from Mammachi to her sister-in-law, Baby Kochamma to her daughter Ammu and then to Rahel.

Elaine Showalter in her seminal book, has propounded three phases of evolution of female tradition: the feminine phase (1840-1880), the feminist phase (1880-1920) and the female phase (1920 onwards) which postulate women as imitator and assimilator, as rebel and as seeker of self and identity respectively. Roy's female characters reflect these phases either imitating patriarchy or rebelling against it or sometimes a blend of both. They are depicted under clutches of patriarchy but simultaneously they keep blowing on its face overtly or covertly. The first generation character under study is Mammachi who is subaltern to the extent that she has assimilated the norms of patriarchy. In her earlier years she faces the extreme physical violence at the hands of her husband Pappachi who beats her every night with a brass flower vase leaving scars on her skull, "the beatings weren't new. What was new was only the frequency with which they took place." (Roy, 47-48). Her son Chacko takes over the charge of pickle factory run by his mother after the death of his father and dominates his mother. He even asks her, "Mamma! That's Enough! Enough violin!" and she stops in quite submissive way by saying, "I think I'll stop now. (Roy, 183) In this way, Chacko follows Manu and his tradition in asserting the son's domination over mother in old age. Her sister Ammu gets exiled and dies exiled while her so called Marxist brother exploits women labourers sexually and get supported by his mother Mammachi as Man's needs. It exposes her double standard as the carnal desire of her son are needs while the same desires of her daughter defile the generations!. In spite of being a passive sufferer and assimilator of male chaunism she undercuts the caste conventions and employs the untouchable Velutha as carpenter inviting the wrath of touchable workers.

Ammu, a middle class Syrian Christian divorcee reflects the spirit of a rebel depicts the transformation from suppression to assertion. Her rebelliousness is the outcome of her extreme exploitation since childhood to youth. The whole novel is replete with her tragic saga. In her childhood she was deprived from the education as her father Pappachi, "insisted that a college education was an unnecessary expense for a girl" (Roy, 38). The domestic violence was unbearable for her so she wanted to escape from the, " clutches of her ill-tempered father and bitter, long suffering mother (Roy, 39). Unfortunately her marriage also proves to be a disaster for her as her husband is an extreme alcoholic and he compels Ammu to satisfy the lust of his English boss, Hollick. It shows his height of cruelty and Eurocentric ideology of exploitation. When Ammu denies he even beats her. Unlike Mammachi who bears her fatal marriage, Ammu breaks her wedlock and takes divorce and thus weakens the roots of male domination by choosing single parenting. After divorce, her bridal photographs seem to her as if she was, "painstakingly decorated before being led to the gallows. It seemed so absurd. So futile. Like polishing firewood." (Roy, 44) She not only transgresses the boundaries of her gender but also shakes the boundaries of caste and class by her sexual relations with Velutha an untouchable worker. When she goes to police station in favour of her low caste lover Velutha who was accused for Sophie's drowning she not only gets disappointment but also bears visual rape and vulgar comments and harassment from the police officer Thomas Matthew. Roy depicts the scene of policeman as—

> "He started at the Ammu's breast as he spoke... then he tapped her breast with her baton. Gently tap. As though he was choosing mangoes from a basket. Pointing out the ones that he wanted packed and delivered. Inspector Thomas Mathew seemed to know whom he could pick on and whom he couldn't. Policeman has that instinct" (Roy, 8).

By depicting this incident where the police, the so called savior of society having 'that instinct', Roy has exposed the vulgur patriarchal structure. Ammu left no moment to vent up her resentment against patriarchy. She also questions Chacko's presumed cleverness and satirizes her mother's blind preferences for her son, "...all Indian mothers are obsessed with their sons and are therefore poor judges of their abilities" (Roy, 56). She rejects another patriarchal discourse of surname and chooses reverting to her maiden name as, "choosing between her husband's name and her father's name didn't give a woman much of a choice" (Roy, 37). Murari Prasad also depicts, "Ammu's rebellion against maternal and marital conventionality and finally her liaison with dark skinned and untouchable Velutha (ironically meaning white) constitutes a violation against a determine social order, sponsoring the immutable 'love laws'" (Prasad, 16).

Another woman under study is baby Kochamma, Mammachi's unmarried sister-in-law who is an amalgam of passivity and rebelliousness which distorts her life, leaving her in self chosen claustrophobic room to spend hours on watching television. Every now and then she can be seen speaking English or mimicking the

English which further reveals her colonized state of mind. Like Mammachi she too assimilates the conventions of patriarchal society. She whole heartedly believes in the commonly held view that a married daughter had no position in her parents' home. Thus, the novelist exposes the prevalent inheritance laws in the Syrian Christian community through the mentality of baby Kochamma. But if probed deeply, it can be noticed that she also violates love laws by falling in love with a catholic father Mulligan. In order to win his love she converts to Roman Catholic against her father's consent. In love for unattainable father Mulligan an Irish monk she stays unmarried all her life. Although she never outcrosses the boundaries of class, caste and gender but her conversion of religion and resolution for celibacy place her in the category of rebel.

Rahel, the daughter of a divorcee mother Ammu, deprived of father's love is the biggest rebel in the novel. She bears the hatred of her maternal family and shows the signs of resistance since her childhood. She was blacklisted in her convent school for decorating the fresh cow dung with tiny flowers outside her housemistress's garden gate. In spite being a polite girl she was expelled from school three times: for colliding with her senior girls, for smoking and third time for stealing and burning the hair bun of her housemistress. This is the outcome of her suppressed desires and neglect. She also takes divorce from her husband and comes to regain her identity in her twin brother Estha. She not only rebles against patriarchy but also transgresses its moral standard by committing incest with her brother and thus reveals the extremity of rebellion, which although being an act of self-assertion on her part, can't be justified in a balanced society.

Thus this gyno-centric text draws attention to women and pleads for social order based on reason, granting equal treatment to both the genders as rational beings and not merely one inferior to other. The writers criticize the moral code of conduct of the societies, its false values and also authors like Rousseau, who in his book 'the social contract' (1762) has mentioned a place for women but has to spend her life under the kind control of man. Similarly, Plato's 'the Republic' where he has though recommended equal treatment to men and women yet he recommends philosopher kings. As post colonialism exposes not only the hegemonic ideologies and center-periphery oppressive relationship but also the decent ring or the reversal of power-positions, similar is the reversal of postcolonial women who turn from subaltern to rebel and further the seeker of self and identity. Through this novel

Roy has pinpointed the attempts of women to derive sense out of the senseless and absurd world by portraying them: calming rights, denying peripheral positions, asserting existence and emancipating demands by challenging andocentric notions and is able to portray the odyssey of women from suppression to assertion. It is the best way for creating a sense for the emancipation of women and one of the most important forms of 'socialization' since it provided role models that sought to awaken a sense of individual responsibility among women to create their own trajectory.

References

Muller, Max. Trans. and Ed. (1887), 'Laws of Manu' *Sacred Books of East*. Oxford: Clarendon Press. Print.

Prasad, Murari. Ed. (2006), *Arundhati Roy: Critical Perspectives*. New Delhi: Pencraft International. Print.

Roy, Arundhati (1997). *The God of Small Things*. New Delhi: Penguin. Print.

Showalter, Elaine (1977). *A Literature of Their Own: British Women Novelists from Bronte to Lessing*. Princeton UP. Print.

PART VII
Gender and Sexuality: Unexplored Dimensions

16

Recognition of 'Transgender' as 'Third Gender'

Some Reflections

Sanjiv Kumar

According to the American Psychological Association (APA), Gender refers to the attitudes, feelings, and behaviours that a given culture associates with a person's biological sex. Behaviour that is compatible with cultural expectations is referred to as gender-normative; behaviours that are viewed as incompatible with these expectations constitute gender non-conformity (APA). Therefore, any initiative or development that questions the existing gender identities is considered as misplaced and incompatible. The set of beliefs, perceptions and presumptions about the gender-specific roles get defined with the entirety of the gender construct which is deeply rooted and manifested in the psyche and behaviour of the people. It is widely accepted that Gender identity refers to an individual's self-identification as a man, woman, transgender or other identified category. In this context, Judith Butler, a widely known American continental philosopher and gender theorist, has rightly elaborated the concept of gender as a subtle and strategic project which only rarely becomes manifest to a reflective understanding. For her,

> Becoming a gender is an impulsive yet mindful process of interpreting a cultural reality laden with sanctions, taboos and prescriptions. The choice to assume a certain kind of body, to live or wear one's body a certain way, implies a

> world of already established corporeal styles. To choose a gender is to interpret received gender norms in a way that organises them anew (Butler, 40).

Next to the Gender is the question of sexual orientation which refers to the sex of those to whom one is sexually and romantically attracted. This orientation may classify the people in various categories including homosexuals (gay or lesbian) who are oriented towards the members of their own sex; heterosexuals who are attracted to the members of the other sex; and bisexuals who get attracted to members of both sexes. Different categories based on sexual orientation are provided an appropriate theoretical framework by Gay Studies and Queer Theory. In the postmodern world, the categories determined by the sexual orientation are not fixed as there are the chances that a heterosexual woman turns into a homosexual and *vice-versa* in due course of time. This sexual fluidity is defined by Lisa M. Diamond as the "situation-dependent flexibility in women's sexual responsiveness. This flexibility makes it possible for some women to experience desires for either men or women under certain circumstances, regardless of their overall sexual orientation (Diamond, 3). Gay Studies and Queer Theory address the political ramifications, social predicaments, advantages and dangers of culturally fixed categories of sexual identities and the ways in which they may be performed, transgressed and queered while 'Queer Theory' has been claimed as giving voice to those elided or marginalised by 'gay' and 'lesbian' studies—bisexuals, trans-sexuals, sadomasochists (Goldman, 525-26). The term Queer includes those who openly wear sexual identities like lesbian, gay, bisexual and trans-gender (LGBT) and those who use indigenous terms like *hijra*, *kothi*, *panthis* to describe themselves. (Kumar, 8)

The comprehensive document of historic Supreme Court judgement pronounced on April 15, 2014 explicitly defines 'trans-gender' as an umbrella term for persons whose gender identity, gender expression or behaviour does not conform to their biological sex. It also includes the persons who do not identify with their sex assigned at birth, which include *hijras*/Eunuchs who, in this writ petition, describe themselves as "third gender" and they do not identify as either male or female. The *hijras* are not men by virtue of anatomy, appearance and psychologically, they are also not women, though they are like women with no female reproduction organ and no menstruation. Since *hijras* do not have reproduction capacities as either men or women, they are neither men nor women and claim to be an institutional "third gender". Among *hijras*, there are emasculated (castrated, *nirvana*) men, non-emasculated men (not castrated/*akva/akka*) and inter-sexed persons (hermaphrodites). TG also includes persons who intend to undergo Sex Re-Assignment Surgery (SRS) or have undergone SRS to align their biological sex with their gender identity in order to become male or female. They are generally called trans-sexual persons. Further, there are persons who like to cross-dress in clothing of opposite gender, i.e. transvestites. Resultantly, the term "trans-gender", in contemporary usage, has become an umbrella term that is used to describe a wide range of identities and experiences, including but not limited to pre-operative, post-operative and non-operative trans-sexual people, who strongly identify with the gender opposite to their biological sex; male and female. (SC)

Going back to the historical paradigms of the issue, the transgenders were accorded the position of immense respect in the Hindu Mythology, Vedic and Puranic literatures and they also played prominent roles in the royal courts of the Islamic world. Tracing the history of eunuchs, Ina Goel remarks:

> History is replete with stories of their non-threatening bodies because of which they were entrusted with guarding the royal harems during the rule of the Mughal dynasty. The king of course ensured that the *hijras* were castrated and therefore unable to impregnate the women in the harem. (Goel, 78)

Similar views are held by Serena Nanda in her ethnography, *Neither Man nor Woman: The Hijras of India* where she emphasizes *hijras* as a 'third sex'. She argues that the *hijras* are an *institutionalized third gender* that has its roots in ancient India, and that has been strengthened by the historical role of the eunuchs in the Mughal Courts. She further asserts that "I believe... ancient Jain and Hindu texts supports the view that the *hijras* are a separate sex/gender, which is, however, marginal rather than equal to male and female" (Nanda, 144). The Supreme Court judgement records the ancient past of the trans-genders as portrayed in *Ramayana*, *Mahabharata*, Jain texts, Vedic and Purana literatures and royal courts of Mughal period.

Paradoxically, the most inhuman and heartrending part of the story was that the Criminal Tribes Act 1871 notified the *hijras* as one of the criminal tribes though numerous dedicated initiatives were introduced to restore the lost respect of the transgenders in the post-independence period. *Wolfenden Committee Report on Homosexuality and Prostitution* in September 1957 was pioneering as it set out to rectify the English criminal law by implementing rationalising views of John Stuart Mill who argued passionately for a private space, free from state interference, even if it involves activities that members of a society don't like, as long as they don't harm anyone—popularly known as the Harm test (Gupta, 4817-18). Similarly, Delhi High Court's ruling in 2009 that overturned Section 377 and decriminalized homosexuality came as a great sigh of relief for the trans-genders. In the recent past i.e. in the year 2009, Election Commission of India took a first step towards bringing the trans-genders in the mainstream when trans-genders were allowed to choose their gender as "other" on ballot forms. Most importantly, in 2006, in response to well-documented patterns of abuse, a group of international human rights experts met in Yogyakarta, Indonesia to outline a set of international principles relating to sexual orientation and gender identity and *the Landmark Supreme Court judgement* studies and considers *the* Yogyakarta principles which largely address a broad range of human rights standards and their application to the issues concerning sexual orientation and gender identity. These twenty-nine principles are based on the sublime democratic vision where—

> All human beings are born free and equal in dignity and rights. All human rights are universal, interdependent, indivisible and interrelated. Sexual orientation and gender identity are integral to every person's dignity and humanity and must not be the basis for discrimination or abuse. (Yogyakarta Principles)

With the pronouncement of the judgement upholding the rights of the transgenders and eunuchs by the Supreme Court of India the debate over the issues concerning gender has intensified in India. The verdict has come as a blow to the established notions defining the binaries of gender. The landmark judgement has been hailed as a human rights document as it addresses the concerns of the transgenders and eunuchs in India who have been struggling for recognition and identity in a democratic country guided by the sublime vision of justice for all. Highlighting the relevance of the judgement as a judicial initiative towards protecting the human rights of the minorities, K.S. Radhakrishnan and A.K. Sikri, the judges observed:

> We are of the firm opinion that by recognizing such Transgenders as third gender, they would be able to enjoy their human rights, towhich they are largely deprived of for want of this recognition… Recognition of trans-genders as a third gender is not a social or medical issue but a human rights issue. (SC)

Further, the judgement records the robust commitment of the judges for the cause of sustaining the constitutional values enshrined in the Constitution of India and, therefore, it is emphatically remarked:

> "… there seems to be no reason why a transgender must be denied of basic human rights which includes Right to life and liberty with dignity, Right to Privacy and freedom of expression, Right to Education and Empowerment, Right against violence, Right against Exploitation and Right against Discrimination…. Now it's time for us to recognize this and to extend and interpret the Constitution in such a manner to ensure a dignified life of trans-gender people. All this can be achieved if the beginning is made with the recognition that TG as third gender. (SC)

The judges were quite conscious of the fact that the trans-genders cannot realise the human rights unless they are assigned their proper 'sex' and the existing gender construct doesn't leave any space for the recognition of the trans-genders as it is limited to either male or female. Considering the trans-genders as either male or female is improper as well as indignified because it deprives them of their right to be recognised with their appropriate sex categorization.

One hundred thirteen page judgement records the predicament of Laxmi Narayan Tripathy, a *hijra* applicant who was born as a male and growing up as a child, she felt different from the boys of her age and was feminine in her ways. On account of her femininity from an early age, she faced repeated sexual harassment, molestation and sexual abuse, both within and outside the family. She was constantly abused by everyone as a *'chakka'* and *'hijra'* leading her to join the *Hijra* community. The ambivalent gender-identity of Tripathy didn't permit her to be the part of mainstream life; rather, she was perpetually subjected to serious discrimination throughout her life. Tripathy was aware that the non-recognition of the identity of *hijras*/trans-gender persons by the State has resulted in the violation of most of the fundamental rights guaranteed to them under the Constitution of India. Therefore, on the pronouncement of judgement, Tripathy observed "Today, for the first time I feel very proud to be an Indian ... today, my sisters and I feel like real Indians... because of the rights granted to us by the Supreme Court." (Tripathy)

However, the Supreme Court judgement is just like a Pandora's Box as it has raised many perplexing questions concerning the validity and relevance of the previous Supreme Court judgement upholding the colonial provisions of section 377 of IPC. In its judgement on 11th December, 2013, the Court pronounced that "Section 377 IPC does not suffer from the vice of unconstitutionality..." (SC 2013). The Indian Penal Code, 1860 provides that "... whoever voluntarily has carnal intercourse against the order of nature with any man, woman or animal, shall be punished with [imprisonment for life].... Penetration is sufficient to constitute the carnal intercourse necessary to the offence described in this section" (IPC, 1860). Paradoxically, both of the judgements cite the constitutionality of the provisions of the verdict, though contradictory in nature. We are currently faced with a situation where the 'third gender' has been given recognition, but homosexuality continues to be criminalised. If one can determine his or her gender, why can't the same person also determine his or her sexual orientation? Besides, trans-gender people can also be homosexuals. (Ghosh)

Here, the two categories seem to have been confused as one and the same i.e. one that of trans-genders and eunuchs performing consensual sex and another that of those who are sexually oriented towards homosexual relations. Similarly, the criminalisation of unnatural sex prevents the consensual sexual relationship among the eunuchs and it is perceived as the failure of the courts to distinguish between two very different situations—of non-consensual sex and consensual sexual relations which implies that male adult seducers or abusers of young boys, men who forcibly rape other men, and male homosexuals (who indulge in consensual sexual activities) are all considered as one. It has made homosexual sexual relationship synonymous to rape and equated homosexuality with sexual perversity and, therefore, Section 377 is considered as the biggest affront to the dignity and humanity of a substantial minority of Indian citizens. Reflecting on human tendency for homosexual behaviour as a natural phenomenon since the evolution of human civilization, R.C. Kirkpatrick observes that "Homosexuality is an emergent quality of individual selection for same-sex affiliation and has been a part of the human experience, perhaps all primate experience, since its inception" (Kirkpatrick, 398).

No doubt, the affiliation and recognition of the transgenders in India has sent a positive signal across the world regarding India's commitment to protect and sustain the democratic human values. It has significantly added to the enthusiasm and excitement of the human rights activists who dream of a utopian situation where the fundamental rights of the marginal sections are savoured and valued.

The two landmark judgements on gender and sex issues have engaged the academia in the pursuit of finding a viable solution to the emerging contradiction. The recognition of trans-genders as 'third gender' is hard to be digested by those who have deeply internalised the notion of absolutely binary gender propositions. For them, the idea of 'third gender' is a remotely imagined concept and any democratic move to accept the trans-genders in the mainstream is considered by them as a serious threat to the entire sociological structure. So, sociology in India lacks 'sexuality' as a separate sub-field and even the engendered sociology recognizes only men and women as legitimate subjects. The presence of gender identities beyond heterosexual binary is rendered invisible (Kumar, 4).

Obviously, the Hon'ble Supreme Court has given sufficient reasons for celebrations to the minority community of trans-genders who are now in a position to determine their identity beyond the existing gender binaries. The impact of the verdict might be assessed with the fact that the international media published this news with the most spirited and high-sounding idioms. The international news agencies, UNDP and human rights agencies hailed the initiative as a historic milestone towards realising the vision of inclusive democracy. The Lesbian, Gays, Bi-sexual and Trans-gender (LGBT) groups are in celebration mode and expect to have a sustainable and viable solution to the questions concerning the free choice of sexual orientation also. Long live our faith in robust Indian democracy!

References

Butler, Judith. "Sex and Gender in Simone de Beauvoir's Second Sex." *Yale French Studies*, No. 72, Simone de Beauvoir: Witness to a Century. (1986), pp. 35-49.

Diamond, Lisa M. (2008), *Sexual Fluidity: Understanding Women's Love and Desire*. London: Harvard University Press, Print.

Goel, Ina, (2014). "Beyond the Gender Binary." *Economic and Political Weekly*. April 12, Vol. XLIX, No. 15. pp. 77-78.

Goldman, Jane. (1999), "Introduction: Works on the Wild (e) Side-Performing, Transgressing, Queering." Ed. Julian Wolfrey. *Literary Theory: A Reader and Guide*. Edinburgh: Edinburgh University Press, pp. 525-536.

Gupta, Alok. (2006), "Section 377 and the Dignity of Indian Homosexuals." *Economic and Political Weekly*. November 18. pp. 4815-23.

Ghosh, Rudroneel. (2014), "Right to live as third gender or homosexual should be recognised as a natural right." *The Times of India*. September 12.

Kirkpatrick, R.C. (2000), "The Evolution of Human Homosexual Behaviour." *Current Anthropology*. Vol. 41, No. 3 (June 2000), pp. 385-413. http://www.jstor.org/stable/10.1086/300145.

Kumar, Pushpesh. (2014), "Queering Indian Sociology: A Critical Engagement." *CAS Working Paper Series*. Centre for the Study of Social Systems, Jawaharlal Nehru University, New Delhi, May 2014, CAS/WP/14-7. pp. 1-29.

Nanda, Serena, (1999), *Neither Man nor Woman: The Hijras of India*. London: Wadsworth Publishing House, Print.

http://www.apa.org/pi/lgbt/resources/sexuality-definitions.pdf.

The Indian Penal Code, 1860, Act No. 45 of 1860, 6th October, 1860. http://districtcourtallahabad.up.nic.in/articles/IPC.pdf.

The Supreme Court of India, Civil Appellate Jurisdiction, Civil Appeal No. 10972 of 2013. 11th Dec. 2013.

The Supreme Court of India, Civil Original Jurisdiction, Writ Petition (Civil) No.400 of 2012 with Writ Petition (Civil) No. 604 of 2013, 15th April 2014. http://supremecourtofindia.nic.in/outtoday/wc40012.pdf.

Tripathy, Laxmi Narayan. (2014), India now recognizes trans-gender citizens as 'third gender'. *The Washington Post*. April 15.

Yogyakara Principles: The Application of International Human Rights in Relation to Sexual Orientation and Gender Identity. http://www.yogyakartaprinciples.org/principles_en.htm.

17

Does Pornography Challenge the Social Status of Women in India?

Satish Kumar

Introduction

The Supreme Court issued notices to various ministries of the Central Government on a PIL seeking modification of internet laws to make watching pornography a non-bailable offence. A bench of Chief Justice Altamash Kabir and Justices A.R. Dave and Vikramjit Sen issued notice on Kamlesh Vaswani's petition saying existing laws had failed to prohibit proliferation of internet pornography and alleged that it was affecting the younger generation and resulting in increasing sexual assaults on women. This has led to a situation where more than 20 crore porn videos/porn clippings are available in the Indian market, which have been downloaded from the internet.

India already has the third largest internet user base, just behind China and the USA. Pornography is widely available, with a recent Google survey declaring that Indians are ranked number six in the world for online porn views. Homosexuality was decriminalized in 2009 for the first time in a hundred years. Statistics say that three in five Indian men approve of pornography and the proportion of those actually watching porn is higher, with nearly three in four declaring that they watch porn. Indian women too are watching porn, and over 55 per cent of all women say their sex partners approve of pornography.[1]

Though the publishing, possession, making, selling or distribution of pornography (including transmitting of obscene material in electronic form) has been banned in India since 1969, with a penalty of imprisonment up to three years, today's technology allows anyone with an internet connection access to porn. The pioneers of porn were southern film-makers from Tamil Nadu and Kerala in the late 1970s and early 1980s.[2] The liberal censors in these states and the availability of infrastructure to support cheap film production led to the birth of the Indian porn industry. India has its first playboy bunny Chopra, who rose to national fame after its appearance on the cover of Playboy magazine and Sunny Leon,[3] a porn star of India origin. She is of India origin making debut in Hindi film and has become the household name in schools and colleges.[4]

The banning of pornography is not an easy going exercise. The Central Government has intimated to the Supreme Court that carpet ban of pornography is not feasible. The general understanding of people raised the question: is it possible to ban the porn sites in India. China has done it in 2013-14.[5] It was possible not because of technical glitch but because of political control of the Communist Party of China. Is it possible for India to do the same? There are two ways of blocking porn. One is by actually removing the content from the internet. The other method, which the government has largely relied on in the past, is getting internet service providers to block access to a particular' website's URL—its address on web URL. Savitabhabi.com was banned in 2009; the site simply changed URL and continued to operate. However, technically, it is nearly impossible to have a blanket ban. A Virtual Private Network (VPN) used for remote working and data protection also allows access to content that has been blocked by the ISP and won't leave a trail.[6]

Beginning of Pornography

The word pornography is derived from the Greek terms for 'prostitute' and 'to write'. Literally translated, it means 'depictions of acts of prostitutes'. The pornography was first introduced in the sixteenth century in Italy. Most early works in pornography were used as a political weapon, for instance, to attack the French aristocracy. Though it is very easy to blame pornography, especially the ones which upset our sensibilities for the increasing number of sexual offenders, statistics often tell a different story. In 1969, the Danish Government took an unprecedented step of decriminalising pornography, and surprisingly, statistics show that in the years following the decriminalisation sexual offences fell in number in Denmark.[7]

The depiction of explicit acts is as old as the civilization itself. However, the modern concept of pornography can be traced back to the Victorian era. Interestingly, the Victorian era was known for repression of human sentiments. In addition, the Victorians were the first to compose laws that restricted the viewing of sexually offensive images and objects. The first law that criminalized pornography was incorporated by the United Kingdom Parliament in 1857 under the Obscene Publications Act. The legal status of the modern porn industry varies from country to country. Most countries permit some degree of adult entertainment. The porn industry is a major component of the world economy, generating large scale revenue and employment. According to top ten reviews.com, over $3,000 is spent every second across the world on pornography. However, it is difficult to estimate the accurate statistics for the entire industry as a large part of the industry operates underground.[8]

Pornography may use a variety of media including books, magazine, photos, animations, videos out of which the most prevalent media is internet. The introduction of home videos and internet saw a boom in a worldwide porn industry that generates billion dollars annually. Talking about India, here watching and possessing a pornographic material is legal but distributing it is illegal and banned. Law for pornography or obscenity is laid down in Section 292 of IPC by Act 36 of 1969. As this industry thrives by getting more extreme each day, sociologist has correspondingly begun to note that violence has risen, age of both victim and violator has fallen and the worst part, violence is much more brutal today.

Dichotomy of Values, Religion and Sexual Behaviour in India

The temple of Kamakhya Devi is just one example of India's rich sexual past. From the time of the *Rig Veda* (1500-1000 BC) to the age of the *Kamasutra* (300 CE) and to the court of the Rajput and Mughal Kings many centuries later, from the elite down to the present in ancient Indian culture, sex was not taboo. It was discussed openly in books, religious and fictional and depicted in paintings, hymns and folktales, which celebrated women with breasts like mangoes. Many Hindu Gods and goddesses were depicted as romantic couples, and ancient Indian Temples, such as Khajuraho in Madhya Pradesh and Ajanta and Ellora in Maharashtra are full of images often erotic and sexually explicit of sacred gods, goddesses and *apsaras*. Form the earliest times, Hinduism has been characterized by two simultaneous forces: erotic and ascetic. The early religious texts the *Upanishads* were the first text to introduce the dichotomy the path of the householder where the goal is the worldly pursuit of family, work and so on and the other path that of the enunciate where the focus is on spiritually and attaining liberation from the cycle of life, death and reincarnation. This tension, between sex and celibacy, between the sensual and the spiritual, appears throughout the vast realm of Hinduism and manifests itself in a multitude of forms.

The *Shiva Lingam*, perhaps the mostly widely worshipped and venerated Hindu symbol illustrates this tension. The *lingam* or the sexual organ of Shiva first appears in the *Mahabharata* (300 BC to 300 CE). The same phallus is seen as both as a potentially procreative phallus and a pillar-like renounce of sexuality. In Hinduism, Shiva is seen as the perfect husband to his wife Parvati, the adulterer who chases the divine Mohini as well as the ultimate renunciation. He is worshipped, celebrated and accepted in all these forms.

Krishna is the ultimate lover and the greatest of erotic literature in ancient India deals with his stories. His *ras-lila* with *gopis* the cowherdeness of Vrindavan described to be sexual congress is mentioned in the *Harivamsha*, which was composed before the fourth century CE. The Sanskrit classic, *Gitagovinda* written by Jayadeva in the twelfth century CE was the most important landmark in the development of Krishna's role as lover. As Pavan Verma writes in the book of Krishna, the cumulative result was that the love lore of Kriahna and Radha moved out from the sanctum sanctorum of the temple to the dust and din of daily life. Their erotic love play made a transition from the refined if passionate milieu of Sanskrit poetics to the earthy and seductive medium of the lingua franca of the masses.

Ancient India was a highly sexualized society, and the erotica depicted in art was an integrated part of our past. Sex continued to be a major part of the philosophical and religious life of the country well into the middle Ages, from around the tenth century to the sixteenth—a period of renaissance in erotic art and literature. During this time, the Sun Temple of Konark, the temples of Khajuraho in Madhya Pradesh and many other structures celebrating sex as a joyful union with the divine, were built across the country. One of the worst outcomes has been the repression and moral policing of Indian society to an outrageous degree, which has resulted in all sorts of imbalance.[9]

Does Pornography Affect the Status of Women?

Does pornography demean the social status of women in India? The feminist debate is also divided into different clusters. Some of them vouch for sexual liberations of women through pornography. Some of them castigate of leading sexually violent social order which germinates social exploitation of women in India. Government reports or other literatures may not connect between the rape cases and unregulated web pornography open for all. Some of the points are pondered which depict the low status of women because of pornography.

One of the factors is that women are depicted in almost all the porn as a sex object, a nymph who is always dying of sex. Women are presented dehumanized as sexual objects, things or commodities; women are presented as sexual objects who enjoy pain or humiliation; women are presented as sexual objects who experience sexual pleasure in being raped; or women are presented as sexual objects tied up or cut up or mutilated or bruised or physically hurt. It might be statistically impossible to directly link the viewing of pornography to such violence but it is undeniable that its mainstreaming is actively encouraging and endorsing a culture of abuse of women and children. The problem with pornography is not much about erotica, it is about extreme violence, degradation and subjugation of women. This objectification in the pornography shape the young male psyche as if female is born to perform only sexual acts and satisfy the male desires. This downplays the social status of women where ever there is competition between the two.

Second, the pornography is market driven. It moves along with the interests of male driven fantasies. Most of the pictures or acting of the scenes are directed to fulfil the lustrous desires of male. The Black market of pornography or obscenity has become a multi-billion dollar industry even outside India. A strong attack has also been levelled by feminists who view pornography as a male weapon used for the establishment and maintenance of a paternalistic society. Feminist arguments against pornography focus on its role in reinforcing sexist views and attitudes, which, on one level, simply fail to treat women as serious human beings and, on another level, sanction and perhaps promote violence against women. Anti-pornographic feminists focus on its ideological role in maintaining gender relations that harm the status of women generally as well as individual women victimized by the violence that is sanctioned and encouraged by the violence materials.

Third, decline of value from the social order targets female more than male. Indian society is reeling under western pressures. The contours of its inbuilt structure are being tampered by western design. Despite sex being a controversial subject in India, but its customary wrapping is intoned with a strong moral fiber which protects the young generations from dipping into unholy pond. Since, the affordability and accessibility of these materials due to technological advancement, has enabled them to skip and loop the custodian eyes. The worst victims are young girls. Every year hundreds of sex scandals are uploaded of innocent teenager girls by their classmates, friends and others, it leads to spoil their future. Some of them commit suicides.[10]

Does Pornography Trigger Rape

No one argues that if pornography disappeared then rape would disappear. We understand that pornography alone doesn't make men do it, but that pornography is part of a world in which men do it and, therefore, the production, content, and use of pornography are important to understand in the quest to eliminate sexual violence. There is evidence that force and coercion are sometimes used to secure women's participation but the contemporary mainstream/corporate industry has no problem finding women (and men) who are willing to perform The primary domination/subordination dynamic eroticized in pornography is of course gender. It is also important to recognize that pornography is but one aspect of a huge sex industry, which includes not only mass-media sex but phone sex, strip clubs, massage parlors, escort services, street prostitution, and sex tourism. People who raise critical questions about pornography and the sex industry often are accused of being prudish, anti-sex, or repressive, but just the opposite is true. Such questions are critical not only to the struggle to end sexual and domestic violence, but also to the task of building a healthy sexual culture. Activists in the anti-violence and anti-pornography movements have been at the forefront of that task.

Feminist Approach to Pornography

Feminist positions on pornography currently break down into three rough categories. The most common one—at least, in academia—is that pornography is an expression of male culture through which women are co modified and exploited. A second view, the liberal position, combines a respect for free speech with the principle "a woman's body, a woman's right" and thus produces a defense of pornography along the lines of, "I don't approve of it, but everyone has the right to consume or produce words and images." A third view—a true defense of pornography—arises from feminists who have been labeled "pro-sex" and who argue that porn has benefits for women.

Little dialogue occurs between the three positions. Anti-pornography feminists treat women who disagree as either brainwashed dupes of patriarchy or as apologists for pornographers. In the anthology *Sexual Liberals and the Attack on Feminism* (1990), editor Dorchen Leidholdt claims that feminists who believe women make their own choices about pornography are spreading "a felicitous lie" (p. 131). In the same work, Sheila Jeffreys argues that "pro-sex" feminists are "eroticizing dominance and subordination." Wendy Stock accuses free speech feminists of identifying with their oppressors "much like concentration camp prisoners with their jailors" (p. 150).[11] Andrea Dworkin accuses them of running a "sex protection racket" (p. 136) and maintains that no one who defends pornography can be a feminist.

Some feminists argue that pornography is an important from sexual expression that does not harm women, and may even benefit them by liberating women and womens, sexuality from the oppressive shackles of tradition and sexual conservatism. Pornography may have a vital role to play in challenging traditional views about femininity and female sexuality and empowering women, both homosexual and heterosexual, to shape their own identities as sexual beings. The entire gamut of Indian legislations dealing with obscenity has been upheld as valid under Article 19(2) of the Constitution of India which allows for the state to impose reasonable ristrictions on the Right to speech and expression on grounds of *inter alia* public order, decency and morality. The only judicial pronouncement on the issue of the clash between obscenity and freedom of speech and expression recognized that the cherished right on which our Democracy rests is meant for the expression of free opinions to change political or social conditions and for the advancement of human knowledge. Lastly, neither the expression of pornographic opinions, nor the indulging of a private taste for pornography, causes significant harm to others in the relevant scene of "harm". Hence, the publication and voluntary private consumption of pornography is none of the state's business. A famous and influential passage by J.S. Mill, which read as follows: The court also stated that the freedom of speech and expression as envisaged in Act 19 of the Constitution of India is subject to reasonable restrictions on the grounds of public interest of public decency and morality and therefore 292 which promotes public decency and morality cannot be held to the unconstitutional. It has been argued that the morality that is being considered in the IPC has little to do with any Indian tradition, but has been influenced by British rules, Christian morality. According to this morality, sex is a sin and is inherently dirty and the only kind of permissible, yet unmentionable sex is that within marriage and that too for procreation alone.

The only principle for which power can be rightfully exercised over any member of a civilized community, against his will, is to prevent harm to others. His own good, either physical or moral, is not a sufficient warrant. He cannot rightfully be compelled to do or forbear because it will be better for him to do so, because it will make happier, because in the opinion of others, to do so would be wise or even right. These are good reasons for remonstrating with him, or reasoning with him, or persuading him, or entreating him, but not for compelling him, or visiting him with any evil in case he do otherwise.

Pornography vs. Individual Freedom

The most glaring instance of obscenity laws being used to subvert individual freedom was found in the Ranjit Udeshi case where the sale of Lady chatterley's Lover was banned and the appellants who were selling the books were imprisoned. *Kamasutra: A True Love Story*, a film by Mira Nair, had 40 cuts from the original version as prescribed by the Indian Censorship Board because of its "sensuous" contents before it could be shown in Indian theatres. Sex is a controversial subject in the social fabric of India, often being linked to immoral and prurient values. The current laws criminalise selling, distributing publicly displaying obscene or pornographic material.

The primary concern underlying this is safeguarding of public morality and decency. But such also lead to the violation of individual liberty and moral independence of a person who wishes to enjoy pornography as his right to view, read or enjoy pornography. Substantively, however, this article undertakes an exercise in achieving a balance between arguments of public morality and individual liberty and to also address the larger question of whether legislation of pornography is a viable option in the present Indian society.

How Big is Pornography Industry in India?

Subsequent growth of the pornography industry, fuelled by the recent advances in information and technology, has also further shaped the sex culture in India. The pornography industry is involved in the production and distribution of sexually explicit materials including literature, photos, audio, animation, movies, toys, and video games. The most popular modes of access are magazines, compact discs, digital versatile discs, and the internet. It is estimated to be a $57 billion/year industry worldwide with its revenue being larger than the combined revenues of all the professions, even football, baseball, and basketball franchises put together. India's growth rate is the third highest in the Asia Pacific region. Alongside this, accessing pornographic material has also increased with 12 per cent of internet websites being related to pornography, and viewers being estimated to spend roughly 3000 to 4000 dollars per second. Against this background, the well-known feminist dictum: "Pornography is the theory—rape is the practice" has raised serious concern, especially among parents and policy makers. Defining what constitutes pornography plays a crucial role in research, policy, and law making. *Pornography* is a Greek word, which originally meant 'writing about prostitutes'.

Why Pornography Need to be Controlled

Pornography, as an industry is gigantic in the country. Legalizing it would probably make government aware of all the black money and tax evasion practices that are abundant in such underground industries. Being closely linked to prostitution, pornography would help keep a check on illegal prostitution in various parts of the country. Making distribution of porn legal would only bring to the front what has always existed behind the backs. Local markets like Palika Bazaar in New

Delhi are knows for selling sex toys—the sale of which incidentally, is not allowed in the country. The open flouting of these rules undoubtedly makes them words written on paper and never implement. On the other hand, legalizing porn will have a disparaging effect on society. Not many people will be comfortable with the idea of a separate section catering to interested crowds in a store selling CDs and DVDs. Moreover, legalizing porn may have a negative externality of increasing the number of women who are illegally trafficked from the neighbouring countries of Nepal and Bangladesh in the name of provision of roles in Indian film industry.

Conclusion

The world of online pornography is overwhelmingly affordable, accessible and acceptable, a fact corroborated by seven Indian cities ranking amongst the top ten in the world for online porn traffic. Google trends reported that the search volume index for the word 'porn' has doubled in India between 2010 and 2012, which makes sense, given that one in five mobile users in India wants adult content on their 3G-enabled phones. Sex toys are latest craze in India and Chinese products have flooded the black market. The adult market in India is estimated to be 221 US Million Dollar. The sale of sex toys is illegal as defined by Section 292 of the Indian Penal Code which defines 'obscene' as 'book, pamphlet, paper, writing, drawing, painting, representation, figure or any other object if it is lascivious or appeals to the prurient interest', so sex toys are only sold on the black market. Prices for sex toys are unregulated so profit margins on these products can be huge. One of the biggest centres of the sex toy trade in the world is Palika Bazar in Delhi. Sex products associated with sexually active behaviour are also becoming popular. For example, vaginal beautification is becoming increasingly important to Indian women. Lingerie market has taken India by storm. Its market has doubled from 780 crore in 2003 to 1,645 crore today. Sex clininics have mushroomed. The trend is dangerous. If the largest young generation of the world is glued to the wrong side of the road, the young India will remain unproductive and beset with multiple social disorders. That will also affect the economy. The status of women is linked with the growth of nation. The virus of pornography is spreading from cities to rural areas that would lead to extreme kind of sexual exploitations. The large part of rural India is still has feudal structure. In such a moribund social order sexual abuse will be widespread.

Notes

1. *India Today*, Sex Survey, 2008.
2. Madhu Kithwar and Ruth Vanita, Using Women as a Pretext for Repression: Indecent Representation of Women (Prohibition) Bill, available at http:// w,w,w, cscsarchive.org.
3. Ruth Vanita, ed. *Quering India: Same Sex Love and Eroticism in Indian Culture and Society* (London Routledge) 2002.
4. Ashish Sinha, 'In hard times, pills, condoms sold most', *Indian Express*, 16 June, 2012.
5. The Report in *Times of India*, 25th July, 2014.
6. Anastasia Guha, 'The Beatitudes of Bountiful Bhabhi', *Tehelka*, May, 2012
7. Jason Overdorf, 'India: soft-core porn makes a comeback' *Global Post*, 7 September, 2011.
8. *Ibid.*
9. Arindam Mukharjee, 'A Sniff and A Heave' *O Outlook*, December, 2012.
10. Tusha Mittal, Bhabhi Anticlimax', *Tehelka*, July, 2009.
11. Pat Califa, '*Whoring in Utopia' from Public Sex: The Culture of Radical Sex*, Cleric Press.

Wrapping up Notes

18

Women Empowerment in India

Why and How?

Ajai Pal Sharma

> "To awaken the people, it is women, who must be awakened, once she is on the move, the family moves, the village moves and the nation moves". —Jawaharlal Nehru

When women are economically and socially empowered, they become a change agent. Woman is considered the nucleus of the family and plays an important and vital role not only in running day to day household activities but in other areas too. Despite many efforts made by the governments, the inequalities still exists in the areas of education, health, sharing the property, control over the resources and more which requires utmost attention of one and all.

In India women are generally and traditionally delegated mainly to household duties. Married women usually take her husband status and live with his family with a little recourse even in case of ill treatment and non-support. Also in matters of sex and child bearing, women often do not have the ability to oppose the wishes of their husband especially in rural areas.[1] A majority of women in our country do not have sustainable economies to support a better life for themselves. They are even being deprived of proper education, employment opportunities, modern healthcare facilities, and many other primary necessities of life. Being the core concept of the preamble of our Constitution, gender disparity, social injustice, economic disparity and many more like issues still exists in our society. What is empowerment then?

Empowerment as a concept was first introduced at the International Women's Conference at Nairobi in 1995. The conference defined empowerment as a redistribution of social power and control of resources in favour of women. The empowered women become agents of their own development, able to exercise choices to set their own agenda and be strong enough to challenge and change their position in the society. Empowerment is self-governance, self-sufficiency and self-maintenance. Another important meaning of women's empowerment is economic independence through information, knowledge, and necessary skills.[2] Urban women may be more aware and empowered about their rights in comparison to rural women who have the history of living depressed life in the hands of the male members. Talking about the women empowerment may be easy but it becomes very difficult when it comes to meaningful implementation of the concept in real sense. India might have taken many steps to empower women and 73rd and 74th Amendments in the Constitution is the milestone in this direction ensuring better access to the women in decision making and power sharing at par with the men.

Empowerment is one of the key factors in determining the success, development, status and position of women in the society.[3] Women empowerment is an on-going process that enhances women's ability to change those structures and ideologies that keep them subordinate and suppressed.[4] A special focus on empowering women is desired to bring long-lasting success and social changes in the communities. We need to augment our efforts with a united approach and continued stewardship for empowering and enhancing their progress. This will enable women to gain access to resources, better control over their lifestyle, effective role in household decision-making, ability to develop self-esteem, confidence, realise their potential and even greater autonomy. Gaining access to societal resources like education, employment, political power, and household resources like income, property, health, nutrition and decision making can be the important pathways in this direction.[5]

Friedman (1992) has presented a model of women's empowerment. It explains the interrelationships between the four forms of empowerment. *Organizational Empowerment*: it emphasises new knowledge and awareness about new benefits for development of the society, *Political Empowerment*: influences other governmental policies and decisions that affect communities, changing town-based people's beliefs, and other women to discuss issues affecting women, *Psychological Empowerment*: influences an increase in self-confidence and self-esteem, greater motivation, inspiration, enthusiasm and interest to develop new services for rural people and *Community Empowerment* which refers an access to new and useful knowledge and awareness, developing new skills, abilities, confidence and competence obtaining the friendship and support of other women, participating in various activities.[6] But this model is yet to be implemented effectively for the empowerment of women.

It is a matter of happiness and joy that The United Nations International Day of Rural Women is being celebrated on 15th October every year in the honour and the role of rural women in enhancing agricultural and rural development worldwide. We all know that women contribute more than men in terms of labour inputs in farming even when they are solely responsible for household management duties; however, that is not being considered the part of family income and hence household income distribution is skewed in favour of men which make the men to believe that they play important role in the rural development than women. This mentality of men needs to be changed with the time.

We know that a woman is the nucleus of the family in all the spheres of life and no work, irrespective of its nature, is considered completed without the presence of women. If we specially talk about the rural women, she gets up first early in the morning, collects water from the tap, wood to burn the *chullah*, fodder for the cattle and what not for others. She manages all the household activities and works for almost more than 15 hours a day and always the last one to eat and sleep in the family. She also plays vital role in preserving the culture of the society along with grooming the children for their bright future. Women may be representing nearly 50 per cent of the population but contribute more than that in the development of the society, despite that their contribution is being ignored by the male dominated society since generations. Rural women constitute nearly 77 per cent of total female population in our country and after contributing 2/3rd of total working hours earn only 1/3rd of the total income with an ownership of only 1/10th of the total resources. Generally the work of women is not recognized in terms of money and hence very less recognition is given to their hard work. Women are even ignored in the matters which are exclusively concerned to them like; giving birth to a child, acquiring education, access to health and many others.

The development of the society is not only increase in the per capita income but increasing the living standards of both men and women, which generally depends upon the status of nutrition, health, sanitation, education, social security, etc. But in real life situations it is not the same what we expect from the society because of various disparities shown towards the women in the society especially in rural areas where women are less informed in comparison to urban areas. It is general perception in the society that male child should be given priority in comparison to female child and forget the nucleus status of the women in the family. We should not forget that when women are economically and socially empowered they become the potent force to bring change not only in their own family but in the whole society. But the agony of the time is that the inequality which resides in our minds makes it difficult for women to fulfil their potential and as a result women have rarely access to the resources that would make their work more productive and ease their work load.

A successful agenda for the empowerment of women requires dismantling of values, structures and processes that maintain women's subordination and that are used to justify inequality in access to political, social, and economic resources. The realization of full potential, the most fundamental prerequisites for women empowerment could be attained through education. Amartya Sen also agrees with the above statement and makes a compelling case for the notion that societies need to see women less as passive recipients of help, and more as dynamic promoters of social transformation, view strongly buttressed by a body of evidence suggesting that the education, employment and ownership rights of women have a powerful influence on their ability to control their environment and contribute to economic development (Augusto, Lopez-Claros, 2005)[7].

The Beijing declaration and Plan for Action (PFA) was an agenda for women's empowerment. There are many issues and challenges which need to be tacked properly if we want to empower women in real sense. These are Gender Equality, Social Injustice, Health and Safety of women workers, Education, training and professional development for women, Entrepreneurship development, women and power in decision making and many more[8].

Some Indicators of Women Empowerment

There are many known indicators which show the empowered status of the women in the society. One important indicator of women empowerment is participation in domestic affairs and the ability to make decisions within the household. Empowerment in this context refers to women's capacity to define their own life choices and to pursue their own goals. This is attributed to the fact that they can work and earn money and therefore, they are being valued and given importance and equal status in the house and the society. Improved education of their children, improved household consumption, savings for the rainy days and improved health of the members of their family are also important indicators. Visible decrease in violence on women and girl child, visible changes in women's participation in decision-making and increase in bargaining and negotiating power at home and in the community are also some other indicators of women empowerment.[9]

Pathways to Women Empowerment

Education

The National Policy of Education (NPE), 1986 viewed education as a premier instrument for promoting equality of status and opportunity between men and women and between groups divided by class, caste and other forms of historic oppression. It regarded education as an agent of basic change in the status of women.[10] Women's education is extremely important as it is human right too and required for the flourishing of many of their capacities. It is, however, noticed that most programmes for education of girls and women in India have reinforced gender roles. In the olden times either girls were not allowed to go to schools or used to sit in last rows in classes and rarely courage enough to come close to the board where the male teacher usually occupies seat. Past experiences have taught us that attempts to control the number of children through behavioural changes in men have failed because of poor economic status and lack of education for both men and women. Education and economic status of the family plays a major role in family planning, birth control and health of women. Until this reality is accepted, the desired changes may not be attainable in the foreseeable future.

Also education plays an important role in bringing about awareness on women's rights. When both boys and girls grow up with mutual respect and understanding of their capabilities and roles in the society, women are more likely to find their rightful place within the family and the community. Education is essential in dismantling of values, structures and processes that maintain women's subordination and that are used to justify inequality in access to political, social and economic resources.[11]

With the efforts made by the government to promote equality and social justice through various educational policies like Sarva Shiksha Abhiyan (SSA), the inequalities in the areas of education have achieved some results but still disparity between male and female is noticeable. Even after sixty-seven years of our planned efforts in this direction we are not able to achieve the goal of 100 per cent literacy in our country. No doubt overall literacy rate has gone up to 74.04 per cent but the disparity between male and female education still persists (82.14% for males and 65.46% for females) as reported in census 2011.[12]

The government might have many plans and facilities towards educating the girl child but despite all we have not been able to uplift the standard of the women education as expected. Education plays an important role in increasing the awareness level on women's rights. As per the Census of India as on January 2012, female literacy rate in rural areas is 58.75 per cent in comparison to 79.92 per cent in urban area. If we bifurcate the education level of rural female then as per the NSSO June 2010, 46.7 per cent are not at all literate, 31.8 per cent are literate up to primary level, 11.1 per cent up to middle level and only 10.3 per cent are educated up to secondary level. This shows the miserable status of the women education which requires immediate attention.

Repercussions of Educational Ignorance: Real Life Cases

1. The George Foundation based in Bangalore, India and founded in 1995, was established to help alleviate poverty, promote health and a clean environment, and to strengthen democratic institutions and values in India. The first case involves a young pretty mother, not having any formal education, who was living with her son in a small hut. Her husband had earlier abandoned her, and she was not able to

return to her parents as they considered her "unworthy." One morning, she accompanied two men from the city who promised employment for her in the Middle East following an interview at an office somewhere, only to be gang raped and then returned to her village after a few days. Her absence was noticed by her neighbours, who only blamed her for the outcome and accused her for the separation from her husband. Feeling shame, and finding that she could no longer live in the community, she set herself on fire with kerosene.[13] If she would have had education to some extent she should have find some ways to live in this cruel society.

2. The second story is about a middle-aged woman whose husband had more than one "wife," a common practice in rural India though not officially allowed. One of his wives contracted AIDS somehow, and while her illness had become generally known, he continued to have sexual relationship with his other wives. He made no effort to medically test or to take adequate protection measures for himself or his other women, and soon all involved contracted the disease.[14]

These two real life stories represent the endless number of lives lost from ignorance, the low status of women and their inability to control their destiny and this can be overcome if we provide ample opportunities to women to have formal education which may give them awareness about the various aspects of the society.

This type of cases can be resolved only when behavioural changes can be initiated and promoted by those who have earned the trust of the people they claim to serve. When people realise that they are the real beneficiaries of the schemes, they begin to trust and have confidence in those providing the services. This then opens the opportunity to educate people on delicate issues such as sexual behaviour, use of condom, family planning, abuse of women and girl child and others. The institutions best suited for communicating these messages are the village health clinics, schools and community centres.

Employment Opportunities

Today we find that with the availability of educational facilities girl child are being educated but not getting the proper employment.

Opportunities for employment at all levels should be created and women should be made aware of these opportunities. They are also to be informed about the resources how to get skills for those opportunities. More and more women should be recruited for the jobs by enforcing and ensuring non-discriminatory hiring policies. They should be retained and supported for their needs in workplace. With the induction of MNREGA government has provided opportunities to all the needy women in rural areas which have been a fruitful experience for many but monitoring process need to be strengthened more. But care should be taken that the safety and security remains the responsibility of the employer and utmost attention should be paid that women are not being harassed at work places.

Eradication of Inequality

There is big argument that in society where men control the destiny of women, how it is possible to empower women? Simply encouraging women to resist the wishes of men would not only fail, but would create mistrust of any goodwill attempts made by the government. Women will get benefit only when both men and women begin to respect and accept the contribution of women. This is only possible when the inequality at home as well as workplace is eradicated from the minds of the men and the society at large. Gender equality refers to that stage of human, social development at which "the rights, responsibilities and opportunities" of individuals will not be determined by the fact of being born male or female. This is only possible when both boy and girl are given equal opportunities and proper education for understanding their rights, privileges and responsibilities. If the gender disparity is not being tacked properly it will create social imbalances. Hence government is required to make more efforts to provide equal opportunities to men and women.

Entrepreneurship Development

According to Jeffrey Timmons (1995), "Entrepreneurship is the ability to create and build something from practically nothing. It is initiating, doing, achieving and building a small enterprise or organization, rather than just watching, analysing or describing one. It is the ability to build a team according to your skills and talents.[15] Micro credit facilities are available for innovative and hard working women entrepreneurs to start small business such as making handicraft items. Self-Help Groups (SHGs) are available in rural parts of the country to help women from the villages to start their business. These groups receive loans from banks for understanding various generation-income activities. From the income of these small businesses the women (borrower) can enjoy better life, food, shelter, healthcare and education for their families and above all this small income will provide a hope for better future. Through small businesses they can cater the demands from local markets. But this all is possible only when all these schemes are being known to the needy women; this can be made possible through community centres at different places.

Population and Health Control

Through education women can be educated regarding need for controlling the size of the family because population increase has posed a serious problem in the country. It is estimated that by 2050 the population will be almost two billions then it will be very difficult to maintain such huge population with such limited resources; therefore, it becomes most important to educate women in regard to population control so that they can realize the benefits of birth control and less children.[16] It will not only increase the life expectancy but also health of women. Hence, both men and women should be educated about the benefits and measures of population control. The women can be educated on delicate topics such as sexual behaviour, use of condoms, family planning and others. Institutions that are best suited for communicating these messages are the local primary health clinics, schools, community centres and others, hence these needs to be promoted and monitored.

Ensuring Better Quality of Life

The formation of more Self-Help Groups and Micro Financing Schemes will enhance the socio-economic position of the women and would help in generating wealth and becoming self-reliant in the society. And since a woman is self-reliant, it would be possible to maintain higher standards of living not only for her but for the children and family. Thus empowering women through proper education and employment will provide important commercial, social and other benefits in improving the living standard of women. Economic empowerment to women will also help in accessing better markets, health, educational facilities not only for their children but for the entire family. With increase in economic status, every woman would be able to lead a quality of life.

Awareness about Health Services

Most of the women especially in rural areas are not aware about different health services like vaccination, immunisation, post and pre-natal care, awareness of sexually transmitted diseases and reproductive tract infection available even their local areas. Women can be made more empowered only if they become enlightened about these health issues. If required need based training may be arranged in all the above said areas to improve the awareness and health of the women. This can be done by arranging suitable training, workshops and exhibitions according the required conditions and it may be possible with the support of school and other institutions.

Most women in the rural areas face severe health problems because of hand to mouth existence and a large family to feed which results in women sacrificing their meals which led them to get anaemic and this manifests into major health issues. Government might be having so many plans to improve the health status in the country especially in rural areas for which NHRM was started in 2005 with an objective of improvement in public health delivery system in the rural areas. Data may be showing some improvement in the various areas like Infant Mortality Rate, Crude Birth Rate, etc. but lot more need to be done especially in rural areas to make sure that the facilities meant for the rural people are reaching to them effectively and timely. Janani Shishu Suraksha Karyakrama (JSSK) is also important initiative in this direction.

Gender Equality

Even many countries have made progress in developing the capabilities of women to empower them but still the inequalities continue to exist between women and men especially in the rural areas. The existing low status of the women in the society is the outcome of our patriarchal system which is in force by traditions. This women's oppression has to be sensitized to improve the gender equality. It should be made compulsory to treat all women and men fairly not only at workplaces but at public places also in order to respect and support human rights and non-discrimination. Addressing gender inequality requires the implementation of gender-sensitive policies and practices, the development of flexible work options and equal representation of women and men in decision-making and governance roles. Equal remuneration including all benefits for work of equal value should be paid to all women and men at work places. This will bring synergy at all levels.

Perception of having Lack of Income Generation Capacity

It has been observed that the contribution of women in household work is not recognized as a part of any economic contribution to the family income. Women are generally not perceived to have any meaningful income generation capacity and hence neglected mainly to household duties and cheap labour and as a result without power to work and earn good income their voices are also silenced. The mentality of men needs to be changed and the doubt on the capacity of women to generate revenues should also be removed from the society and women should be given equal opportunities and remunerations at par with the men.

Control by Men

Especially in rural areas everything is being controlled by men only and women are ignored for any participation and giving their opinion in the family matters even if it is related to their interest. So in a society where men control the destiny of women, it is quite difficult to empower women. Even in the matters of sex and child bearing rural women do not have the permission to oppose the wishes of their men and if they are encouraged to do so it will create mistrust rather helping among the communities. Women can gain power only when men start respecting the feelings of women and accept their contribution what they are devoting to the family matters and involve them in the decision making for all the issues.

Unequal Access to Economic Opportunities

Women are more likely than men to work as unpaid family labourers or in the informal sector. Women farmers tend to farm smaller plots and less profitable crops than men. Women entrepreneurs operate in smaller firms and less profitable sectors. As a result, women everywhere tend to earn less than men. If we see the status of employment of rural women than 54.2 per cent are self-employed, 40.3 per cent are casual labourer and only 5.5 per cent are regular employer in different sectors. This type of mentality of men require drastic changes and all women be given equal chances of earning so that they can uplift their own economic status in addition to uplifting the economic status of the family and ultimately of the society.

Less Voice in Households and in Societal Decision Making

All over the country, especially poor and less educated women have less say over decisions and less control over resources in their households. And even they are not allowed to participate in formal politics and are under-represented in its upper echelons too. As per the World Development Report 2012, 1/5th of married women in India are not involved in spending decisions, even about their own incomes. Women's ability to own, control, and dispose of property still differs from that of men–sometimes legally, often in practice. This type of disparity between men and women should not be allowed and they should be treated at par in all the matters either related to household or societal decisions.

Social Empowerment

Especially rural women are deprived in all the areas whether it is health, nutrition, sanitation, education, etc. Addressing all these gender gaps in human capital endowments requires fixing the institutions that can deliver public services in timely manner to expectant mothers and improving the availability of clean water and sanitation to households will go a long way to closing these social gaps. Other areas where rural women suffer most are female mortality and skewed sex ratios at birth which need to be addressed at the earliest. There is no doubt that in present time rural women have become more aware about these sensitive issues but lot more is required to be done.

Capacity Building

Capacity building and empowerment are two important attributes complementary to each other. There should be separate agency to provide skills and capacity building in various areas particularly to rural women. SHG is the core areas where rural women can have their own business through micro-financing to have economic liberty. In this direction government has taken many initiatives like STEP (Support to Training and Employment Programme) to encourage rural women so that their productivity can be increased and they can keep themselves abreast of the various changes occurring in the competitive environment. Training is such programme which can enhance the knowledge, skill and abilities firstly on need basis and then can be provided on essential needs.

Role of Private Institutions in Empowering Women

Issues of poverty, health, education and many more have traditionally been the concern of governments. In the past and even today, most programmes designed to benefit women are funded and managed exclusively by the governments to preserve its power. For example, modern healthcare for all the rural India is a free government service, but the reality is that the delivery of primary health care has failed miserably. It is well-known fact that private sector is the major recruiter of women employees which has also benefited from their engagement. Hence the role of private institutions also become evident in supporting the government is this social cause.

As per the report (McKinsey, 2009) 72 per cent of the organizations agreed that they had generated higher profits for the company after having engagement with women.[16] It is revealed from their study that engagement with women employees benefits the organizations in increasing in the pool of skilled and accessible labour, increase in employee productivity, enhanced brand reputation of the organization, creation of new markets or expansion of existing market, improved relationship between company and government officials and many more. The same report revealed that 67 per cent of the organizations have said that their engagements with women especially in developing countries have increased over the years in the areas of additional value generation, stated needs of local communities, performance improvements, corporate culture and giving global trends to the organization. This is the evidence which shows that women are not at all less than men for their involvement and commitment in bringing out the results for any organization, hence appeal to men that women need support and empowerment at all levels.

Some Popular Flagship Programmes Initiated by Government for Rural Development

Mahatma Gandhi National Rural Employment Guarantee Act

The MGNREGA was passed in 2005 with an aim at enhancing the livelihood security of people in rural areas by guaranteeing hundred days of wage-employment in a financial year to a rural household whose adult members volunteer to do unskilled manual work. As on date this scheme is in operation in 632 districts in the country. In 2012-13, the scheme provided the employment to more than 4.8 crore households, generating more than 213 crore person days of employment at a total expenditure of Rs. 39,000 crore. The average rate per day has been increased from Rs. 65 to Rs. 128 in 2012-13. A provision was also made to provide more than 100 days of work in the draught affected areas. It has been reported by the government data that every 5th household in the rural area is the beneficiary of the scheme and half of them are women with a large part of the allocations reaching to disadvantaged sections. The scheme might have provided opportunities to all the needy women in rural areas but strict monitoring process need to be implemented to make it more success and bring transparency in the disbursement of the funds.

National Rural Livelihood Mission (NRLM)

The NRLM was established in June, 2010 by the GoI, to be implemented in all States of the country to establish efficient and sustainable institutions of the rural poor that enable them to increase household income through livelihood enhancements and improved access to financial and selected public services. This is mainly an approach interrelated to four tasks:

(a) Mobilizing all rural poor households into effective Self-Help Groups (SHGs).

(b) Enhancing access to credit and other financial, technical and marketing services.
(c) Building capacities and skills for gainful and sustainable livelihood, and
(d) Improving the delivery of social and economic support services to poor.

This has been proved a very useful arsenal to remove the poverty and women empowerment especially in rural areas of South India where this scheme is running successfully. Now, the government has plans to implement it at the national level as revealed by the UPA Chairperson on the occasion of the Livelihood Day on June 03, 2013. It was further disclosed that under this scheme the women who are running SHGs will be given loan at the interact rate of 7 per cent and shall be given a rebate of 3 per cent to those who re-pay their loans in time. Presently, this scheme is running in 600 districts covering 6,000 blocks and has benefited 2,50,000 Gram Panchayat (BPL). In the next 10 years, government has the target of covering nearly 7 crore BPL households through the NRLM. This scheme is expected to remove the poverty especially to rural women by helping them either through micro-financing or other schemes.

Swarnjayanthi Gram Swarozgar Yojana

SGSY was launched by GOI on 1st April, 1999 as a poverty alleviation programme. The programme aims at establishing a large number of micro-enterprises in the rural areas, building upon the potential of the rural poor. The poor can fight poverty only collectively, not individually and therefore, the people with homogenous background can come together and get organized into SHGs to attain a collective goal for a common cause for the benefit of group members. The major objective is to bring the assisted poor rural families above the poverty line by providing them with income generating assets through a mix of bank credit and government subsidy by ensuring appreciable sustained level of income over a period of time. It also aims at establishing a large number of micro enterprises in rural areas based on the potential and competencies of the rural poor. This scheme has been very successful at national level and has increased the level of rural women socially as well as economically especially in South India where a number of SHGs are working under this yojana.

Support to Training and Employment Programme for Women

STEP was started in 2003-04 to increase the self-reliance and autonomy of women by enhancing their productivity and enabling them to take up income generation activities. Further, the scope of this programme was to mobilize rural women in small viable groups and make facilities available through training to upgrade their skills and access to credits at various levels for starting their own business at small scales. This programme also provides the opportunity to women to learn from each other in the group and share solutions to common challenges when they are being delivered various training programmes.

Conclusion

In the history of human development women has contributed substantially in all the areas where men can contribute but her contribution has not been recognized as expected by them. This has been happening because of low level of women education especially in rural areas where male child is given preference to female child even today when the results (education) shows that female students are outperforming the male students at all levels including civil services examinations. Government may be taking many initiatives to empower the women but what is most important is to change the mentality and attitude of the male members of the society who are engulfed in the patriarchal system. Women constitute half of the population but owns only one tenth of the resources which shows the skewed attitude of men towards women. This can be done only through the mode of education which can help them to improve their knowledge and skill level for improved contribution in the developmental activities especially in rural areas. We need to have rural women like Chhavi Rajawat, a management graduate who ditched her corporate career to become Sarpanch of her ancestral village in the desert of Rajasthan and working ever since to bring better water, solar power, paved roads, toilets and banks to the village. This is real women empowerment especially at village level which is the result of better education and commitment to contribute to the development of the society. All the women especially rural women need to get motivation from Chhavi Rajawat to uplift themselves and contribute to the rural development.

There is no quick solution to women's empowerment. The real solution lies in a holistic approach that deals with all the major interrelated issues of economic welfare, social justice, education, health, education, traditions and many more. Though government has taken various steps for empowering women but some where it is lacking in implementing the schemes properly and perfectly. Some more concrete steps need to be taken for supervision, monitoring and controlling the implementation of plans whether it is purely with the government or through public private partnership.

Notes

1. Jan & Hayat, *World Review of Business Research*, Vol. 1. No. 3, July, 2011.
2. International Women's Conference, Nairobi, 1995.
3. *University News*, 43(47), November 21-27, 2005.
4. *Kurukshetra, A Journal of Rural Development*, January, 2012.
5. Lingam Lakshmi (2009), Enabling Women Empowerment, *University News*, November 21-27.
6. *Kurukshetra, A Journal of Rural Development*, January 2012.
7. *Ibid.*
8. Fourth World Conference on Women Empowerment, Beijing, 1995.
9. *Ibid.*
10. National Policy of Education, 1986.
11. Ministry of Human Resource Development, *National Policy on Education* (1986), Government of India, New Delhi.
12. *Census Survey*, 2011.
13. Text of Speech delivered by Dr. Abraham George at the conference on women empowerment, Santa Fe, New Maxico, USA on 26-27 April, 2001.
14. Timmons, Jaffrey (1995), *New Venture Creation* (4th Ed.), Boston.
15. Singh, S.K. (2009), Role of Education in Upliftment of Women, *University News*, February 02-08.
16. McKinsey Report, 2009.

Index